Civil Society and Governance in Europe

Civil Society and Governance in Europe
From National to International Linkages

Edited by

William A. Maloney

Professor of Politics, University of Newcastle upon Tyne, United Kingdom

and

Jan W. van Deth

Professor of Political Science and International Comparative Social Research, University of Mannheim, Germany

Edward Elgar
Cheltenham, UK • Northampton, MA, USA

© William A. Maloney and Jan W. van Deth 2008

All rights reserved. No part of this publication may be reproduced, stored in a retrieval system or transmitted in any form or by any means, electronic, mechanical or photocopying, recording, or otherwise without the prior permission of the publisher.

Published by
Edward Elgar Publishing Limited
Glensanda House
Montpellier Parade
Cheltenham
Glos GL50 1UA
UK

Edward Elgar Publishing, Inc.
William Pratt House
9 Dewey Court
Northampton
Massachusetts 01060
USA

A catalogue record for this book
is available from the British Library

Library of Congress Control Number: 2007942981

ISBN 978 1 84720 758 6

Printed and bound in Great Britain by MPG Books Ltd, Bodmin, Cornwall

Contents

List of figures vii
List of tables viii
List of contributors x
Preface xiv

PART I INTRODUCTION

1. Introduction: from bottom-up and top-down towards multi-level governance in Europe 3
   Jan W. van Deth and William A. Maloney
2. Bringing society back in: civil society, social capital and the third sector 19
   Annette Zimmer and Matthias Freise

PART II BOTTOM-UP: CIVIL SOCIETY AND VOLUNTARY ASSOCIATIONS

3. The associational impact on attitudes towards Europe: a tale of two cities 45
   William A. Maloney and Jan W. van Deth
4. The political opportunity structure for civil society organisations in a multilevel context: social movement organisations and the European Union 71
   Marc Hooghe
5. Bringing the citizens closer to the EU? The role of civil society in Wales in the European Convention 91
   Deborah Cook
6. Europeanisation as empowerment of civil society: all smoke and mirrors? 109
   Cristina Elena Parau and Jerry Wittmeier Bains
7. Citizenship, welfare and the opportunities for political mobilisation: migrants and unemployed compared 127
   Didier Chabanet and Marco Giugni

PART III TOP-DOWN: INTEREST MEDIATION AND
         DECISION MAKING

8. Addressing the 'communication gap': the difficult
    connection of European and domestic political spaces   151
    Cécile Leconte
9. The role of interest groups in fostering citizen engagement:
    the determinants of outside lobbying   170
    Christine Mahoney
10. Coalition structures in national policy networks: the domestic
    context of European politics   193
    Silke Adam, Margit Jochum and Hanspeter Kriesi
11. European Union support for civil society in the Baltic states   218
    Susan Stewart

PART IV IN CONCLUSION

12. Conclusion: Europeanization, multi-level governance and
    civil society   241
    William A. Maloney and Jan W. van Deth

Index   253

Figures

1.1	A schematic overview of relationships in a multi-level system of governance in Europe	10
2.1	Civil society as a point of reference	29
3.1	Methodology and response rates	50
3.2	Attachments towards various objects among respondents in Aberdeen and Mannheim	56
3.3	Interest in politics at various levels among respondents in Aberdeen and Mannheim	57
3.4	Confidence in political institutions among respondents in Aberdeen and Mannheim	58
3.5	A typology of attachments and interest towards Europe	60
3.6	Confidence in the European Union among different types	61
5.1	Chronological spread of Welsh newspaper coverage of the Convention on the future of Europe, October 2001–July 2003	99
7.1	A theoretical framework for the analysis of claim making by migrants and unemployed people	128
10.1	Typology of policy networks	195
10.2	EU integration	203
10.3	Agriculture	204
10.4	Immigration	205
10.5	Policy networks as determinants of policy change	212

Tables

3.1	Distributions of associations and respondents among various types of associations in Aberdeen and Mannheim	53
3.2	Socio-demographic characteristics of respondents in Aberdeen and Mannheim	54
3.3	Attitudes towards Europe in Aberdeen and Mannheim	60
3.4	Distribution of types of European attachment	61
3.5	Distributions of different types among various associations in Aberdeen and Mannheim	64
3.6	Distributions of different types among associations of various size in Aberdeen and Mannheim	65
3.7	Distributions of different types among various levels of associational involvement in Aberdeen and Mannheim	66
7.1	Overall summary scores for the two dimensions of citizenship	136
7.2	Average discursive positions towards migrants by issue field (1990–1998)	137
7.3	Average discursive positions towards unemployed people by issue field (1995–2002)	138
7.4	Predictions about the extent of claim making by migrants	139
7.5	Predictions about the extent of claim making by unemployed people	140
7.6	Share of migrant actors in claim making in immigration and ethnic relations politics by issue field (1990–1998)	141
7.7	Share of unemployed actors in claim making in employment politics by issue field (1995–2002)	142
9.1	Outside tactics by institutional system	180
9.2	Percentage of advocates using outside tactics by issue characteristics in the US	183
9.3	Percentage of advocates using outside tactics by issue characteristics in the EU	185
10.1	Power distribution among coalitions	200
10.2	Composition of coalitions and average power	200
10.A1	Power distribution among coalitions	213

10.A2	Density ratios of conflict/cooperation and bargaining/cooperation by country and policy domain	213
10.A3	Complex image matrices for three policy domains in each country	214

Contributors

Silke Adam is Senior Researcher at the Department of Communication Science at the University of Hohenheim (Germany). She studied communication science at the University of Hohenheim (Diplom) and at Boston University, USA (MSc) and participated in summer schools on network analysis (Tilburg, Constance, Lisbon). Recent publications include: *Symbolische Netzwerke in Europa* (Cologne: Halem, 2007); 'Domestic adaptations of Europe' (*International Journal of Public Opinion Research*, 2007); 'Comparative analysis of policy networks in Western Europe' (with Hanspeter Kriesi and Margit Jochum, *Journal of European Public Policy*, 2006). E-mail: adamsilk@uni-hohenheim.de

Didier Chabanet is Research Fellow at Ecole Nationale des Travaux Publics de l'Etat, and Associate Research Fellow at Ecole Normale Supérieure Lettres et Sciences Humaines in Lyon, France. He is also currently Fernand Brandel Senior Research Fellow at the European University Institute in Florence, Italy. He has established himself as a well-known international scholar in the field of social movements, collective action and European integration. He has extensively advanced research and knowledge on the mobilization of the unemployed. His books include *European Governance and Democracy. Power and Protest in the EU* (with Richard Balme, Lanham, Rowman and Littlefield, 2008). E-mail: didierchabanet@hotmail.com

Deborah Cook is a Fast Streamer at the Welsh Assembly Government, and was a researcher in the Scottish Executive's International and Europe Social Research Team. She completed her doctorate from the University of Glamorgan, Wales, on the role of civil society in Wales in European Union policy making in 2006. Recent publications include: 'Wales and the European Convention: any scope for civil society?' (*Contemporary Wales* 19(1), 2007) and *Participation and engagement in politics and policy making: Building a bridge between Europe and its citizens' Evidence review*, papers One and Three (with Kesi Mahendran, Edinburgh Scottish Executive, 2007). Email: Deborah.Cook@wales.gsi.gov.uk

Matthias Freise is a Research Associate at the Institute of Political Science, University of Münster (Germany) where he heads the research group European Civil Society and Multilevel Governance in co-operation with

Annette Zimmer. His fields of research are European studies, civil society theory and third sector research. Recent publications include *European civil society* (Baden-Baden: Nomos, forthcoming 2008). E-Mail: freisem@uni-muenster.de

Marco Giugni is a researcher and teacher at the Department of Political Science, University of Geneva (Switzerland). He has authored or co-authored several books and articles on social movements and contentious politics. He has directed and collaborated in a number of comparative projects on topics relating to social movements and contentious politics, social exclusion, and social and political integration. His research interests include: social movements and collective action, immigration and ethnic relations, unemployment and social exclusion. E-mail: marco.giugni@politic.unige.ch

Marc Hooghe is Associate Professor of Political Science at the Catholic University of Leuven (Belgium), and Visiting Professor at the Universities of Lille and Darmstadt. He has published mainly on social capital, political participation and political socialisation. Recently, his work has appeared in the *European Journal of Political Research*, *British Journal of Political Science*, *Scandinavian Political Studies* and *Canadian Journal of Political Science*. He is president of the Belgian Political Science Association and editor of *Acta Politica*. Email: Marc.Hooghe@soc.kuleuven.be

Margit Jochum works as a scientific collaborator at the Centre for Legislative Studies, Techniques and Evaluations (CETEL), Faculty of Law, University of Geneva (Switzerland). Her current research focuses in particular on the pre-parliamentary stages of the legislative process and on political communication in the field of agricultural policy. She is a PhD candidate in comparative politics at the Department of Political Science of the University of Zurich (Switzerland). She previously worked at this same institution as a research assistant in the Europub.com project. E-mail: margit.jochum@droit.unige.ch

Hanspeter Kriesi holds the Chair in Comparative Politics at the Department of Political Science of the University of Zurich (Switzerland). Previously, he has taught at the universities of Amsterdam and Geneva. He is a specialist in Swiss direct democracy, but his wide-ranging research interests also include the study of social movements, political parties and interest groups, public opinion, the public sphere and the media. He has recently co-edited *The Blackwell companion to social movements* (together with David Snow and Sarah Soule; Oxford: Blackwell, 2004). His books include *Direct democratic choice: The Swiss experience* (Lanham: Lexington, 2005). He is now the Director of a Swiss national research programme on 'Challenges to democracy in the 21st century'. E-mail: hanspeter.kriesi@ipz.uzh.ch

Cécile Leconte earned her PhD in political science at Sciences Po Paris (France) and the University of Innsbruck (Austria) in 2003. In 2004 she was a visiting scholar at the Minda de Gunzburg Center for European Studies, Harvard University, US. She is Senior Lecturer in European Politics at the Lille Institute of Political Studies, where she heads the European studies programme, and at Sciences Po Paris. She is also a researcher at the CNRS Lille Centre for Politics and Administration and associate researcher at the Centre d'Etudes Européennes (Sciences Po Paris). Recent publications include *L'Europe face au défi populiste* (Paris: Presses Universitaires de France, 2005; preface by Jacques Delors). E-mail: cecile.leconte@iep.univ-lille2.fr

Christine Mahoney is Assistant Professor in the Department of Political Science at Syracuse University (United States). Her book *Brussels vs the beltway: advocacy in the United States and the European Union* is forthcoming (Washington: Georgetown University Press, 2008). She has also published in *European Union Politics*, the *Journal of Public Policy* and the *Journal of European Public Policy*, as well as a number of edited volumes. Her work has been supported by a Postdoctoral Fellowship at Syracuse University's European Union Center of Excellence, a Fulbright Fellowship to the European Union, a Martz Award and an RGSO Fellowship. She has been an affiliated researcher at the Free University of Brussels and a visiting junior scholar at Oxford University. E-mail: chmahone@maxwell.syr.edu

William A. Maloney is Professor of Politics in the School of Geography, Politics and Sociology, University of Newcastle upon Tyne (United Kingdom) and in 2004 was elected an Official Fellow of the Mannheim Centre for European Social Research (MZES), Germany. His main research interests are in the areas of interest group politics (internal and external dynamics), social capital and (non-)participation. His recent publications include *Social capital and associations in European democracies* (edited with Sigrid Rossteutscher, London: Routledge, 2006) and *Interest groups and the democratic process: Enhancing participation?* (with Grant Jordan, Basingstoke: Palgrave, 2007). E-mail: william.maloney@ncl.ac.uk

Cristina Elena Parau is a British Academy Postdoctoral Fellow at the European Institute, London School of Economics (United Kingdom). Her research focuses on the making of independent judiciaries in Eastern Europe. In 2007 she earned a doctorate from the Government Department of the London School of Economics for her thesis on the EU's impact on the domestic opportunity structures of civil society and the state in the accession country of Romania. Between 2002 and 2007 she held research posts at Westminster University, Queen Mary University of London and the London School of Economics. E-mail: C.Parau@lse.ac.uk

Susan Stewart is a Research Fellow in the research unit on Russia and the CIS at the German Institute for International and Security Affairs in Berlin. She was previously a lecturer at the Faculty of Social Sciences of the University of Mannheim (Germany), as well as a research associate at the Mannheim Centre for European Social Research (MZES). Her recent publications on democracy promotion include 'EU democracy promotion in the Western Balkans' (in Michèle Knodt and Annette Jünemann (eds), *The EU as an external democracy promoter*, Baden-Baden: Nomos, 2007). E-mail: susan.stewart@swp-berlin.org

Jan W. van Deth is Professor of Political Science and International Comparative Social Research at the University of Mannheim (Germany). He was Director of the Mannheim Centre for European Social Research (MZES) and is a Corresponding Member of the Royal Netherlands Academy of Arts and Sciences. He was convenor of the international network 'Citizenship, Involvement, Democracy' (CID) of the European Science Foundation and is national coordinator of the German team for the European Social Survey. His recent publications include *Foundations of comparative politics* (with Kenneth Newton, Cambridge: Cambridge University Press, 2005). E-mail: jvdeth@uni-mannheim.de

Jerry Wittmeier Bains holds a juris doctor from the University of Miami and a Master's in Political Theory from the London School of Economics. He is an independent researcher, and in his spare time does philosophy in the classical mould. Email: j.bains-alumni@lse.ac.uk

Annette Zimmer is Professor of Social Policy and Comparative Politics at the University of Münster (Germany). She was affiliated with the Program on Nonprofit Organizations at Yale University (USA), served as the DAAD Visiting Professor at the University of Toronto (Canada), and co-ordinated the EU-funded Research and Training Network 'Women in European Universities'. She serves on the Board of the German Political Science Association and on the Advisory Board of the German Volunteer Survey. Recent publications include *Gendered career trajectories in academia in cross-national perspective* (with Renate Siemienska, Warsaw: Scholar 2007) and *Future of civil society* (with Eckhard Priller, Wiesbaden: VS Verlag, 2004). E-Mail: zimmean@uni-muenster.de

Preface
Jan W. van Deth and William A. Maloney

Ongoing specialisation in the social sciences has made the study of rapid social and political developments in modern societies more challenging. Even broad and wide-ranging processes such as globalisation, individualisation or modernisation do not normally draw together scholars from different (sub-)disciplines. Europeanisation and the rise of a multi-level system of governance in Europe are two further examples of apparently closely linked processes that are studied separately by many scholars. In 2005 – through the CONNEX network (see below) – we had the opportunity to bring together a number of social scientists with different backgrounds, research interests and perspectives on political and social developments in Europe. At a conference in Bled (Slovenia) we discussed the various ways decisions in Europe were made and the success or otherwise of attempts to improve the engagement of citizens, voluntary associations, lobbyists, national 'gatekeepers' and interest groups within the complex European system of growing sub-national, national and supranational interdependencies.

The participants at the Bled conference all shared their ideas about how to approach the study of decision making in Europe from a variety of angles and perspectives. Furthermore, all shared the goal of basing conclusions on empirical analyses and not simply theory (or speculation) alone. The considerable differences between the results of the various empirical analyses presented appeared to have more in common than we initially thought. Systematic comparisons turned out to be highly fruitful by distinguishing between 'bottom-up' (that is, focusing on the consequences of Europeanisation for civil society at the local level) and 'top-down' approaches (that is, focusing on the consequences for civil society of the process of European integration and democracy in the European Union). At our second meeting in Mannheim (Germany) in autumn 2005 colleagues refined and expanded their papers and after lengthy discussions about the distinctive and shared aspects we decided to publish this volume.

The meetings in Bled and Mannheim were organised within the framework of the Network of Excellence CONNEX ('Connecting Excellence on European Governance') funded by the European Union under the 6th Framework Programme. This network is dedicated to the analysis of efficient and democratic multi-level governance in Europe (see http://www.connex-network.org). We are very grateful to Beate Kohler-Koch (Network Coordinator) and Fabrice Larat (Network Manager) for their enthusiastic support during all stages of our work on this project.

Discussing and developing contributions to a volume like this is only feasible with the help and assistance of many colleagues and institutional support. In addition to the resources provided by CONNEX we gratefully acknowledge the support of the Mannheim Centre for European Social Research (MZES) and the British Academy (Visiting Professorship award) that enabled William Maloney and Jan van Deth respectively to work on this volume in Mannheim and Aberdeen. For assistance in organising the meeting in Bled we thank Igor Bahovec and for the meeting in Mannheim Tobias Prellwitz. The time consuming tasks of converting a set of heterogeneously formatted papers into uniformly formatted book chapters was carried out by student assistants Christoph Kleeberg, Christian Schnaudt and, in particular, Benjamin Engst. Finally, from the outset Felicity Plester of Edward Elgar Publishing encouraged and guided us through the production process with much enthusiasm and great competence. We are very privileged to be surrounded and supported by many generous people who all shared their expertise, time and patience with us.

PART I

Introduction

1. Introduction: from bottom-up and top-down towards multi-level governance in Europe

Jan W. van Deth and William A. Maloney

As every small-town politician knows, strengthening democratic decision-making processes is not an easy matter – most citizens are hard to motivate to engage in public policy debates. And as every small-town politician or local political entrepreneur knows, most citizens are also unwilling to engage actively in the formal or institutionalised political life of their communities. On both counts citizens can find better things to do with their time. Simultaneously however, there are a wide variety of groups and associations actively seeking to advance their specific interests. When we look to more complex political systems like major cities, regions, states and national states we find these polities are 'plagued' by the virtually unsolvable problems and dilemmas that come with any serious attempt to base political decisions on the active engagement of citizens and citizens' organisations. Finally, if we travel one further political level to the multi-layer system of the European Union (EU) – the central focus of this volume – then finding a solution looks like a 'lost cause' before we have even truly begun our search. Put simply and logically, the more numerous the governmental tiers, the further decision-making processes are from citizens, the weaker their potential influence and the smaller the 'incentives' to participate.[1]

Given the above, how does the EU seek to involve citizens more fully and to increase identification with its political institutions? How does the EU seek to improve the transparency, legitimacy and accountability of decision-making procedures? These questions have become central in the enlarged EU. With the continuing expansion of the Union, a complex system of national, sub-national, international, trans-national and supra-national institutions has emerged with multiple recursive linkages. In other words, political decision making within Europe is increasingly characterised by the further development of Europeanisation (see Graziano and Vink, 2007). Two approaches ('top-down' and 'bottom-up') can be used to analyse the increasingly complex and interdependent relationships in this area. The traditional Truman (1951) demand-side or bottom-up approach that relies on the initiative of citizens to act spontaneously in the face of a political threat or to advance a common interest through organisational mobilisation faces many barriers. And even if such mobilisations are successful, it is likely that in many cases it would take a long time before such voices were audible to EU decision makers – if they were heard at all! For these reasons, the European Commission instigated several top-down approaches, trying to stimulate the active involvement of civil society organisations, most notably citizen groups, in EU decision-making processes. As Greenwood (2007: 343) highlights, the Commission has played an 'active role in funding regimes for citizen interest groups and in empowering citizen interest groups through (various) policy initiatives'.

Although the links between civil society and democracy have been established at the local and national level, not much is known about the extent to which associations contribute to European integration or the functioning of democracy at the (complex) EU level. How do local and national associations empower civic actors to 'get engaged' in the European and/or international arena? Are there positive or negative feedback loops? Do civil society organisations at various levels contribute to good governance in terms of democracy and efficiency?

1.1 CIVIL SOCIETY AND MULTI-LEVEL GOVERNANCE: THE DEMOCRATIC CHALLENGE

Civil society is now at the core of EU thinking on bridging the 'democratic deficit'.[2] The European Commission increasingly refers to civil society and social capital in order to promote good governance in terms of democracy, accountability and efficiency. As Saurugger (2007: 388) reminds us, organised civil society is attractive to policy makers because it is a 'product of the right of free association' and these bodies are primarily seen 'as bottom-up, citizen-initiated phenomena, part of the voluntary process of people's coming together to govern themselves'. Civil society is seen as comprising a vast number of associations such as interest groups, voluntary associations, social movements, social movement organisations, non-governmental organisations (NGOs), clubs, political initiatives, foundations and so on. At the EU level, many of these associations are large; more crucially however, they are also 'supposed' to be encompassing and representative, with grassroots involvement and an accountable leadership (Saurugger, 2007: 388). The EU believes that such a 'civil society' could and should play a major role in increasing the density, diversity, breadth and depth of the links between citizens and decision makers in Europe.³ As Warleigh (2001: 620) notes, 'Civil society has been championed by both right and left' as a means to either 'defeat "big government"' or bring citizens back in, and there is a broad consensus among EU policy makers 'that a greater role for civil society must be a central feature of European governance in the future'.

Accordingly, the EU White Paper on Governance (Commission of the European Communities 2001) issued a rallying call for a more engaged and vibrant European civil society, not as a desirable add-on, but an urgent and immediate necessity. In its decision to establish a 'Community action programme to promote active European citizenship (civic participation)' the Council of the European Union specified as one of the main objectives its aim 'to bring citizens closer to the European Union and its institutions and to encourage them to engage more frequently with its institutions'. Besides, all kind of 'civil society bodies' are invited to specify their needs for support to become actively involved in reaching these goals.⁴ These formulations reflect the much more general goals formulated in the White Paper. Thus the Commission aimed to make the policy-making process in Europe more open, transparent and participatory, and involve a wider range of actors in it from varying institutional and territorial levels – that is, from Eurogroups to local groups. The key objective is to encourage citizens 'to engage more frequently with its institutions . . . [and] to stimulate initiatives by bodies engaged in the promotion of active and participatory citizenship' (Commission of the European Communities 2001). However, as Friedrich (2007: 6) argues, the modern perspective on encouraging a more participatory democracy is no longer rooted in the classic democratic theory (of Rousseau or Mill) 'about the participation of individuals . . . [S]ince the 1960s (Blühdorn 2007), the term participatory democracy is increasingly used together with participatory governance, referring to the participation of collective actors of the organised civil society'. He further notes, as does the Commission, that civil society is not a panacea for all the democratic pathologies associated with the European policy-making process. Civil society does, however, open 'the possibility for thoughts about additional, complementary institutionalisations that are capable of rendering policy-making process more democratic which cannot (and perhaps even should not) rely predominantly on representative mechanisms' (Friedrich, 2007: 9).

The EU White Paper on Governance (Commission of the European Communities 2001) should also be set in the context of the post-Putnam social capital debate that (re-)emphasised the importance of the internal aspects of associational life for the proper functioning of democracies and societal integration. Working in the spirit of Alexis de Tocqueville, many authors have stressed the importance of civil society for the proper functioning of democratic political systems. In his seminal work on Italy, Putnam concluded: 'Good government in Italy is a by-product of singing groups and soccer clubs' (1993: 176). Consequently, the problems encountered by many democracies are – at least partly – the result of a decline in membership of many types of associations, clubs, groups and organisations; that is, a decline in civil society (Putnam, 1995, 2000). Claims made about the benevolent aspects of civil society and social capital are not restricted to 'good government' and they are not modest. To quote Putnam once more: 'social capital makes us smarter, healthier, safer, richer, and better able to govern a just and stable democracy' (Putnam 2000: 290). Notwithstanding the attractiveness of the social capital concept and the lines of reasoning, it is clear that even the most evangelical adherent would not consider it to be a panacea for all democratic pathologies. What is widely accepted, however, is the notion that modern democracies are dependent on an active and vibrant civil society and a healthy stock of social capital. In the current epoch (and from the Commission's perspective) groups are seen as delivering for democracy on two main counts (and several other subsidiary but important ways). First, they are perceived as (effective) representative vehicles delivering public policy outcomes that match citizens' preferences. Second, the internal social capital experiences within groups are seen as democratically crucial. In general, groups are seen as generating the pro-democratic values that bolster democracy and, in the specific EU context, they have the potential to enhance the quality of the political linkage between citizens and decision makers. Additionally, they may even increase citizens' attachment to, trust and confidence in, and identification with, the EU and European institutions among citizens across Europe (compare Noll and Scheuer, 2006).

However, even a cursory glance at the 'standard operating procedures' of the decision-making process in Brussels or Strasbourg would make even a mild sceptic perceive the general recommendation to mobilise more associations as little more than laudable but symbolic rhetoric. According to the Commission, about 2600 lobbying groups and over 15 000 representatives of various groups are active in Brussels alone. Interestingly, and importantly for the normative aspects of the civil society debate outlined above, the distinction between the lobbying activities of commercial bodies and interest groups on the one hand, and activities of non-profit associations with more general concerns on the other, has gradually been eroded by the rise of so-called non-governmental organisations (NGOs) – a new type of association which places itself explicitly between authorities or institutions and the citizenry. The result of these various developments is the formation of a 'lobby-cracy' consisting of 'merchants of influence' offering a mixture of conventional lobbying and more up-to-date forms of politicking.[5] As Saurugger (forthcoming 2009), Michalowitz (2004), Sudbery (2003) and Warleigh (2001) have argued, NGOs cannot really be viewed as normatively superior to 'grubby' old-fashioned interest groups (see below for a more detailed discussion). Accordingly, the challenge for democratic decision making cannot solely focus on an unconditional increase in the role and competences of various groups. It must take into account the specific developments of the interactions between decision makers and interest groups in Europe and both the changing nature of citizen mobilisation and citizen involvement in the policy-making process.

For example, chequebook participation is widely accepted by many citizens. Besides, it is seen by groups as the most efficient way to mobilise and – more crucially from a civil society perspective – many citizens see such limited involvement as attractive. As Jordan and Maloney (2007: 160–61) note, on the demand-side, most members or supporters 'are content to embrace a politically marginal role and contract-out their participation' to groups and many do not see membership of groups as a means of being 'active in politics'. Indeed, quite the reverse. Many citizens perceive passive involvement as a 'benefit' and would consider leaving organisations that sought to impose the 'cost' of active involvement in group activities.[6] In his study of NGOs in the development policy area, Warleigh (2001: 623) found that these bodies were staff-dominated and made 'little or no effort to educate their supporters about the need for engagement with EU decision-makers . . . Moreover – and perhaps more worryingly – I found no evidence that supporters are unhappy with this passive role, displaying at best little interest in the EU as a focus of campaigning or locus of political authority'.[7] Later he notes that several group leaders conceded that a lack of membership 'participation was a problem for their credibility' (Warleigh, 2001: 634). Sudbery (2003: 89) quoted a Senior Policy Officer, European Platform of Social NGOs, as stating that 'we do not have direct contact with supporters, but rely on member organisations to bring the issues to our attention'. She (2003: 90) also found that with limited resources, groups preferenced 'effective results' over raising awareness. A senior representative of the European Environment Bureau (EEB) said that 'While ideally it would be good to get people involved . . . my role is not to encourage the most participatory governance, but to ensure the best results for the environment'. Even members of the European Commission Governance team were candid about the tension between efficiency and citizen participation. 'We simply do not have the resources to deal with all civil society organisations . . . Perhaps the most effective way to link with the citizen . . . is by more effective results . . . The issue about bringing in the citizen is for speeches, for the rhetoric' (Sudbery 2003: 91f).

From the group perspective, the best way to produce effective results clearly has a significant impact on the nature of the 'demands' it makes of its membership. There are clearly tensions – felt by groups and policy makers – between democratic efficiency and more participatory *modus operandi*. This of course is a generic problem not confined to the political system of the EU. Crenson and Ginsberg (2002: 147) argue that in the US the new politics of policy making advantages expertise and technical knowledge over the mobilisation of large numbers of citizens. As they conclude, this new politics is open ' "to all those who have ideas and expertise rather than to those who assert interest and preferences". Those admission requirements exclude the great mass of ordinary citizens'. Similarly, Chaskin (2003) – who focused on attempts at fostering neighbourhood democracy – highlighted the importance of expertise and argued that this was partly driven by the professionalisation of public agencies. Skocpol (2003: 134) summarises the recent general trends:

> the very model of what counts as effective organization in US politics and civic life has changed very sharply. No longer do most leaders and citizens think of building, or working through, state and nationwide federations that link face-to-face groups into state and national networks. If a new cause arises, entrepreneurs think of opening a national office, raising funds through direct mail and hiring pollsters and media consultants . . . Organizational leaders have little time to discuss things with groups of members.

Directly at the EU level, Saurugger (2007: 397) more than hints at the tension that exists between being representative, responsive and accountable on the one hand and acting as an efficient policy-making partner on the other. The more efficient groups are:

> representing their interests in a constructive, precise and coherent manner, the more influence they exert. These activities, however, require major expertise on the group's and movement's side which contributes to modeling the style of militancy and leads to greater internal professionalization. Thus, the organizational structures of civil society have reformed to match better the perceived access structure of the European political system . . . Organized civil society – organized as groups or social movements – has a tendency to become increasingly professionalized to represent the interests of their constituency in an efficient way (Saurugger 2007: 397–398).[8]

Notwithstanding the scepticism above, the EU has provided significant levels of funding to many civil society organisations. At least the Commission could credibly argue that laudable rhetoric has also been matched by significant financial commitment. As Greenwood (2007: 343) notes 'the Commission's role in stimulating the emergence of citizen interest groups, and in funding and nurturing them ... really catches the eye'. It spends approximately 1 per cent (€1bn) on funding groups and almost the entire (300) citizen interest group universe (excluding Greenpeace) mobilised at the EU level receives some EU funding. Some groups are close to being almost entirely solvent on the basis of EU money (for example, 80–90 per cent of the funding of the European Network Against Racism and the European Social Platform comes from EU institutions and Social Platform organisations receive 60–90 per cent of their funding from EU sources) (Greenwood 2007: 343f). Without being mean spirited, this funding is not all aimed at extending participatory democracy and 'bringing citizens in', and in some respects such patronage can be seen as counterproductive. First, some funding is designed to engender lobbying that will strengthen the bargaining positions of DGs. Greenwood (2007) cites Bauer's (2002) example of the DG Employment, Social Affairs and Equal Opportunities (DG EMP) and the European Anti-Poverty Network relationship as a 'lobby sponsorship'. Bauer (2002) presented this as a case of the Commission 'creating its own constituencies with the clear intention of raising support for particular policy solutions and, thus, of influencing deliberations and indirectly setting political priorities' (Bauer 2002: 389; cited in Greenwood 2007: 344). Secondly, there is also a negative externality to patronage – it can obviate the need for members.[9] If institutional sources are prepared to fund organisations to operational levels of 80–90 per cent, then members become a luxury, or as Skocpol (2003: 134) acerbically put it 'Members are a nonlucrative distraction'. Why spend a great deal of organisational resources seeking and servicing members, when patronage permits fully focused professional lobbying?

1.2 THE HORIZONTAL AND VERTICAL DIMENSIONS

It is clear from the discussion above that establishing and improving democratic decision-making processes at the EU level is not straightforward. At the core of these debates are links between groups and institutions at various levels in Europe. As outlined, this dimension can be analysed in two directions: top-down (that is, the consequences of Europeanisation for civil society at national or regional levels) and bottom-up (that is, the consequences of civil society for the process of European integration and democratic governance in the EU). The exploration of these recursive linkages requires a rethinking of the relationships between (local, regional, national and trans-national) civil society on the one hand, and multi-level governance at the European level on the other.[10] In addition to this, the key role that NGOs play in the various links between the conventional sub-national levels and the trans-national level has to be analysed. By dealing with the roles and functions of NGOs, the crucial problems and prospects of democratic decision-making processes in complex multi-level systems become evident.

As noted above, the average citizen is somewhat distant from EU institutions. This is illustrated in the schematic overview of relationships in a multi-level system of governance in Europe (Figure 1.1). It is also evident in such a rudimentary scheme that a number of relationships exist between: (i) citizens and activists within all kinds of civil society associations; (ii) these associations and other associations at other levels (local, regional and so on); (iii) these associations and national state institutions; (iv) these associations and 'their' European federations active at the EU level; and

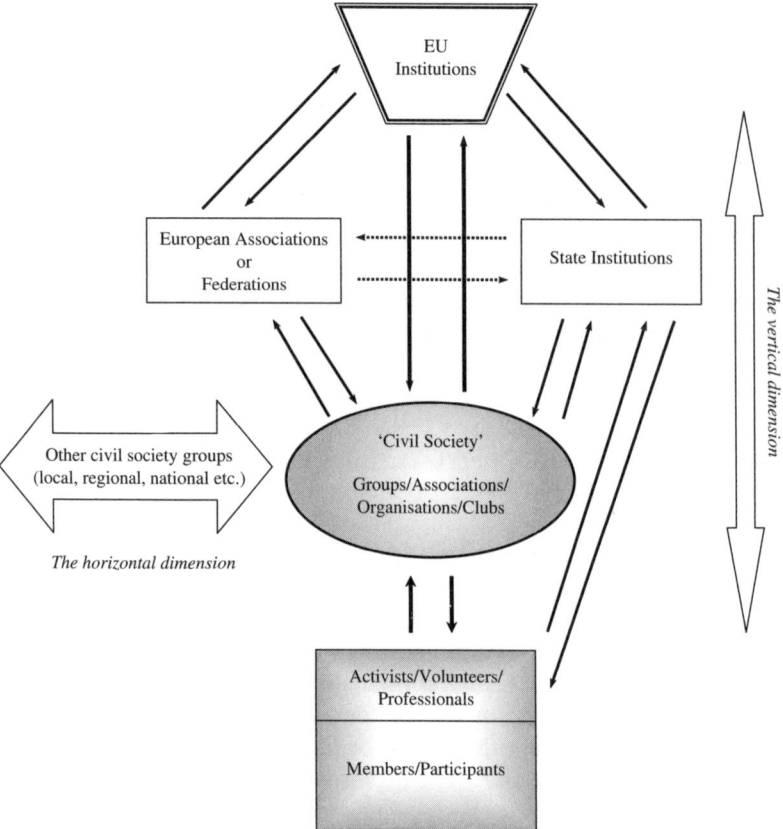

Figure 1.1 A schematic overview of relationships in a multi-level system of governance in Europe

(v) these associations and EU institutions.[11] Two dimensions can be discerned in this network of relationships vis-à-vis civil society associations. First, a horizontal dimension entails the relationships between various actors at the same level: in Figure 1.1 the relationships between associations and other associations – for example between sports clubs and youth clubs in some region – are depicted as horizontal relations. In general, the horizontal dimension consists of cross-sectional relationships such as connections between associations, or between regions or local communities, or between state governments. Although these relationships are worthy of study and generate some interesting research questions, this dimension is of limited analytical value for our purposes because greater inclusion in European decision-making processes is difficult to attain here. The second, vertical dimension is more relevant for our focus and consists of all the relationships between actors at different levels irrespective of the specific nature of these contacts or the relevant actors. Of the five main relationships outlined above, the second example (ii) refers directly to the horizontal dimension; the rest can be seen as cases on the vertical dimension.

In the bottom-up approach, the relationships between the various actors on the vertical dimension that begins with the individual citizen are followed. Direct links between citizens and EU institutions are very rare beyond voting for the European Parliament or possibly obtaining information on EU regulations and procedures. The indirect links via national institutions or civil society associations appear more important. State institutions represent the 'national' interests of citizens and civil society associations offer opportunities to represent the wishes and demands of particular areas such as sports, safety regulations or cultural exchanges. Given that national and area-specific interests are not mutually exclusive, many associations have founded European associations or federations that unite various national interests in specific areas. These national and European entities might engage in a competitive struggle for resources at the European level or they may join forces to further their common interests' vis-à-vis EU institutions. From a bottom-up perspective, voluntary associations and national institutions appear as linkages, transmitters, amplifiers or barriers in the relationships between citizens and decision-making processes at the EU level.

On the vertical dimension, a top-down approach starts with high-level decision-making processes. Political themes and issues originate and are defined by the actors involved in decision making at the EU level. Linkages with national institutions, associations and federations of voluntary associations are highly relevant since they conceal the interdependencies and powers of various actors. By mobilising these institutions and associations, demands and interests can be strengthened. Information is transmitted from arenas in Brussels and Strasbourg to actors not directly involved in decision-making procedures at that level. As with the bottom-up perspective, the top-down perspective locates citizens at some distance from decision-making processes. In a similar way, voluntary associations and national institutions can be seen as linkages, transmitters, amplifiers or barriers in the relationships between decision-making processes at the European level and individual citizens. It was on this basis that the European Commission launched its plan to increase citizens' engagement in European affairs through voluntary associations as representative and participatory vehicles, as indicated in the White Paper.

While the top-down and bottom-up directions on the vertical dimension are clearly very different, they share the assumption that national institutions, associations and federations of voluntary associations play a crucial linkage role between citizens and decision-making processes at the European level. Furthermore, the two perspectives see these intermediary actors as playing similar roles by either strengthening and encouraging these linkages (by articulating and transmitting demands or by channelling information) or by frustrating the relationships (by filtering, manipulating or stopping demands and information). National institutions, associations and federations of voluntary associations, then, form the main objects when researching the challenges facing democratic decision-making processes in the EU.

1.3 THE ROLES AND FUNCTIONS OF NGOS

Akin to many other social science research areas, there are several normative debates and other controversies centring on civil society and the role of groups, organisations and associations, especially NGOs. What should be the proper role of civil society or NGOs in a democratic system? What functions do civil society or NGOs actually perform in specific democratic systems? There are, of course, the almost obligatory definitional, labelling and counting debates surrounding the distinguishing characteristics of the entity, the accuracy of the labels we attach to certain phenomena and the question of which type of bodies qualify as belonging to civil society or the NGO sector and how they are distinctive from other kindred (sometimes almost identical) phenomena. In some cases the labels chosen are used by scholars to indicate some normative desirability (or pathology). Thus labelling an organisation as an NGO rather than an 'interest' or 'pressure group' or part of some 'lobby' may accord it a more normatively desirable status. As Grant (2002: 5) highlights, 'civil society' – of which NGOs are a key component – can be seen as providing a positive conferral of greater legitimacy on what others might perceive as an interest group system. In this respect, interest groups might be viewed as democratically damaged goods and NGOs as democratically superior vehicles. However, in many cases empirical research uncovers greater commonality than the diversity suggested by the labelling. Friedrich (2007: 11) cites Nanz and Steffek's (2005: 382) deliberative-tradition type of definition of a civil society organisation as:

> a non-governmental, non-profit organization that has a clearly stated purpose, legal personality and pursues its goals in non-violent ways. Apart from activist organizations this definition includes social partners (i.e. trade unions and employers associations), consumer associations, charities, grass roots organizations and religious communities.

As Friedrich (2007: 12) argues, 'On purely empirical grounds there seems to be no reason not to call these organizations "interest groups" as pluralists would probably do'.

The Commission's (2000: 3) discussion paper on NGOs struggled to find a 'common definition' and described the sector as 'extremely diverse, heterogeneous and populated by organisations with hugely varied goals, structure and motivations'. Nevertheless, the paper argued that the NGO term could be seen as shorthand for entities that shared certain characteristics: non-profit-making, voluntary, independent, a formal body with some sort of constitution that is accountable to members and/or donors, and not rent-seeking – that is, not in pursuit of sectional interests, such as 'the commercial or professional interests of their members' (Commission of the European Communities 2000: 4). In addition to this, NGOs vary in size (a handful of members to hundreds of paid staff and millions of members) and scope (advocacy and service delivery).[12] Similarly Grant (2002) also noted that the United Nations (UN) states that NGOs must have aims and purposes in conformity with the spirit, purposes and principles of the UN Charter; a formal organisation and a democratically adopted constitution; and appropriate mechanisms of accountability (UN Regulation 1996/31 quoted by Grant 2002: 2). Grant points out that, in practice, sectional and business groups are widely accredited as NGOs and he cites Scholte (1999: 171), who claims that 65 per cent of 'civic organizations' at the Singapore Conference of the World Trade Organization (WTO) were business-based (also see Saurugger forthcoming 2009, Michalowitz 2004, Sudbery 2003 and Warleigh 2001).[13]

The Commission sees NGOs as contributing to EU democracy on a number of fronts.[14] First, 'fostering a more participatory democracy' (Commission of the European Communities 2000: 4). Associational membership provides citizens with a means of participating beyond the confines of elections, political parties and trade unions. They can also act as

Tocquevillian schools of democracy, facilitating the development of pro-democratic values and social integration, and they can also be significant generators of social capital. NGOs are a valuable prop for democracies and are increasingly becoming involved in the policy-making process. Second, representing specific groups (such as pensioners, disabled, ethnic minorities) and interests (such as environment, human rights, animal welfare). NGOs are seen as being able to act as a counterbalance to other societal interests and 'to reach the poorest and most disadvantaged and to provide a voice for those not sufficiently heard through other channels' (Commission of the European Communities 2000: 5). Thus advocacy and counterbalancing advocacy are seen as important attributes, and groups also have a significant surrogate function – that is, they act on behalf of a public that lack the necessary political resources (for example, children or those with specific mental health problems). Much group activity seeks to advance many causes that benefit constituencies and interests beyond the direct interests of participators (for example, human rights, poverty, debt relief). Third, NGOs through their expertise and links at local, regional, national and European levels can contribute directly to the policy-making process and also monitor policy implementation by providing some feedback or evaluation. Fourth, NGOs can contribute to project management by 'monitoring and evaluating projects financed by the EU' (Commission of the European Communities 2000: 5). Finally, they are seen as contributing to European integration 'in a practical way and often at the grassroots level' (Commission of the European Communities 2000: 5). National and European level networks of NGOs help shape 'European public opinion'. The Commission also valorises NGOs as enhancing political linkage and political representation and as vehicles of self-government.

1.4 THE PLAN OF THE BOOK

The contributors to this volume analyse the opportunities for voluntary associations to contribute to European integration and decision making from various perspectives. The two main approaches – bottom-up versus top-down – are represented in the first part on 'Civil Society and Voluntary Associations', and in the second part on 'Interest Mediation and Decision Making', respectively. Before the results of these approaches are presented, Annette Zimmer and Matthias Freise discuss the main similarities and distinctions between the central concepts of civil society, social capital and the third sector (Chapter 2). According to their conceptualisations, the various actors should be discerned on the basis of a distinction between so-called civil society associations and third-sector organisations.

The first part of the volume consists of five contributions dealing with bottom-up perspectives on the relationships between citizens and citizens' organisations and political decision-making processes. As highlighted above, the Commission's valorisation and embracing of civil society was also aimed at increasing European citizens' trust and confidence in, and identification with, Europe and European institutions. The level of confidence in these institutions is usually low (see Maloney and van Deth, Chapter 3). Maloney and van Deth start this part with an analysis of orientations towards Europe among activists and volunteers of all kinds of voluntary associations in Aberdeen and Mannheim. Marc Hooghe expands the scope by explicitly considering the political opportunity structure for civil society organisations in Europe (Chapter 4), whereas Deborah Cook focuses on attempts to strengthen the links between citizens and Europe by analysing the role of these organisations in the discussions on the European Convention in Wales (Chapter 5). Christina Parau and Jerry Wittmeier Bains study the role of domestic actors in complex decision-making processes in Britain and the Czech Republic (Chapter 6). The first part is concluded by Didier Chabanet and Marco Giugni, who compare the various ways in which migrants and unemployed people try to articulate their claims (Chapter 7).

The four contributions to the second part of the volume deal with top-down perspectives and focus on interest mediation and decision making. The development of a European 'political space' is analysed by Cécile Leconte on the basis of her study of the gatekeeping role of national party elites (Chapter 8). Policy making and the role of associations form the topic of the next two contributions. Christine Mahoney presents the results of her research on lobbying groups and discusses the role of interest groups in fostering citizen engagement (Chapter 9). The cake is cut in a different way by Silke Adam, Margit Jochum and Hanspeter Kriesi in their extensive analyses of the development of policy networks in several policy domains in various countries (Chapter 10). The most explicit attempts to introduce top-down approaches are presented by Susan Stewart in her discussions of EU support for civil society in the Baltic states (Chapter 11).

In the concluding chapter, William Maloney and Jan van Deth return to the initial question of multi-level governance and Europeanisation (Chapter 12). The research has demonstrated that the Europeanisation process in terms of civil society actors adapting to the European political space had a somewhat uneven development. Some of the main empirical findings include:

- engagement with and confidence in the EU (compared to national institutions) is relatively weak among the group of citizens that the social capital model predicts would be highest – associational members;

- party elites play a key gatekeeper role in the European space;
- the EU is having a limited success in stimulating the development of civil society and social capital in the Baltic states;
- interest groups – in 'their' role as intermediary associations – have not been particularly successful in fostering citizen engagement.

The social capital being generated within the European space is nation-centred: that is, values and trust are heavily oriented towards national societies and political systems. Consequently, there appears to be a deficit in the stock, or variety, of social capital required that could contribute to 'good' EU governance and enhance political legitimation.

NOTES

1. A rational choice perspective would emphasise that the incentives to 'join in' are not large given that the likelihood that an individual's involvement would be important, crucial or pivotal is negligible. And in cases of collective benefits, individuals might choose to free-ride on the basis that others will incur the costs of participation to secure the good.
2. It is also worth noting that the notion of a democratic deficit is a relatively recent phenomenon. As Majone (1998: 12) highlights, the prevailing view (that is, before the Single European Act and the Maastricht Treaty) was that 'the integration process derives its legitimation from the democratic character of the (sovereign democratic) Member States'.
3. Clearly the civil society concept has much elasticity (for a detailed analysis see Chapter 2, by Zimmer and Freise).
4. Council Decision of 26 January 2004 (2004/100/EC) Art. 1 (b).
5. See the article by Dan Bilefski 'Critics urge openness for merchants of influence' in the *International Herald Tribune* of 29 October 2005.
6. Of course for some, active involvement is a benefit of membership.
7. Jordan and Maloney (2007: 158f) also cite similar evidence of staff dominance and the attractiveness of passivity for members of campaign groups in the UK. A representative of the Council for the Protection of Rural England (CPRE) argued that the council positively encourages active involvement, but many members view this as an additional cost (that may lead to exit). The CPRE representative said the organisation treads very carefully in trying to activate supporters: 'We think we'd lose them if we did that [press for more active membership] because they're people who want to give money and they don't want to do any more than that . . . My remit has been to develop a supporter base as opposed to a member base. It's much easier to recruit people who just want to pay money than recruit individuals into an organisation where they potentially see it as a time-related activity which they don't have time to do basically . . . So the whole task [of recruiting people] has to be geared around saying "oh don't worry, we're not expecting you to come to meetings and things, we just want your support".'
8. Grande (2002: 130) makes the point that professionalised representation in the EU could be 'justified for reasons of system effectiveness, but the democratic quality of their activities is dubious from the perspective of both representative and participatory models of democracy' (quoted in Saurugger, forthcoming 2009).
9. There is also the 'danger' that patronage may affect the tactics, strategies and policy positions of groups. Groups heavily reliant on patronage may not want to engage in activities that may be frowned upon by their sponsor or occupy policy positions too distant from the major funder's standpoint.

10. An extensive discussion of the concept 'European Governance' is presented by Smismans (2006).
11. For extensive overviews of the various approaches to the role of interest groups and civil society organisations in European democratic decision-making processes, see Eising (2000) or Mair (2005).
12. The discussion paper argued that in its broadest sense the NGO term could subsume trade unions and business or professional organisations. However, the document was dealing 'primarily with organisations active in the so-called "Third Sector", i.e. in the non-governmental and non-economic field' (Commission of the European Communities 2000: 4).
13. Warren (2001: 10) cites van Til's (2000) estimate that '77.5 percent of nonprofit expenditures and 64 percent of nonprofit employment [in the USA] are within associations that act as much like for-profit organizations in that they pursue economic interests within competitive markets' (see also Jordan and Maloney 2007).
14. We are well aware that there is a 'dark side to social capital' and that there are other 'democratic pathologies' associated with groups. The aim of this section is simply to outline the potential positive contribution that NGOs could make to democracy in the EU (largely, but not wholly, from the Commission's perspective).

REFERENCES

Bauer, M. (2002) 'Limitations to agency control in European Union policy-making: The commission and the poverty programmes' *Journal of Common Market Studies* 40 (2), 381–400.

Blühdorn, I. (2007) 'The participatory revolution: New social movements and civil society', in K. Larres (ed.) *A companion to Europe since 1945*, London: Blackwell Publishing.

Chaskin, R.J. (2003) 'Fostering neighborhood democracy: Legitimacy and accountability within loosely coupled systems' *Nonprofit and Voluntary Sector Quarterly* 32 (2), 161–89.

Commission of the European Communities (CEC) (2000) *The Commission and non-governmental organizations: Building a stronger partnership*, Commission Discussion Paper, 18 January 2000, Brussels: CEC.

Commission of the European Communities (CEC) (2001) *European governance: A white paper*, 25 July 2001 COM(2001) 428 final, Brussels: CEC.

Crenson, M.A. and Ginsberg, B. (2002) *Downsizing democracy: How America sidelined its citizens and privatized its public*, Baltimore: The Johns Hopkins University Press.

Eising, R. (2000) *Assoziative Demokratie in der Europäischen Union*, Polis 47, Hagen: Institut für Politikwissenschaft.

Friedrich, D. (2007) *Old wine in new bottles? The actual and potential contribution of civil society organisations to democratic governance in Europe*, RECON Online Working Paper 2007/08, July 2007, www.reconproject.eu/main.php/RECON_wp_0708.pdf?.fileitem=5456965, last access: 16 October 2007.

Grande, E. (2002) 'Post-national democracy in Europe', in M.T. Greven and L.W. Pauly (eds) *Democracy beyond the state? The European dilemma and the emerging global order*, Lanham: Rowman and Littlefield, pp. 115–38.

Grant, W. (2002) 'Civil society and the internal democracy of interest groups', paper prepared for the *Political Studies Association of the United Kingdom Annual Conference*, Aberdeen, April.

Graziano, P. and Vink, M.P. (2007) *Europeanization: New research agendas*, Basingstoke: Palgrave Macmillan.

Greenwood, J. (2007) 'Review article: Organized civil society and democratic legitimacy in the European Union' *British Journal of Political Science* 37 (2), 333–57.

Jordan, G. and Maloney, W.A. (2007) *Democracy and interest groups: Enhancing participation?* Basingstoke: Palgrave Macmillan.

Mair, P. (2005) *Popular democracy and the European Union polity*, European Governance Papers, www.connex-network.org/eurogor/pdf/egp-connex-c-05-03.pdf, last access: 16 October 2007.

Majone, G. (1998) 'Europe's 'democratic deficit': The question of standards' *European Law Journal* 4 (1), 5–28.

Michalowitz, I. (2004) 'Analysing structured paths of lobbying behaviour: Why discussing the involvement of "civil society" does not solve the EU's democratic deficit' *European Integration* 26 (2), 145–70.

Nanz, P. and Steffek, J. (2005) 'Assessing the democratic quality of deliberation in international governance: criteria and research strategies' *Acta Politica* 40 (3), 368–83.

Noll, H.-H. and Scheuer, A. (2006) 'Kein Herz für Europa?' *Informationsdienst Soziale Indikatoren* 35, 1–5.

Putnam, R.D. (1993) *Making democracy work: Civic traditions in modern Italy*, Princeton, NJ: Princeton University Press.

Putnam, R.D. (1995) 'Bowling alone: America's declining social capital' *Journal of Democracy* 6 (1), 65–78.

Putnam, R.D. (2000) *Bowling Alone: The collapse and revival of American community*, New York: Simon and Schuster.

Saurugger, S. (2007) 'Democratic 'misfit'? Conceptions of civil society participation in France and the European Union' *Political Studies* 55 (2), 384–404.

Saurugger, S. (forthcoming 2009) 'Associations and democracy in the European Union' *West European Politics*.

Scholte, J.A. (1999) *Global civil society: Changing the world?* Centre for the Study of Globalisation and Regionalisation (CSGR), Working Paper No. 31/99, Coventry: University of Warwick.

Skocpol, T. (2003) *Diminished democracy: From membership to management in American civic life*, Oklahoma: University of Oklahoma Press.

Smismans, S. (2006) 'Civil society and European governance: From concepts to research agenda', in S. Smismans (ed.) *Civil society and legitimate European governance*, Cheltenham: Edward Elgar, pp. 3–19.

Sudbery, I. (2003) 'Bridging the legitimacy gap in the EU: Can civil society help to bring the Union closer to its citizens?' *Collegium* 26, 75–95.

Truman, D.B. (1951) *The governmental process: Public interests and public opinion*, New York: Alfred A Knopf.

van Til, J. (2000) *Growing civil society: From nonprofit sector to third space*, Indiana: Indiana University Press.

Warleigh, A. (2001) ' "Europeanizing" civil society: NGOs as agents of political socialization' *Journal of Common Market Studies* 39 (4), 619–39.

Warren, M.E. (2001) *Democracy and association*, Princeton, NJ: Princeton University Press.

2. Bringing society back in: civil society, social capital and the third sector

Annette Zimmer and Matthias Freise

2.1 INTRODUCTION

There are many reasons why social scientists and policy experts alike are increasingly turning towards society in their search for reform concepts, new ideas and progressive initiatives. In times of globalisation and Europeanisation, traditional nation states have lost power and steering capacity. Those state-centred reform concepts of the 1970s focusing on management and social engineering are therefore outdated. However, the so-called Washington consensus emphasising exclusively the power of the market also proved to be unsuccessful. Despite political rhetoric, the heyday of neo-liberalism and what critical voices called turbo-capitalism are gone, particularly in the countries of the European Union. Against the background of high rates of unemployment, growing societal inequality and an insecure future of the welfare state caused by a combination of market and state failure, society-centred approaches have regained importance in the social sciences.

At least three concepts, all predominately society-centred, have gained momentum during the last decades: the civil society, social capital and third sector approaches. None of these concepts constitutes a 'grand theory' but they claim to be helpful in the sense of a so-called middle-range theory, which specifically draws attention to the innovative capacity of civic engagement and societal activity.

Below, we briefly describe each concept, highlighting its specific background and origin as well as its methodology and acceptance by the scientific community and the public. Against this background we will argue in favour of a closer nexus between the civil society and the third sector approaches by referring to the terminology of the European Union, which defines third sector organisations as 'organised civil society'. We will further argue that civil society organisations might gain importance for the deepening of European integration since they have the potential to bring EU policy making closer to the people.

2.2 THREE CONCEPTS REVISITED

2.2.1 Civil Society

The civil society approach has a long history dating back to classical Greece, when the term was closely connected with the Aristotelian notion of an ideal way of life. 'The history of the term "civil society" is older than the history of the modern world', remarks Sven Reichardt (2004: 35). It is fascinating to follow the various conceptualisations of the term during the centuries. However, its current popularity dates from the 1970s, when the term was used by dissidents and civic movements in Eastern Europe and Latin America in order to express their opposition to the ruling authoritarian regimes. Discussions which took place in these oppositional groups influenced debates on the further development of democratic theory in the Western hemisphere (Klein 2001; Thaa 1996). The re-entry of civil society into political discourse indicated a turning point with respect to democratic theory in political science. Since the late 1950s, democratic theory had been dominated by theories of representative democracy, which, according to Fritz Scharpf, primarily focused on the output legitimacy of democratic systems (Scharpf 1970; 1999: 1.1). With the 'third wave of democratisation', 'input legitimacy', which is closely linked to various forms of participatory democracy, regained momentum in political science (Klein 2001; Schmalz-Bruns 1995; Young 2002).

There is no doubt that the shift from output to input legitimacy of democratic systems has to be judged against the background of the so-called crisis of the welfare state. However, it would be too simple to explain the current attractiveness of participatory democracy by referring exclusively to state failure and thus to the well-documented 'growth to limits' (Flora 1986) of the welfare state. The emergence and popularity of the civil society concept serves also as an indicator for the growth to limits of the rational choice approach. In the meantime, citizens are no longer exclusively conceptualised as mini-computers constantly calculating costs and benefits. On the contrary, they are perceived as societal and political citizens striving for the betterment of their communities. In order to round off the picture, two further societal trends have to be mentioned: first the new social movements of the 1980s, which heavily criticised the routines of participatory democracy, and second the educational reform of the 1960s and 1970s, which had a significant impact on the citizenry. Citizens being able and willing to engage in politics, albeit choosing procedures and initiatives which at that time were unusual, asked for the further development of democracy as a political programme. Against this background, the civil society approach gained momentum.

In other words, the civil society approach is a highly normative concept directed towards a 'utopian program' (Dubiel 1994) which aims at the deepening of democracy and the improvement of the societal status quo. Therefore, some authors argue that the concept of civil society encompasses the capacity of a society to criticise and to be able to confront economic, political and social elites (Sachsse 2002). Besides the future-oriented utopian programme there is a further constitutive element of the civil society concept, which translates into the civic-mindedness of its members. Civil societies are non-violent entities, capable of intensive discourse and able to reach consensus by means of discussions. Thus civil societies are civilised societies in the literary meaning of the term (Reichardt 2004: 36).

Finally, there is a third element encompassed in the civil society concept, which was primarily taken up by historians investigating processes of societal modernisation and democratisation during the 19th century. This element relates to those entities and dynamic forces which constitute the infrastructure of civil society as a 'public sphere' that belongs neither to the market nor to the state but holds an intermediary position. The historian Jürgen Kocka defines the infrastructure of civil society as a 'societal sphere between state, economy and private life populated by voluntary associations, networks and non-governmental organisations' (Kocka 2002: 16 translated by the authors).[1] Focusing on civil society as a societal sphere opens avenues for empirical research. Thanks to the work of historians, we are by now well-informed about those organisations and associations which populated the societal sphere, thus forming the infrastructure of civil society in the 19th century. Amongst those were first and foremost voluntary associations, mutual organisations such as cooperatives, business and professional associations as well as foundations. The flourishing of these organisations, particularly in the second half of the 19th century, tells us an interesting story about societal differentiation and modernisation (Reichardt 2004). In Germany, these organisations were used by the state administration to tackle the so-called social question, providing solutions for the problems of urbanisation and industrialisation (Sachsse 1996).

At the same time, voluntary organisations developed into the basis of social milieus such as the catholic or the social democratic milieu, thus serving as bridgeheads for the formation of modern societally embedded parties. Finally, the cooperative movement constituted a countervailing power against the 19th-century 'turbo-capitalism' and enabled low-income farmers and craftsmen to adapt themselves to the changing conditions of the economy (Pankoke 2004). Historical investigations also highlighted that specific embeddedness is of utmost importance for the flourishing of civil society, its infrastructure and also its civic-mindedness. In short, there is a strong interface between democracy as a state of mind and political behaviour and the strength and civic-mindedness of civil society (Zimmer 2004). There is no doubt that a strong democracy needs an active citizenry; however, an active citizenry, organised in numerous voluntary organisations and societally based groups, does not lead automatically to strong and lasting democracy, as the failure of the Weimar Republic in Germany has clearly proven (Berman 1997).

The linkage between a 'utopian programme' and the real world of organisations was taken up by the European Union in the late 1980s under Jacques Delors' presidency. He became aware of the 'intermediary sphere' between the market and the state (Delors 2004). It is exactly the interaction between a progressive idea and the real world of organisations engaged in various policy fields that makes civil society attractive and has witnessed it becoming a buzzword in current political discourse, particularly in Brussels (Zimmer and Sittermann 2004). From a theoretical point of view, the term civil society provides the possibility of linking policy analysis with participatory democratic theory, thus bridging the gap between output and input legitimacy of democratic governance, and therefore tackling the so-called democratic deficit of European government. Civil society as a utopian programme is thoroughly anchored in political and democratic theory. The term is highly attractive due to its normative dimension, which reflects the current popularity of participatory democratic theory. However, civil society used as an 'analytical-descriptive term' in the sense of Jürgen Kocka (2002) serves as a synonym for voluntary associations and other organisations that populate a societal sphere beyond the state and the market. As outlined later, there is no doubt that the empirical twist of the term provides the common ground for the linkage between civil society and third sector research.

2.2.2 Social Capital

The social capital approach also has a long tradition of scholarly research (Farr 2004; Portes 1998). In essence, 'social capital' has always been linked to the individual citizen. Very well known in the scientific community is the interpretation of social capital worked out by Pierre Bourdieu. Differentiating between very specific forms of capital – economic, cultural and social – Bourdieu developed a sophisticated theory and socio-economic analysis by which he significantly contributed to the explanation of societal stratification. According to Bourdieu, social capital, and thus the 'strength of weak ties', in combination with the two other types of capital demonstrates why social inequality is hard to overcome (Braun 2001). Bourdieu's social capital theory encompasses a harsh critique of the status quo and the ruling societal elites. However, neither Bourdieu's nor Coleman's social capital approach – the latter focusing on the problems of societal coordination – gained as much popularity as Robert Putnam's perspective. Putnam's approach had a major impact on the political science community. In fact, the social capital approach in political science is almost exclusively connected with Putnam's work because, as Sidney Tarrow (1996: 389) highlighted, 'all self-respecting political scientists like to think of themselves as intrigued with what makes democracy work'.

In his seminal work *Making Democracy Work* (1993), Putnam analysed why public administration reforms were successfully implemented in the North of Italy whereas they failed in southern Italy. In sharp contrast to mainstream public administration research, Putnam argued that the success or failure of policy implementation is closely linked to the existence or absence of social capital. This encompasses trust, norms and networks. According to Putnam, it is primarily accumulated by face-to-face contacts in voluntary associations. He came to the conclusion that 'good government in Italy is a by-product of singing groups and soccer clubs' (Putnam 1993: 176). While Putnam's work has been highly criticised, it has nevertheless inspired and provoked much research. Instead of focusing exclusively on the individual and his or her capital, Putnam drew attention to the social capital of communities. He maintained that social capital or 'civicness' reduces transaction costs and contributes to efficiency. Contributing to the social advancement of the individual as well as the betterment of the community, Putnam's social capital is of 'mutual benefit' (1993: 35).

From a theoretical point of view and compared to the civil society discourse, Putnam's social capital approach is far less sophisticated. In *Making Democracy Work* he builds on the work of Alexis de Tocqueville, and with respect to his empirical analysis he significantly draws on the research of Almond and Verba. It is evident that, particularly in his later publications, Putnam (2000; 2002) is thoroughly in accordance with the long tradition of political culture research (Pye 1972) in focusing primarily on the micro-level of the individual. In the context of our argument, it is worth mentioning that first Putnam brought to the fore a societal explanation for good or bad governance. Neither the state nor the market is fully responsible for *Making Democracy Work*: trust, social networks, values and civic-mindedness play a key role. Second, particularly in his 1993 volume, Putnam emphasised the importance of associational involvement and the participatory behaviour of citizens. Similar to the civil society approach, at least in this book, the 'intermediary sphere' of voluntary organisations and networks of cooperation ranked very high in his analysis (Putnam 1993). However, since then, empirical research working with the social capital approach has been predominantly attached to the micro-level of the individual citizen.

2.2.3 Third Sector

The common ground of the two aforementioned concepts and the third sector approach is their reference to the 'intermediary sphere' of non-governmental organisations that work on behalf of the common weal. In accordance with Robert Putnam's 1993 version of the social capital concept, the third sector approach is intrigued with efficiency and societal effectiveness. The term 'third sector', introduced by Amitai Etzioni in his article 'The Third Sector and Domestic Missions' (1973), refers to a societal sphere, 'a third alternative, indeed sector . . . between the state and the market' (1973: 314) which is populated by organisations that, according to Etzioni, are able to combine the entrepreneurial spirit and organisational effectiveness of the business firm with the common good orientation of the state and its public administration. This capacity led Etzioni to refer to the sector as being populated by 'organizations for the future' (1973: 318).

Similar to Putnam's social capital concept, the third sector approach was at the outset linked to public policy considerations and, in particular, welfare state analysis. Despite some vague reference to the work of de Tocqueville, at least in the early years, the third sector approach did not claim any particular linkage to democratic theory or political culture discourse. On the contrary, the development of the third sector approach provides a good example of social science significantly responding to its political and socio-economic environment.

There were two major political events and streams in the United States which had a major impact on the social sciences and which, in the long run, resulted in an intensive analysis of the societal sphere between the market and the state. First, in the late 1960s Washington launched a far-reaching tax reform which aimed to reduce the political power of private independent foundations. In summary, foundations had to improve their transparency by publishing annual reports and financial statements. Moreover, they were forced to spend a considerable share of their assets on grant giving, thus reducing their capital stocks. Second, as soon as Ronald Reagan came to power, his administration started wide-ranging initiatives aiming to reduce the so-called 'big government' of Washington DC. Against that background, government spending on welfare issues was massively cut and Washington officials turned to what at that time was called the 'independent sector' to deliver those social services which were no longer provided or financed by government. Confronted with a neo-liberal and anti-government zeitgeist, some leaders of large private (liberal minded) independent foundations (for example, the Ford Foundation and the Russell Sage Foundation) combined to work against the neo-liberal revolution in Washington.

The goals which the liberal foundations wanted to attain were twofold: first, they tried to keep their wealth and assets. They wanted to demonstrate their value within modern societies (Anheier 2005: 301–27). Secondly, they tried to protect the minimalist liberal welfare state in the United States. In essence, during the following decades, private foundations financed research centres and university programmes which aimed at analysing private organisations working on behalf of the public and the common weal. The outcome of this research provided a fascinating picture of America's third sector (Filer Commission 1975), which by no means merits the title 'independent sector' because, as clearly documented by the research results, it was to a remarkable degree financed by public monies. Furthermore, the research proved to be very valuable for the political goals of US foundations. Tax constraints and financial burdens were loosened in the aftermath of the Filer Commission. From a scientific point of view, this resistance to the neo-liberal zeitgeist resulted in the establishment of the third sector approach, which tries to shed light on those private organisations and initiatives working in the public sphere for the common good. The findings of empirical research using the third sector approach further underlined the importance of societal activity and civic-mindedness for modern societies.

It became clear that third sector organisations defined as belonging neither to the public sector nor to the market constitute a very specific segment of modern societies. Although these organisations are working in different areas fulfilling a variety of societal tasks, the nonprofit or third sector approach underlines that these organisations have specific features in common. They follow the non-distribution constraint that reinvests profits but does not permit their distribution among members and/or the employees of the organisation. They are private organisations operating within the public sphere for the public benefit. Moreover, voluntary participation is a key feature of nonprofit organisations. Thus, there is a clear distinction between nonprofits and communitarian entities, such as families or clans (Priller and Zimmer 2001). Finally, nonprofits stand out for their multi-functional character. In sharp contrast to the logic of functional differentiation as the prime feature of modern societies, nonprofits participate in at least three societal spheres simultaneously. As providers of services for their members and/or the general public, they are part of the market economy. They also participate in the political process through their advocacy activities. Finally, because nonprofits are dependent on voluntary input – donations, membership dues and volunteering – they are also embedded in particular communities where they form an integral part of our *lebenswelt*. They make a significant contribution to processes of empowerment and self-actualisation, while at the same time fostering feelings of solidarity and belongingness. In many ways, the multi-tasking and multi-functional character of nonprofit organisations makes them interesting partners for policy planning. In sum, working with nonprofits might provide avenues to tackle problems of input as well as output legitimacy. However, the multi-functional character of nonprofits did not move into the centre of theory building under the framework of the third sector approach. In contrast, theory building was heavily dominated by economists.

In the 1980s, the study of private enterprises working for the public was primarily taken up by economists, who tried to explain this paradox using concepts and theories based on micro-economics. Without going into detail, their major rationales were developed explaining the existence of third/nonprofit sector organisations in market economies. These organisations were either conceptualised as an outcome of a combined market and state failure, as an initiative of social or religious entrepreneurs or as a joint public–private initiative or public–private partnership. At the very heart of these explanations is the non-distribution constraint whereby these organisations are active in the market place, but are constrained from making dividend payouts. In other words, incentives to engage in third sector or nonprofit organisations are very different from profit maximisation (see Powell and Guerin 1997).

There is little doubt that the start-up incentives and motivations for nonprofit enterprises differ from those operating in the market and state bureaucracies. This is analogous to the social movement literature that also identifies 'solidarity' as a key motivation for collective action. Indeed many nonprofit organisations (NPOs) grew out of social movements (for example, women or ecology). In addition to this, their internal administrative procedures are based on 'solidarity'. According to Streeck, nonprofits may be characterised as organisations situated between 'charismatic leadership' and a fully fleshed bureaucracy (Streeck 1981).

Since the late 1980s, the third sector concept has increasingly been adopted by political scientists and sociologists trying to establish a nexus between this particular approach and their disciplines. These scholars are not primarily interested in the question 'why': that is, trying to explain the existence of NPOs. Rather, they want to know what functions these bodies fulfil in market economies and democratic nations. Generally, sociologists take a bottom-up approach, perceiving organisations as vehicles for participation and social integration as well as societal stratification. In particular, they focus on civic engagement and therefore on micro-level individual activity. In contrast, political scientists follow a more top-down approach, analysing the potential of nonprofit organisations as service providers in different welfare regimes. Each discipline uses the concept of the sector in a functional manner. However, while sociology stresses the added value or organisational function for the individual, political science is interested in the surplus of nonprofit activity for government and thus for societal engineering or, to put it differently, for governance. Although nonprofits are also heavily engaged in lobbying activities, by and large, interest representation and lobbying are not classified as constituting the core of nonprofit/third sector research.

Sociologists, political scientists and economists primarily focus on just one single facet or function of third sector/nonprofit organisations. For economists, the non-distribution constraint is the most interesting feature. In accordance with the Institutional Choice Approach, third sector organisations offer an institutional alternative to social service production by private enterprises or government entities. Sociologists are interested in the potential of third sector organisations to provide avenues for societal integration. They perceive these organisations as bedrocks of social milieus and societal communities and therefore as transmitters of values and norms. Finally, political scientists are also primarily interested in the service delivery function of third sector organisations, perceiving them as actors within public–private partnerships, particularly in the welfare domain. Interestingly enough, research analysing the advocacy function of these organisations is very unlikely to be characterised as third sector research but is more likely to be described as lobbying or interest representation. However, the boundaries between disciplines and approaches are less distinct with respect to those third sector organisations engaged in international activities and called non-governmental organisations (NGOs). In sum, there is definitely a black spot within third sector research. Until recently, policy analyses of nonprofit organisations have not examined the involvement of these organisations within the full circle of the policy process. In other words, third sector research takes a somewhat static view of policy fields mapping their composition or 'welfare mix'. Neither the potential of third sector organisations as transmitters of norms and values and therefore as important actors within processes of framing, nor their capacity to mobilise and engage in advocacy and lobbying has been analysed.

Currently, there is very little cross-fertilisation between third sector and social capital research. On the contrary, each research community follows a distinctive and relatively narrow line of argument. Whereas the third sector approach has become a 'hot topic' in studies portraying the welfare mix of social service delivery in different countries (for example, Anheier and Kendall 2002; Evers and Laville 2004), studies on civic participation and theoretical considerations in relation to the further development of modern democracy draw heavily on the social capital approach (for example, Prakash and Selle 2004). Thus, the third sector approach is closely linked to questions dealing with the so-called output legitimacy of governance arrangements, whereas research referring to the social capital approach is geared towards problems of input legitimacy of democratic governance. Since each approach sheds light on just one facet of governance arrangements, we argue below that they could be grouped under the civil society concept that could serve as a shared point of reference for the third sector and social capital approaches.

2.2.4 Civil Society as an Encompassing Concept

The civil society concept encompasses two distinctive elements: First, a normative perspective that aims at the improvement of democratic participation and social justice: second, a reference to the so-called 'intermediary sphere' of modern societies, populated by voluntary organisations and societal networks in which active citizens are engaged. At least implicitly, civil society addresses the micro-level of civic engagement, which constitutes the prime field of analysis of the social capital approach, as well as the meso-level of voluntary activity that is the arena of third sector research. Against the background that the programmatic-normative element of civil society theories serves as the common reference point of the micro-level concept of social capital and the meso-level concept of the research on third sector organisations, the civil society concept could develop into an umbrella or macro-level approach under which both the social capital and the third sector perspective could be arranged (see Figure 2.1).

Below, we examine specific topics addressed by the social capital and third sector approaches which provide the common ground for mutual understanding and cross-fertilisation. There is no doubt that civic-mindedness plays a crucial role for each concept. As clearly documented in the literature, civic-mindedness translates into civil engagement in voluntary associations. These organisations are of prime importance for the social capital as well as for the third sector approach. Particularly in his early work, Putnam specifically referred to associations in their capacity to provide the social structures of cooperation (Putnam 1993: 89). In accordance with Alexis de Tocqueville, Putnam highlighted that 'civil associations contribute to the effectiveness and stability of democratic government' (Putnam 1993: 89). He furthermore underlined the importance of voluntary associations for 'what

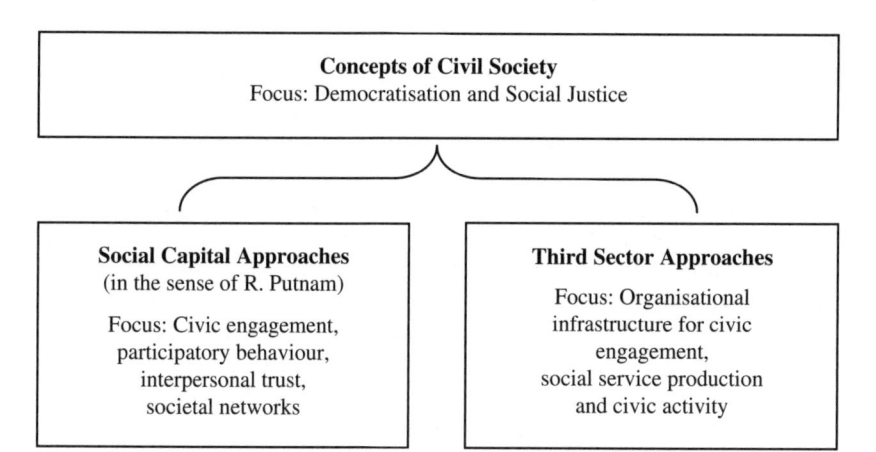

```
┌─────────────────────────────────────────────────┐
│           Concepts of Civil Society             │
│   Focus: Democratisation and Social Justice     │
└─────────────────────────────────────────────────┘
                        │
          ┌─────────────┴─────────────┐
┌──────────────────────┐    ┌──────────────────────┐
│ Social Capital       │    │ Third Sector         │
│ Approaches           │    │ Approaches           │
│ (in the sense of     │    │                      │
│ R. Putnam)           │    │ Focus: Organisational│
│                      │    │ infrastructure for   │
│ Focus: Civic         │    │ civic engagement,    │
│ engagement,          │    │ social service       │
│ participatory        │    │ production           │
│ behaviour,           │    │ and civic activity   │
│ interpersonal trust, │    │                      │
│ societal networks    │    │                      │
└──────────────────────┘    └──────────────────────┘
```

Figure 2.1   Civil society as a point of reference

twentieth-century political scientists have called interest articulation and interest aggregation' (Putnam 1993: 90).

There is a close nexus between the early work of Putnam and the civil society literature, which particularly refers to the 'intermediary sphere' of voluntary organisations, that constitute the 'infrastructure of civil society'. Interestingly however, it makes no difference if the infrastructure of civil society is portrayed from a communitarian, liberal or deliberative perspective. Ralf Dahrendorf, rooted in the classic-liberal tradition, points out that civil society is characterised by 'the existence of autonomous, i.e. non-governmental or not in any other way centrally ruled organizations' (Dahrendorf 1991: 262). These organisations provide the possibility for 'the autonomous declaration of interests, values and preferences' (ibidem). Jürgen Habermas highlights different functions of civil society such as articulation, representation and enforcement of interests. According to his line of argument, 'the core of civil society' is formed by 'a system of associations which institutionalise problem-solving discourses on questions of general interest within the framework of the public' (Habermas 1992: 443f authors' translation). In accordance with Robert Dahl (1998: 15), who perceives democracy as a political project for which governments and citizens have to struggle continuously, Charles Taylor paints a highly differentiated picture of civil society. For him, the quality of (the) civil society depends on the ability 'of all associations to determine and to influence politics significantly' (Taylor 1991: 57).

The 'intermediary sphere', populated by voluntary associations and nonprofit organisations, also constitutes the prime point of reference of the third sector approach that attributes specific features to these organisations. Amongst those, voluntarism is the most prominent. According to the definition used under the framework of the Johns Hopkins Project (Zimmer 2004: 18) the meaning of voluntarism with respect to nonprofit organisations is at least twofold. First, membership has to be voluntary and non-coercive. Second, nonprofit organisations are based to a certain extent on voluntary support that encompasses both the social investment of time (unpaid labour, volunteering and serving on the board of NPOs) and money (corporate and private giving).

However, as outlined above, each concept focuses on just one facet of these multi-functional organisations. Whereas third sector research focuses on the service production function of nonprofits, the civil society concept highlights the programmatic and future-oriented potentials of civic organisations that enable the citizenry to invest time and money in the further development of democracy. Finally, the social capital approach focuses on the integrative potential of voluntary organisations – highlighting their capacity to build networks based on trust and reciprocity. The civil society concept and the social capital approaches are highly normative.[2] The third sector and the social capital approach are based on empiricism and the civil society concept in its programmatic dimension is very much inclined to political theory and, more specifically, to democratic theory. However, despite the common ground, the third sector approach focuses on the meso-level of inquiry, researching nonprofit organisations as corporate actors, whereas the social capital concept centres on the micro-level of inquiry, analysing civic activity and the civic engagement of citizens. The social capital approach investigates the importance and pronounced appearance of civic activity on the input side of government. In contrast, third sector research focuses on the output side of government by analysing the importance of nonprofits as producers of social services in specific welfare regimes. As such, nonprofits are integrated into processes of policy implementation, constituting an institutional alternative of welfare production instead of government.

Against this background, we argue that an integration of the two approaches – social capital and third sector – would definitely enrich empirical research on issues of democratic governance. There are at least some indicators that the European Commission as well as the Economic and Social Committee are trying to follow the path of integrating both perspectives. In our concluding remarks we argue that research based on a perspective that combines the two approaches might be useful with respect to a further understanding of the processes of multi-level governance in Europe.

2.3 MULTI-LEVEL GOVERNANCE AND CIVIL SOCIETY

2.3.1 From Governing to Governance

There is an increasing tendency in the political science discourse to replace the term 'governing' with 'governance' (Kersbergen and Waarden 2004), although, according to Benz, a clear cut definition of the term has not yet been developed (Benz 2004: 130; Wolf 2002). The reasons for the shift from governing to governance are manifold. Amongst them, the decreasing steering capacity of the national state ranks high; in international relations, governance even refers to a special situation in which governing takes place without government. In recent years, the notion of governance has taken a very prominent position in EU research due to the specific policy architecture of the EU: that is, governance is characterised as having horizontal and vertical dimensions (Bache and Flinders 2005; George 2005). The vertical dimension refers to EU governance as a loose coupling of different 'layers of authority – European, national, and sub-national' (Hooghe 1996: 18), whereas the horizontal dimension contrasts the traditional notion of governing: governance arrangements are not restricted to state actors but include private corporate actors, business associations, lobbying and public interest groups.

There is a consensus in the literature on the so-called 'informality' of governance arrangements (see Jachtenfuchs and Kohler-Koch 2004: 94). Numerous studies show that EU governance is at its very core network governance (Eising and Kohler-Koch 1999) that translates into processes of bargaining and deliberation. Recent research analyses the impact of the Method of Open Coordination (OMC) on European governance arrangements (for example, Zeitlin *et al*. 2005). Vertical integration OMC, as a new mode of steering, provides some leeway for flexible adjustment and thus self-organisation on national and sub-national levels of authority without coming into conflict with the overall aims and purposes of a specific policy as defined by EU authorities, the Council of Ministers, the Commission and the European Parliament (Bauer and Knöll 2003).

It is not surprising that governance arrangements moved into the focus of EU research along with the expansion of the competencies of the Union, whereas bargaining processes linked to regulative policies are primarily researched at the policy arena in Brussels. Distributive policies, whose importance has grown significantly under the framework of European social policy and which encompass national and sub-national level actors, require a far more refined and bottom-up analytical approach. Moreover, regulations are primarily put into practice and supervised by governments and public authorities. However, this does not hold true for distributive policies, which are very often implemented via private actors, including nonprofit organizations. In other words, the multi-level governance arrangement of the EU, where policy implementation at the subnational level is not restricted to governments and public bureaucracies, asks for a multi-level research design analysing processes of bargaining, lobbying and decision making at each layer of authority (Heinelt 2005).

From a normative point of view there are two ways of judging governance arrangements. The first one, linked to arguments of efficiency, is closely connected to what Fritz Scharpf (1999) called output legitimacy of governing. The second one, related to concepts of participatory democracy, is very close to the notion of input legitimacy. As outlined elsewhere, governing in Europe is based on the 'community method', which was originally designed as a top-down approach involving the Commission as the policy entrepreneur and the Council of Ministers as the lobby arena of the member states. Whereas the Commission (which is very much in accordance with the Hegelian idea of ideal statehood) conceives its mission as safeguarding the common weal of Europe and its various societies, the Council of Ministers takes care that the national interests of the member states are not sacrificed. In its search for efficiency and effective government, the Commission is accused of lacking transparency, civic participation and thus input legitimacy. At the same time, the Commission is, compared to national standards, a very small bureaucracy that is dependent on external advice and expertise provided by outsiders. From the very beginning it has tried to tackle both problems – the lack of internal expertise and the so-called democratic deficit – by establishing procedures of consultation with private actors, thus setting up governance arrangements or issue-specific networks (Laffan 2002). For some time now the 'social partners' (trade unions and employers' associations) have enjoyed special privileges with respect to consultation and dialogue with the Commission. The 'social dialogue' is perceived as providing a blueprint for the establishment of a 'civic dialogue'. However, it is not clear what 'civic dialogue' means and which organisations will participate. Nevertheless, as clearly documented by the publications of the Commission and the Social and Economic Council, the topic has increasingly gained importance since the late 1990s.

2.3.2 EU Governance Arrangements and Civil Society Organisations

In its communication *Promoting the Role of Voluntary Organizations and Foundations in Europe* of 1997, the Commission highlighted both the economic and social importance of voluntary organisations. These are acknowledged as having a decisive role for democratic societies, so the Commission ascribes an influential role to them in the process of further EU integration (European Commission 1997: 8).

In its opinion *The Role and Contribution of Civil Society Organizations in the Building of Europe* of 1999 the Economic and Social Committee (EESC) introduced the term 'organized civil society' or 'organizations of the civil society' into EU speech. According to the EESC, civil society translates into 'the sum of all organizational structures whose members have objectives and responsibilities that are of general interest and who also act as mediators between the public authorities and citizens' (EESC 1999: 7.1).

The Commission's Discussion Paper of 2000, *The Commission and Non-Governmental Organizations: Building a Stronger Partnership*, co-authored by the President and the Vice-President of the Commission, specifically referred to the multifunctional character of these organisations. It distinguishes between 'operational NGOs [which] contribute to the delivery of services [such as in the field of welfare], whereas the primary aim of advocacy NGOs is to influence the policies of public authorities and public opinion in general' (European Commission 2000: 1.2). Building on the terminology developed by Fritz Scharpf (1999), the Commission argued that these bodies might contribute to an improvement of the input as well as the output legitimacy of European governing. More specifically, the organisations are perceived as contributing to 'participatory democracy', 'interest representation of specific groups and specific issues', 'policy making', 'project management' and last but not least to 'European integration'.

The Commission's White Paper on European Governance of 2001 particularly highlighted the importance of civil society organisations as channels of communication between the EU and its citizens. Again, the White Paper stressed the importance of civil society organisations for providing a 'structured channel for feedback, criticism and protest' and for promoting democracy at the national level.

Finally, the communication (2002) by the Commission *Towards a Reinforced Culture of Consultation and Dialogue – General Principles and Minimum Standards for Consultation of Interested Parties* outlines how civil society organisations are envisaged to participate in those EU-specific multi-level governance arrangements. The communication refers to the establishment of a 'civic dialogue'. Civil society organisations that 'exist permanently at Community level, . . . have authority to represent and act at European level . . ., have member organisations in most of the EU Member States [and] provide direct access to its member's expertise' (European Commission 2002: 2. Footnote 15).

In other words, the Commission is specifically taking into account the so-called Euro-Feds – Brussels-based umbrella organisations of nationally bound associations. Moreover, the Commission perceives the Euro-Feds as transmitters of expertise and as forums for discussion and dialogue. To a certain extent, the lobbying function of these umbrella organisations is also acknowledged. However, the communication lacks any reference to the social capital dimension of Brussels-based governance arrangements. Furthermore, the Commission is vague with respect to the problem of how to organise the flow of communication between the Euro-Feds and their nationally bound membership organisations. In sum, the communication lacks any reference to the vertical dimension of multi-level governance (Heinelt 2002).

2.3.3 Bridging of Concepts

Below we discuss (from a theoretical perspective) how the three different approaches and concepts – the third sector, social capital and civil society approaches – might contribute to the further development of multi-level governance as an analytical model as well as a normative concept. While doing so, we are confronted with the problem that multi-level governance is by no means a coherent approach and concept: it is used in different ways and for different purposes. As Bache and Flinders (2005) argue, there is a need for conceptual clarity with respect to the meaning and content of multi-level governance. As a starting point, Bache and Flinders (2005: 195) distinguish between multi-level governance as an analytical model and as a normative concept.

Current research primarily uses the concept of multi-level governance as an organising perspective and thus as an analytical tool in order to investigate how actors and processes of decision making are interrelated and to what extent there is an overlapping of policy networks at the various territorial levels. Supported by the results of numerous studies, there is indeed no doubt about the growing importance of multi-level interactions. Furthermore, as Bache and Flinders highlight, the common understanding of multi-level governance translates into a situation in which 'decision making at various territorial levels is characterised by the increased participation of non-state actors' (Bache and Flinders 2005: 197). However, the extent to which multi-level governance strengthens or endangers democratic legitimacy and accountability is quite unclear and under-researched. According to Bache and Flinders (2005: 195), 'multi-level governance is emerging as a normatively superior mode of allocating authority'. Simultaneously, there is a growing awareness of the implications of multi-level governance for democratic accountability. In particular, the devolution of state power to non-state actors including civil society organisations raises questions about the role of these actors and more specifically about their democratic legitimacy. In their résumé, Bache and Flinders pinpoint the weakness of the multi-level governance approach. They argue that it is useful for mapping 'how things interrelate' but falls short with respect to addressing the problem of legitimacy. In order to be viewed as a 'fully fledged' theory, multi-level governance 'needs to generate clearer expectations in relation to the influence of . . . non-state actors, as well as highlighting their mobilization and participation' (Bache and Flinders 2005: 204).

There are good reasons to argue that the three approaches – civil society, third sector and social capital – have the potential to contribute to the further improvement of multi-level governance as an analytical model and as a normative concept. As outlined above, the three approaches and the multi-level concept have been used quite ambiguously. The civil society, third sector and social capital concepts stand out from a normative perspective. At the same time, they are used as analytical tools and frames of reference to investigate (and express) the degree of civic-mindedness of societies under study. To a certain extent, the same holds true for the multi-level governance approach, which according to Bache and Flinders is used as an analytical model as well as a normative concept.

We take a closer look below at the normative and analytical contribution of the three approaches and assess the extent to which they can overcome the diagnosed weaknesses of the multi-level governance approach. More precisely, are these approaches able to generate clearer expectations in relation to the influence of non-state actors and, more specifically, civil society organisations involved in settings of multi-level governance? If so, how do they achieve this, and to what extent?

What is the added value of applying the third sector approach in studies investigating EU multi-level governance arrangements? As a starting point, studies should take into account whether, how and the extent to which third sector organisations are integrated or embedded in multi-level governance arrangements. The implications of studying multi-level governance with an eye on the third sector would be at least twofold. First, those policy fields and arenas have to be identified in which third sector organisations play a significant role. Second, an empirical test is needed to verify whether the participation of third sector organisations contributes normatively to an improvement in the accountability and democratic legitimacy of multi-level governance arrangements.

Against the background of third sector research, it can already be stated that the so-called core welfare domain (social and health services), the fields of leisure and sports activities and, depending on the country, education, research, arts and culture are policy arenas heavily populated by third sector organisations. Furthermore, it is already well-known that, depending on the policy traditions of the respective countries, there are decisive differences with respect to the integration of third sector organisations in processes of policy implementation and decision making. While the evolving field of new public management sheds light on the topic of third sector involvement in policy implementation, research investigating the role of third sector organisations as advocacy groups generally follows the tradition of well-established interest group research. Similar to interest group research in federalised countries, there is a need to investigate the vertical channels of communication in multi-level governance arrangements. Thus, the organisational set-up of third sector organisations at each territorial level, and particularly their affiliation with supra-regional or supra-national platforms, plays a decisive role in relation to the mapping of the opportunity structures of non-state actors in multi-level governance arrangements.

However, providing a picture of third sector organisations acting as service providers and interest groups at the various territorial levels does not contribute to a normative assessment of the contribution these organisations make to accountability and democratic legitimacy in a multi-level governance setting. According to the literature (for example, Evers and Laville 2004), third sector involvement in service delivery provides efficiency gains, as well as reductions in transaction costs and increases in civic-mindedness derived from volunteering. Moreover, it is said that, compared to public entities, they are closer to citizens because they are less formalised, and, in contrast to companies, profit making is not their prime incentive. In sum, from a theoretical point of view it makes sense to incorporate third sector organisations into welfare production. However, the question of efficiency and civic-mindedness gains remains open, requiring empirical verification.

But there are also good reasons to underline the importance of third sector organisations acting as pressure groups in multi-level governance arrangements. Generally, these organizations represent so-called weak interests that are not easily organised. Cosmopolitan policy entrepreneurs and favourable circumstances such as established channels of communication between the various territorial levels are necessary in order to facilitate the integration and incorporation of third sector organisations as lobbyists and pressure groups. However, there is little doubt that the policy community of third sector organisations has struggled with the well-known problems of pluralistic interest representation. Those organisations with access to resources and information are able to set up far more professionalised lobby structures compared to their 'resource poor' counterparts. As Bache and Flinders (2005: 205) argue:

participation does not equate power and the emergence of multi-level governance does not necessarily enhance the position of weaker social groups and may indeed concentrate power in the hands of those groups and actors with the necessary resources to operate most effectively in the context of complexity.

From a theoretical point of view, incorporation and integration of third sector organisations as pressure groups and policy entrepreneurs has the potential to bring policy making in multi-level governance arrangements closer to the people. However, this remains an empirical question. In many settings it is not clear to whom third sector organisations as pressure groups are accountable. Furthermore, third sector organisations in neo-corporatist arrangements suffer from a lack of legitimacy since they enjoy a privileged position granted by the state. Indeed, the incorporation of third sector organisations in multi-level governance arrangements might be due to strategic considerations. Faced with the dilemma that there is no way to 'negotiate' the democratic deficit in multi-level governance arrangements, third sector organisations might simply be used as a cloak of respectability to cover the deep-seated problem of a lack of democratic accountability.

From a theoretical standpoint, the social capital approach provides the opportunity to contribute to the discussion by drawing attention to the degree of civic-mindedness of selected societies as well as to the representativeness of those third sector organisations that are members of policy networks in multi-level governance arrangements and thus acting as pressure groups. According to Bache and Flinders (2005: 205), in multi-level governance arrangements there is a decisive need for 'new means . . . to connect citizens more effectively with the shifting locations of power'. They further emphasise that 'the diffusion of competencies and the changing patterns of participation demand additional mechanisms of accountability beyond those provided by representative institutions'. The social capital approach used as an analytical tool provides the know-how and the significant indicators for analysing the civic-mindedness of societies. Against this background, third sector organisations are not perceived as an alternative in service provision vis-à-vis the market and the state. On the contrary, besides informal networks and the family, third sector organisations provide the infrastructure for the accumulation and flourishing of social capital.

At least implicitly, there is a nexus between the degree and structure of the social capital of a selected country and the representativeness and accountability of its third sector. Building on a neo-Tocquevillian tradition of democratic theory, third sector organisations as voluntary associations provide important channels for societal integration and political participation, and as such they are characterised as being 'schools of democracy'. Unfortunately, the social capital approach focuses exclusively on the individual level of participation. Accordingly, it fails to take into account the embeddedness and thus the environment of the third or voluntary sector in which civic activity primarily takes place. However, there are significant differences between a pluralistic and a neo-corporatist setting for civic participation. Interest representation backed by third sector organisations operating in a pluralistic environment might be less powerful than interest representation by third sector organisations with a neo-corporatist background due to a lack of resources and professionalisation. In order to use the potential of the social capital approach for tackling the lack of accountability and legitimacy of multi-level governance arrangements, it is not sufficient simply to measure the degree and structure of social capital in a selected country. Further information is needed which addresses the way social capital is stabilised and represented by civic organisations. Theoretically, it makes a great difference whether membership in third sector organisations is compulsory, based on church or party affiliation or organised on a straightforward voluntary basis. Accordingly, it is important to know if the organisation is rich in social capital and represents citizens or if it enjoys a privileged position as a member of a neo-corporatist policy arrangement. In sum, the social capital approach provides avenues for facilitating third sector research that focuses primarily on organisations. By drawing on the results of social capital research, it might be possible to judge whether third sector organisations acting as pressure and advocacy groups in multi-level governance arrangements represent a legitimate and accountable voice of their constituency in the respective policy field.

Finally, there is the question of what the civil society approach might add to the further development and democratic underpinning of multi-level governance. As outlined earlier, civil society as an analytical concept has much in common with the third sector and the social capital approach. In sum, there is no additional or added value with respect to multi-level governance from an empirical point of view. However, there is a decisive need for further research in relation to theory development. As Bache and Flinders (2005: 205) argue, there is a need for 'new and innovative conduits between the public and the institutions involved in complex networks. In essence, this may involve a fundamental reappraisal of the meaning of democracy and the role of representative institutions within nation states'. In other words, the civil society approach faces the challenge of developing the bedrock and thus the democratic rationale and legitimisation for multi-level governance arrangements that are necessarily dependent on the involvement of third sector organisations that are backed and legitimised by social capital.

2.4 CONCLUSIONS

Comparing concepts of EU governance arrangements envisaged by the Commission and outlined in EU documents with those approaches and concepts favoured by the social science research community, we are confronted with a paradox. On the one hand, the Commission emphasises the meso-level, thus conceptualising 'civil society organisations' as corporate partners within processes of European policy making. On the other hand, social science research focuses almost exclusively on the micro-level of civic engagement and activity by relying on the social capital approach.

Against this background, we make a strong plea for the integration of the micro- and meso-level approaches linking the social capital concept with the third sector approach. This nexus might facilitate research on the vertical dimension of multi-level governance arrangements, whereas research conducted with the social capital concept primarily seeks to investigate the extent to which EU policy making is accepted and has an impact on European integration. Third sector research focusing on the organisational level provides the tools and techniques to follow those channels of vertical communication within associational groups or families of civil society organisations that are active at the national and sub-national levels in the various member states. As outlined above, EU (Commission) documents advance two main types of reason for the benefit of cooperation with civil society organisations. The first is closely linked to output legitimacy (that is, efficiency and effectiveness gains). The second, in sharp contrast, focuses on democratic theory ideas and input legitimacy. Indeed, due to the multi-functional character of civil society, organisations provide the opportunity to combine policy making with elements of participatory democracy that make them very attractive for any approach trying to strengthen multi-level democratic governance. However, until now there has been a paucity of research investigating the horizontal as well as the vertical dimension of European multi-level governance including civil society organisations.

NOTES

1. German original: 'Zivilgesellschaft meint damit einen spezifischen Bereich, einen gesellschaftlichen Raum, den Raum gesellschaftlicher Selbstorganisation zwischen Staat, Ökonomie und Privatheit, die Sphäre der Vereine, Zirkel, sozialen Beziehungen und Nichtregierungsorganisationen' (Kocka 2002: 16).
2. The so-called dark side of civic engagement and voluntary activity has not been addressed for some time. However, Putnam distinguishes between 'bridging' and 'bonding social capital', of which the latter does hinder societal integration. Those authors following the civil society approach have also become quite cautious about their judgement with respect to voluntary action.

REFERENCES

Anheier, H.K. (2005) *Nonprofit organizations: Theory, management, policy*, London: Routledge.
Anheier, H.K. and Kendall, J. (2002) *Third sector policy at the crossroads: An international nonprofit analysis*, London: Routledge.
Bache, I. and Flinders, M. (2005) 'Multi-level governance: Conclusions and implications' in I. Bache and M. Flinders (eds) *Multi-level governance*, Oxford: Oxford University Press, pp. 195–206.
Bauer, M. and Knöll, R. (2003) 'Die Methode der offenen Koordinierung: Zukunft europäischer Politikgestaltung oder schleichende Zentralisierung?' *Aus Politik und Zeitgeschichte* (B 01–02/2003), 33–8.
Benz, A. (2004) 'Einleitung: Governance – Modebegriff oder nützliches sozialwissenschaftliches Konzept' in A. Benz (ed.) *Governance: Regieren in komplexen Regelsystemen*, Wiesbaden: VS Verlag, pp. 11–29.
Berman, S. (1997) 'Civil society and the collapse of the Weimar Republic' *World Politics* 49 (3), 401–29.
Braun, S. (2001) 'Putnam und Bourdieu und das soziale Kapital in Deutschland: Der rhetorische Kurswert einer sozialwissenschaftlichen Kategorie' *Leviathan* (3), 337–54.
Dahl, Robert (1998) *On Democracy*, New Haven: Yale University Press.
Dahrendorf, R. (1991) 'Die gefährdete Civil Society' in K. Michalski (ed.) *Europa und die Civil Society: Castelgandolfo-Gespräche 1989*, Stuttgart: Klett-Cotta, pp. 247–63.
Delors, J. (2004) 'The European Union and the third sector' in A. Evers and J.-L. Laville (eds) *The third sector in Europe*, Cheltenham: Edward Elgar, pp. 206–15.
Dubiel, H. (1994) *Ungewissheit und Politik*, Frankfurt am Main: Suhrkamp.
Eising, R. and Kohler-Koch, B. (1999) *The transformation of governance in the European Union*, London: Routledge.
Etzioni, A. (1973) 'The third sector and domestic missions' *Public Administration Review* 33 (4), 314–23.
European Commission (1997) *Promoting the role of voluntary organizations and foundations in Europe* COM(1997)0241 final.
European Commission (2000) *Discussion Paper: The Commission and non-governmental organizations: Building a stronger partnership* COM(2000)11 final.
European Commission (2001) *European governance: A white paper* COM(2001)428 final.
European Commission (2002) *Towards a reinforced culture of consultation and dialogue: General principles and minimum standards for consultation of interested parties by the Commission: Communication from the Commission* COM(2002)704 final.
European Economic and Social Committee (1999) *The role and contribution of civil society organizations in the building of Europe* OJ C329, 17 November 1999.
Evers, A. and Laville, J.-L. (eds) (2004) *The third sector in Europe*, Cheltenham: Edward Elgar.
Farr, J. (2004) 'Social capital: A conceptual history' in *Political Theory* 32 (I), 6–33.
Filer Commission (Commission on Private Philanthropy and Public Needs) (1975) *Giving in America: Toward a stronger voluntary sector*, Washington DC: The Commission.

Flora, P. (ed.) (1986) *Growth to limits: The Western European welfare states since World War II*, Berlin: de Gruyter.
George, S. (2005) 'Multi-level governance and the European Union' in I. Bache and M. Flinders (eds) *Multi-level governance*, Oxford: Oxford University Press, pp. 107–26.
Habermas, J. (1992) *Faktizität und Geltung*, Frankfurt am Main: Suhrkamp.
Heinelt, H. (2002) 'Civic perspectives on a democratic transformation of the EU' in J. Grote and B. Gbikpi (eds) *Participatory governance: Political and societal implications*, Opladen: Leske und Budrich, pp. 97–120.
Heinelt, H. (2005) 'Konzeptionelle Überlegungen zur Entwicklung der Strukturfonds als kumulativer Politikprozess' in H. Heinelt, J. Lang, T. Malek and B. Reissert (eds) *Die Entwicklung der EU Strukturfonds als kumulativer Politikprozess*, Baden-Baden: Nomos, pp. 17–44.
Hooghe, L. (1996) 'Building a Europe with the regions: The changing role of the European Commission' in L. Hooghe (ed.) *Cohesion Policy and European Integration: Building Multi-Level Governance*, Oxford: Oxford University Press, pp. 89–126.
Jachtenfuchs, M. and Kohler-Koch, B. (2004) 'Governance in der Europäischen Union' in A. Benz (ed.) *Governance: Regieren in komplexen Regelsystemen*, Wiesbaden: VS Verlag, pp. 77–102.
Kersbergen, K.v. and Waarden, F.v. (2004) 'Politics and the transformation of governance: Issues of legitimacy, accountability, and governance in political science' *European Journal of Political Research* 43 (2), 143–71.
Klein, A. (2001) *Der Diskurs der Zivilgesellschaft*, Opladen: Leske und Budrich.
Kocka, J. (2002) 'Das Bürgertum als Träger von Zivilgesellschaft: Traditionslinien, Entwicklungen, Perspektiven' in Deutscher Bundestag (ed.) *Enquete-Kommission 'Zukunft des Bürgerschaftlichen Engagements', vol 2: Bürgerschaftliches Engagement und Zivilgesellschaft*, Opladen: Leske und Budrich, pp. 15–22.
Laffan, B. (2002) 'The European Commission: Promoting EU governance' in J. Grote and B. Gbikpi (eds) *Participatory governance: Political and societal implications*, Opladen: Leske und Budrich, pp. 121–40.
Pankoke, E. (2004) 'Voluntary associations and civic engagement: European traditions, discourses and perspectives for voluntary and intermediary networks' in A. Zimmer and E. Priller (eds) *Future of civil society*, Wiesbaden: VS Verlag, pp. 57–76.
Portes, A. (1998) 'Social capital: Its origin and application in modern sociology' *Annual Review of Sociology* 24 (1), 1–24.
Powell, F. and Guerin, D. (1997) *Civil society and social policy*, Dublin: A.A. Farmer.
Prakash, S. and Selle, P. (eds) (2004) *Investigating social capital: Comparative perspectives on civil society, participation and governance*, London: Sage.
Priller, E. and Zimmer, A. (2001) 'Wachstum und Wandel des dritten Sektors in Deutschland' in E. Priller and A. Zimmer (eds) *Der dritte Sektor international: Mehr Markt – weniger Staat?* Berlin: Edition Sigma, pp. 199–228.
Putnam, R.D. (1993) *Making democracy work: Civic traditions in modern Italy*, Princeton: Princeton University Press.
Putnam, R.D. (2000) *Bowling Alone: The collapse and revival of American communities*, New York: Simon and Schuster.
Putnam, R.D. (ed.) (2002) *Democracies in flux: The evolution of social capital in contemporary society*, Oxford: Oxford University Press.

Pye, L.W. (1972) 'Culture and political science: Problems in the evaluation of the concept of political culture' *Social Science Quarterly* 53 (2), 285–96.
Reichardt, S. (2004) 'Civil society: A concept for comparative historical research' in A. Zimmer and E. Priller (eds) *Future of civil society*, Wiesbaden: VS Verlag, pp. 35–56.
Sachsse, Ch. (1996) 'Verein, Verband und Wohlfahrtsstaat: Entstehung und Entwicklung der dualen Wohlfahrtspflege' in T. Rauschenbach, C. Sachsse and T. Olk (eds) *Von der Wertgemeinschaft zum Dienstleistungsunternehmen: Jugend- und Wohlfahrtsverbände im Umbruch*, Frankfurt am Main: Suhrkamp, pp. 123–49.
Sachsse, Ch. (2002) 'Traditionslinien bürgerschaftlichen Engagements in Deutschland' *Aus Politik und Zeitgeschichte* (B 9/2002), 3–5.
Scharpf, F.W. (1970) *Demokratietheorie zwischen Utopie und Anpassung*, Konstanz: Universitätsverlag.
Scharpf, F.W. (1999) *Regieren in Europa: Effektiv und demokratisch?* Frankfurt am Main: Campus.
Schmalz-Bruns, R. (1995) *Reflexive Demokratie*, Baden-Baden: Nomos.
Streeck, W. (1981) *Gewerkschaftliche Organisationsprobleme in der sozialstaatlichen Demokratie*, Königstein and Taunus: Athenäum.
Tarrow, S. (1996) 'Making social science work across space and time: A critical reflection on Robert Putnam's "Making democracy work"' *American Political Science Review* 90 (2), 389–97.
Taylor, C. (1991) 'Die Beschwörung der Civil Society' in K. Michalski (ed.) *Europa und die Civil Society: Castelgandolfo-Gespräche 1989*, Stuttgart: Klett-Cotta, pp. 52–81.
Thaa, W. (1996) *Die Wiedergeburt des Politischen: Zivilgesellschaft und Legitimitätskonflikt in den Revolutionen von 1989*, Opladen: Leske und Budrich.
Wolf, K.-D. (2002) 'Governance: Concepts' in J. Grote and B. Gbikpi (eds) *Participatory governance: Political and societal implications*, Opladen: Leske und Budrich, pp. 35–50.
Young, I.M. (2002) *Inclusion and democracy*, Oxford: Oxford University Press.
Zeitlin, J., Pochet, P. and Magnusson, L. (eds) (2005) *The open method of coordination in action: The European employment and social inclusion strategies*, Frankfurt am Main: Peter Lang.
Zimmer, A. (2004) 'Civil society organizations in central and Eastern European countries: Introduction and terminology' in A. Zimmer and E. Priller (eds) *Future of civil society*, Wiesbaden: VS Verlag, pp. 11–27.
Zimmer, A. and Sittermann, B. (2004) *Brussels civil society*, ISTR Conference Working Papers Series: www.istr.org/conferences/toronto/workingpapers/zimmer. annette.pdf, last access: 7 July 2007.

PART II

Bottom-up: civil society and voluntary associations

3. The associational impact on attitudes towards Europe: a tale of two cities

William A. Maloney and Jan W. van Deth

3.1 INTRODUCTION

The EU White Paper on Governance CEC, 2001, outlined the need to stimulate a more engaged and vibrant European civil society.[1] The policy-making process is to be made more open, transparent and participatory, and is to involve a wider range of actors from varying institutional and territorial levels – that is, from Eurogroups to local groups. The key aim is to 'bring citizens closer to the European Union and its institutions and to encourage them to engage more frequently with its institutions . . . [and] to stimulate initiatives by bodies engaged in the promotion of active and participatory citizenship' *Official Journal* 2004: 30/7–37/8). Sloat (2003: 130) cites a speech from Commissioner Prodi to the European Parliament in February 2000 in which he 'called for a civic participation in all stages of the policymaking process'.[2] The Commission believes that the legitimacy of the EU would be greatly enhanced through the encouragement of greater and more meaningful citizen involvement (CEC, 2004b: 12) – and it has idealistic (strong democracy-type – Barber, 1984) expectations. As Michalowitz (2004: 152) notes:

> the Commission demands a certain 'inner democracy' including the expectation of a civil society organisation to 'itself follow the principles of good governance'. The expectation is that groups should be open and internally democratic purely to enhance a thriving EU democracy. This requirement essentially means having transparency of internal decision-making processes and a guarantee that all members have the opportunity to have some input into a decision.[3]

In short, the EU has joined the emerging consensus that a revival of patterns of civic engagement and citizenship will compensate for the assumed deficiencies of modern democracies.

However, given much of the contemporary focus on the (alleged) associational impact on members, there is a paucity of research that actually links the citizen to the association, and of course the local association or local supporters, members, activists and/or volunteers[4] to EU institutions. This chapter seeks to make a contribution to that research gap by connecting the (local) organizational context in Germany and the UK (see below) to various attitudes towards Europe. The main questions driving our analysis, include: What types of organizations do European citizens join? Does associational type have any impact on the levels of attachment, confidence or engagement? How does the EU compare to other local, regional and national political (and other state) institutions? Of course, it is also interesting to note which citizens are active locally. The EU is likely to face the same problem of skewed participation and representation distortion (Verba et al., 1995) as national and region governments. This chapter also assesses the impact of organizational size and levels of membership involvement on attachment to, and interest in, the EU. In order to obtain empirically based answers to these questions, we present data from a comparative study of associational life in Aberdeen (UK) and Mannheim (Germany). This study includes extensive mapping of all voluntary associations in these two cities, and interviews with selected supporters.[5]

3.2 SETTING THE CONTEXTS[6]

This chapter is set in two contextual layers. First is the city/country where the associations and 'their' members are located. Second is the association universe itself. With regard to the first layer it is, of course, crucial to recognize that associational universes are located in specific cultural, economic, social and political contexts that impact on their shape, structure and modus operandi. Aberdeen and Mannheim share certain basic characteristics – both cities are: regional centres with populations in excess of 200 000; have a mixture of industry and services (locally and internationally focused) and have mutated from being industrially based to service-oriented cities; have a fully fledged educational system (with at least one university); have a major hospital; and have a cosmopolitan city centre. This is where the similarities dissipate. In Aberdeen unemployment is low (2.3 per cent); in Mannheim it is relatively high (10 per cent). The religious and ethnic dimensions are important and vary in both locales. Mannheim exhibits a greater degree of ethnic and religious heterogeneity – over 16 per cent of the Mannheim population is non-indigenous, whereas the Aberdeen figure is under 2 per cent. Aberdeen is a confessionally homogeneous city; Mannheim is divided between Protestantism (Diakonie) and Catholicism (Caritas). Such (religious and ethnic) heterogeneity may engender a denser and more diverse associational universe: that is, it may stimulate the founding of various organizations (from sports, recreation and leisure clubs to welfare-based groups) along ethnic or religious lines. (However, it is important to note that in both cities religious organizations make a significant contribution to associational vibrancy and are heavily involved in the delivery of welfare services.)

The democratic development of both countries has followed divergent paths and impacted differentially on the associational universes. The British transition has been relatively smooth compared to Germany. Most notably the National Socialism (1933–1945) interruption ended Germany's first democratic experiment and associative freedom. Following the collapse of the Nazi regime, the first 20 years of the *Bundesrepublik* were characterized by a largely passive German citizenry. The ethos and practice of the day was predominately *Ohne mich* (without me) (Scheuch 1993: 143). From the 1960s, voluntary activity in Germany recovered and membership and volunteer numbers began to rise. We are also dealing with a unitary and a federal state. The potential effects of federalism are complex. However, in short, federalism exerts strong pressures on associations to organize along the lines of the political system (Kriesi and Baglioni 2001). Finally, the British and German welfare regimes differ. The British regime has mutated (1948) from a system characterized by universal provision (a universal and egalitarian tax-funded British system that aims at equal but minimal care for all in need), to one increasingly predicated on neo-liberal tenets (since the late 1970s). Associations have become increasingly involved in the delivery of welfare services throughout this period. The German corporatist model is predicated on a generous insurance-based system that focuses on the (male) full-time employee who seeks to maintain differentials and traditionally recognized status ('insiders') and relegates redistribution to the margins by restricting coverage to wage earners only, not all citizens ('outsiders') (see Svallfors 1993: 91–93).

This very brief sketch of the first contextual layer has identified several areas where the local (and national) context might potentially impact on the associational universe. (In fact, given that in many areas the differences are large, the expectation is that these will have a significant impact on the structure and operation of these associational universes.) Notwithstanding this, the second contextual layer – the organizational universe – is the primary context for our analyses. Aberdeen and Mannheim were selected primarily to assess associations' social capital building potential and their impact on individual activity profiles and democratic and civic attitudes. These locales possess the full range and diversity of associative forms and activity: that is, covering the entire scope of organizational interests; formal and informal groups; a mixture of (large) groups that number members in thousands and (small) associations that count them on one hand; autocratically controlled associations as well as virtuous paragons of participatory democracy;

groups that bridge and/or bond, and so on. The aim is to assess the impact of organizations on members (that is, an assessment of the link between specific organizational characteristics and demographics and the attitudes, skills, social capital equipment and so on of activists and members). In short, the research context is predicated upon the assumption that these cities provide much variation of organizational types, albeit within varying historical, institutional and cultural settings.

3.3 MAPPING, THE RESEARCH DESIGN AND THE SECTORAL TAXONOMY

3.3.1 Mapping and the Research Design

The research design consists of a five-step approach. First, select an appropriate municipality. Second, make a comprehensive inventory of all associational life.[7] Third, mail a questionnaire to all mapped organizations. Fourth, select organizations for the members' survey. Fifth, interview supporters.

Detailed mapping was undertaken in Aberdeen and Mannheim in an attempt to identify as many voluntary associations as possible and to uncover a wide variety of organizational types in terms of relevant characteristics (such as size, internal participation structures, income, source of income, level of institutionalization). A large number of organizations were discovered in these areas: 5002 in Mannheim and 1907 in Aberdeen. These figures delivered high associational densities and impressive per capita ratios: 1 organization per 64 inhabitants in Mannheim. Previous German research reported much lower densities – 1:200 to 1:350 (Zimmer 1996: 94). In Aberdeen the ratio was 1:112 – higher than that reported by Hall (2001: 21) for a medium-size Scottish city (1:165). Such densities are partly explained by the mapping procedure that extended beyond official lists and directories to the less visible and less institutionalized segments of the associational universe. (Although as discussed above, the religious dimension in Mannheim may help to explain the situation there.) Once mapping was completed, all organizations received a short questionnaire which had two main aims: (i) to collect all relevant data about the major organizational features of associations; and (ii) to enable the identification of organizations for the membership survey. The organizational questionnaire sought information on: organizational demographics (organization name, year founded, membership and/or supporter size, staffing levels, income and expenditure); sources of income; main objectives; organizational structure (including management and internal democratic procedures); and external organizational activities (nature, type and frequency of contact with external bodies, organizational outputs – that is, service provision to 'clients', other membership services and benefits).

Following the organizational survey, a sample for the membership survey was drawn on the basis of an empirical typology along the dichotomized variables and dimensions below:

1. Vertical integration (part of peak organization)
2. Horizontal integration (summary measure of 'part of networks' and 'contact with other organizations')
3. Size (summary measure of membership levels, number of volunteers, number of clients and so on)
4. Degree of institutionalization
5. Political contacts
6. Financial strength
7. Source of finance.

The objective was to collect a sub-sample that contained all possible associational variations. A maximum of 20 organizations (if possible) were selected per issue area (for example, in Mannheim 20 of 103 children and youth organizations). At this stage the sample was casually drawn. Extensive data analysis was carried out on both the original total (103) and the sample (20), taking into account the organizational features mentioned above. In cases where the sample did not include all types and organizational variations, it was corrected. It should be noted that the sampling procedure focused less on general representivity, more on representation of variations. This procedure was repeated for all areas whenever the original total comprised more than 20 organizations. The final organizational samples for the study on activists and volunteers were 229 in Aberdeen and 238 in Mannheim.[8] Figure 3.1 provides a description of the various steps and the response rates.[9]

It is important to note that the methodology does not follow the regular design by selecting people randomly and asking them about their organizational experiences, but starts by locating individuals within their specific associational contexts. While there are many studies of voluntary organizations (usually focused on 'big players'), and numerous (representative) surveys of members and activists, few, if any, combined these approaches and tailored empirical data on organizations to that on individuals.

3.3.2 A Sectoral Taxonomy of Associative Activity

Associations are involved in numerous activities, concerns and tasks. In order to study different organizations systematically, the wide range of

MAPPING

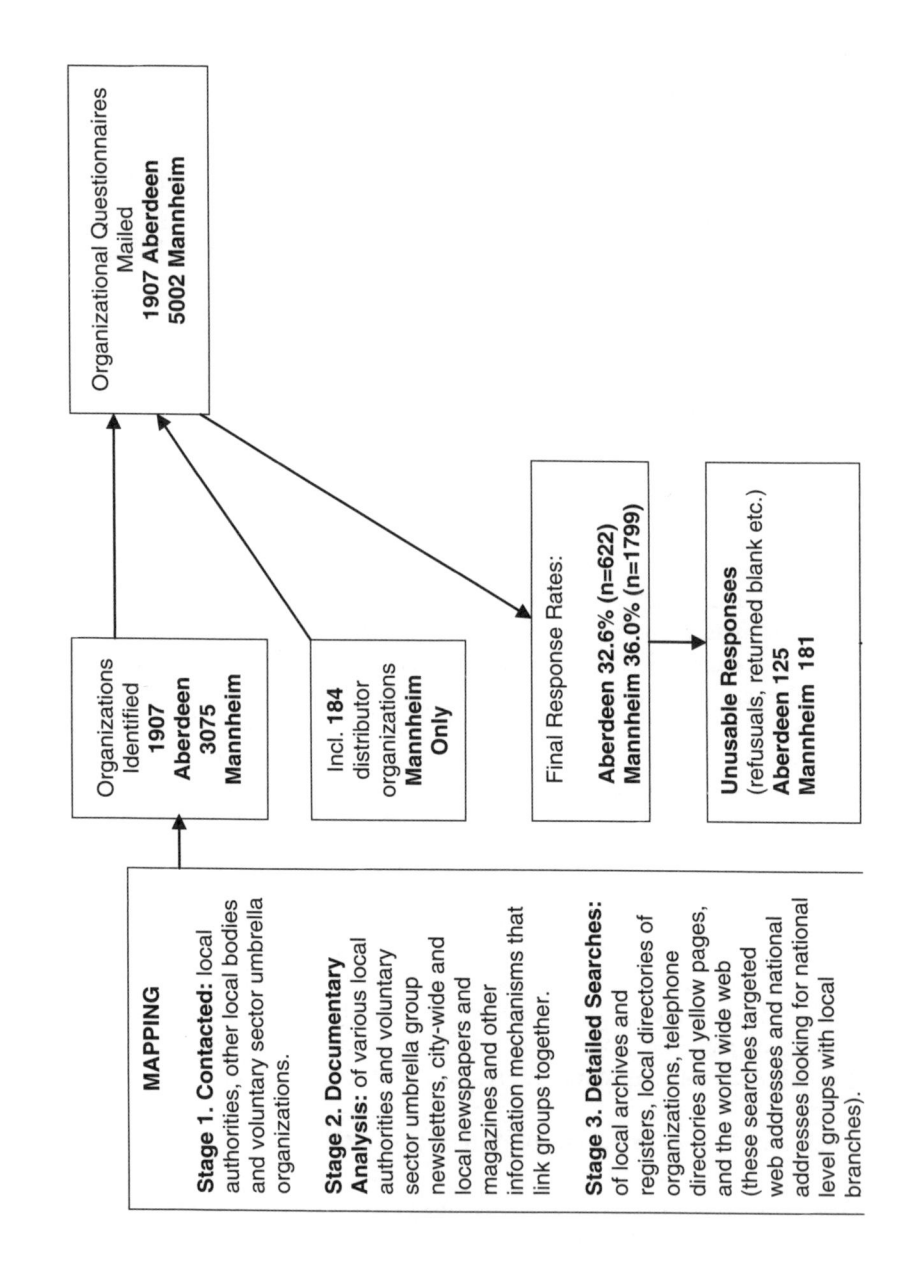

Stage 1. Contacted: local authorities, other local bodies and voluntary sector umbrella organizations.

Stage 2. Documentary Analysis: of various local authorities and voluntary sector umbrella group newsletters, city-wide and local newspapers and magazines and other information mechanisms that link groups together.

Stage 3. Detailed Searches: of local archives and registers, local directories of organizations, telephone directories and yellow pages, and the world wide web (these searches targeted web addresses and national addresses looking for national level groups with local branches).

↓

Organizations Identified
1907 Aberdeen
3075 Mannheim

Incl. **184** distributor organizations **Mannheim Only**

↓

Organizational Questionnaires Mailed
1907 Aberdeen
5002 Mannheim

↓

Final Response Rates:
Aberdeen 32.6% (n=622)
Mannheim 36.0% (n=1799)

→

Unusable Responses
(refusuals, returned blank etc.)
Aberdeen 125
Mannheim 181

50

Stage 4. Final Round-up and Validation: all schools, churches, community centres, community education centres, hospitals were telephoned. Final validation of mapping.

Stage 5. Contact to Distributor Organizations (Mannheim only): all potential distributors were contacted and asked to provide numbers of groups, agreement about distribution process.

Data on **497** organizations in Aberdeen

Data on **1618** organizations in Mannheim

Member Questionnaires Mailed:

Aberdeen: 3196 individuals from **229** organizations

Mannheim: 3497 individuals from **238** organizations

ABERDEEN
Data on **872** individual members

MANNHEIM
Data on **1868** individual members

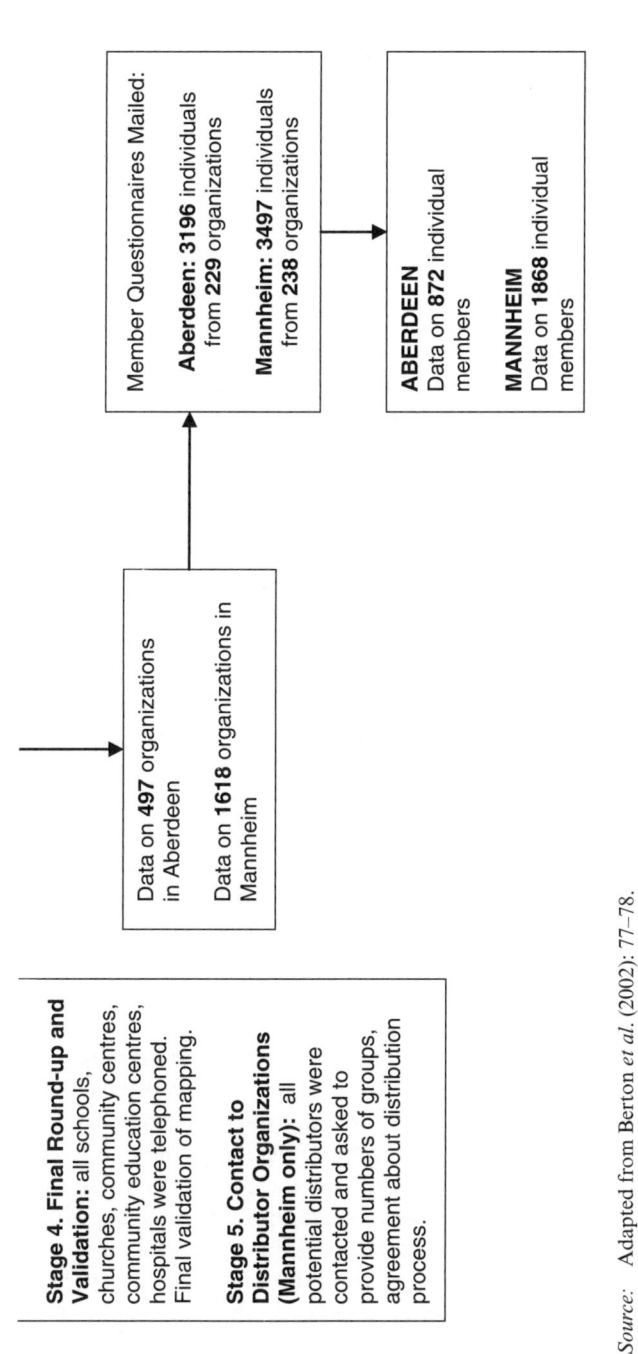

Source: Adapted from Berton et al. (2002): 77–78.

Figure 3.1 Methodology and response rates

issue concerns (37) in Aberdeen and Mannheim were taken as the bases for a taxonomy of different organizations. This empirically based taxonomy was developed through the application of three data reduction and scaling procedures – principal component analyses and two versions of hierarchical cluster analyses[10] – in order to establish stable groups or clusters of associative concerns. Analytically, the taxonomy is based upon the major issue concerns of organizations and is based on the assumption that the associational sector matters. While factor analytical devices are founded upon correlation between variables – that is, correlations between the diverse concerns mentioned by associations – the cluster and scaling methods are predicated on the relationship between the sector that the organizations indicated as 'the most important' and their various complementary activities. These last two methods apply this self-classification of organizations as the baseline for finding associations between associations. In order to apply this distinction, a data matrix was constructed that plotted the most important (core) against all other (complementary) concerns (for a full description of the methodology see Rossteutscher and van Deth 2002).[11] The three methods were applied to the organizational data in both cities and a similar number and types of concerns emerged across all methods.

The taxonomies provided by the various data-reduction techniques, however, resulted in a relatively substantial loss of cases. Apparently, associational life in the two cities is similarly structured, but several additions to the taxonomy are required in order to deal with 'real world' peculiarities. The most important extension of the taxonomy concerns religion. The inclusion of religion contradicts the empirical scaling results, but, from an empirical perspective, religion is an idiosyncratic (and interesting) case: 'wildly' oscillating around the universe of associational activities. In both cities, some 167 organizations claimed that religion was their most important concern. However, the factor and scaling analyses illustrated that there was no strong empirical basis for including religious organizations because the sectoral space occupied varied in each city. The apparent inconsistencies in the positioning of religious concerns reflect the fact that religion is a sub-unit of civil society that – to a very large extent – reproduces the diversity of civil society itself. Thus the wide range of complementary concerns is the major cause of religion's mutating position in the universe of associations. However, the religious sector was included as an additional and independent type for several reasons: its omnipresence; the important literature that posits religious organizations within civil society and provides a theoretical justification for its inclusion (for example, Banner 2002; Wuthnow 1996); and empirical research such as, Verba et al. (1995: 282f) which found that religious institutions were generators of civic skills and

Table 3.1 Distributions of associations and respondents among various types of associations in Aberdeen and Mannheim (percentages)

	Aberdeen		Mannheim	
	organizations	respondents	organizations	respondents
Family	3	1	8	9
Sports	18	11	16	9
Culture	5	5	12	7
Community concerns	1	0	4	8
Politics	2	1	3	3
'New' politics	1	0	1	1
General welfare	7	8	4	9
Group-specific welfare	13	14	9	10
Economic interest	2	–	4	3
Religion	15	29	9	5
Other concerns	36	31	31	37
N-valid:				
organizations	393	–	1202	–
responses	–	713	–	1677
N-total:				
organizations	497	–	1618	–
responses	–	872	–	1868

Note: The figures do not total to 100 per cent because of rounding.

engendered political involvement. The final composition of this taxonomy and the relative distribution of types across cities represent the fuzzy empirical 'real world' that is (unhelpfully) not neat and tidy (see Table 3.1).[12]

3.4 ASSOCIATIONS AND THEIR SUPPORTERS

As usual, the two contexts briefly indicated (cities and countries versus associations) are characterized by a number of similarities and differences. Although the structure of associational life in the two cities appears to have a lot in common, the actual distributions of different types of group varies widely (see Table 3.1). Looking at the distributions of the organizational types (columns 'organizations' in Table 3.1), Aberdeen has relatively more associations dealing with welfare and religion; in Mannheim there is a greater emphasis on families and children, and culture concerns. In broad terms, however, the distributions are similar, with approximately one-third of the associations dealing with 'other concerns', sport clubs being the

Table 3.2 Socio-demographic characteristics of respondents in Aberdeen and Mannheim (percentages and years)

	Aberdeen	Mannheim
Male (%)	40	53
Age (average)	55.0	52.5
Education (% Diploma or % Realschule)	51	51
Income (% under £20 000 or 48 000DM)	41	37
Employed (%)	47	52
Married/cohabiting (% living together)	68	72
Religion (% no religion)	16	16
Associational membership (average years)	13.7	14.2
Associational commitment (% very committed)	68	58
Most important association (% yes, this one)	74	72

largest category in both cities, and very few organizations engaging in politics or economic matters. Thus the general conclusion of 'minor' variations and broad similarities is also visible in the distributions of the supporters in various groups (see columns 'respondents' in Table 3.1).[13] These differences are clear in the religious sector: 29 per cent of the respondents in Aberdeen belong to a religious group, while the corresponding Mannheim figure is 5 per cent. Likewise, the relative numbers for respondents for other types of associations differ. In spite of the attempts to obtain a more even distribution of respondents of different types of associations (see Section 3.1), the figures presented in Table 3.1 show substantial differences between the types of associations in the two cities.

Table 3.2 summarizes some of the main socio-demographic characteristics of respondents in Aberdeen and Mannheim. A cursory glance at the figures clearly shows that the respondents in both cities are – on average – remarkably similar. People in their early to mid-50s comprise the majority of supporters, with a clear overrepresentation of women in Aberdeen. In the two cities, citizens with organizational affiliations have almost identical educational attainment levels and comparable incomes, and approximately half are employed. Two-thirds of the respondents are married or live with their partner and a large majority are religious. In both cities the average length of membership or affiliation to the association is about 14 years. Somewhat more people in Aberdeen are 'very committed' to the association than in Mannheim, but in both cities about three-quarters consider the actual organization the most important group they are affiliated to. Table 3.2 highlights a staggering congruity. The 'typical' supporter is easy to identify – not even the very apparent differences between the cities and the skewed distributions of types of associations (presented in Table 3.1) result in clear differences between respondents in Aberdeen and Mannheim!

If we compare some of these demographic findings with statistical information about the populations in Aberdeen and Mannheim, clear differences emerge. The average age of the population in Mannheim is 41.2 years, just over 23 per cent are non-religious (and those who are religious are largely divided between Protestantism and Catholicism), about half of them are employed (and unemployment is currently 10 per cent) and ethnic minorities comprise some 16 per cent of the population.[14] In Aberdeen, the corresponding figures are 38.5 years of age, 42.4 per cent non-religious (and for those who are religious, Protestantism is dominant), 55.4 per cent employed (unemployment is 2.3 per cent) and ethnic minorities are only 2 per cent of the population (Registrar General for Scotland 2003). These data show that while the cities differ substantially, the characteristics of our respondents in the voluntary sector are surprisingly similar. Neither the evident bias in the selection of associations and respondents, nor the apparent differences between the populations in Mannheim and Aberdeen are reflected in the socio-demographic characteristics of our supporters! Although it is too early to draw firm conclusions from these figures, the findings suggest that the first contextual layer – the two cities/countries – is less relevant for the characteristics of supporters than expected.

3.5 ATTITUDES TOWARDS EUROPE

Following the fashionable interpretations of the communitarian or social capital perspectives, we expect to find positive attitudes towards Europe among the supporters in both cities. However, it is unclear whether the relative position of European attitudes differs among the respondents, even if supporters are characterized by higher levels of attachment, engagement and confidence than the average citizen. How do attitudes towards Europe fit into this scheme? Does active involvement in voluntary associations imply positive attitudes towards Europe? The scant empirical evidence points in the opposite direction. For example, Erlach (2005: 199) reported a negative correlation between active involvement in voluntary associations and interest in international political affairs. In this section we assess attitudes towards Europe across three dimensions: (1) attachment – the relative importance of Europe compared to other areas, regions or countries; (2) political engagement – the level of political interest in Europe in contrast to other political systems; and (3) confidence – the level of trust in the European Union compared to other local, regional and nation political (and other state) institutions.

3.5.1 Attachment

People develop feelings of attachment towards various objects. How does 'Europe' rank when we asked our respondents to indicate their level of attachment? Figure 3.2 shows the mean levels in Aberdeen and Mannheim. It is immediately evident that supporters in the two cities differ significantly. Generally, the Scottish respondents exhibit high levels of attachments with all of the objects with the clear exception of Europe! In Mannheim there is a clear split between city, neighborhood and Germany on the one hand, and the other items including Europe on the other. In short, in both cities Europe comes out at, or close to, the bottom.

The difference between the level of attachment to Europe of supporters in Aberdeen and Mannheim is particularly noteworthy – one full point on an eleven-point scale. There are two basic explanations for this. First, geographical location. Aberdeen is very much on the European periphery and the physical distance from the political institutions may depress attachment levels. Second, UK citizens have consistently exhibited higher levels of

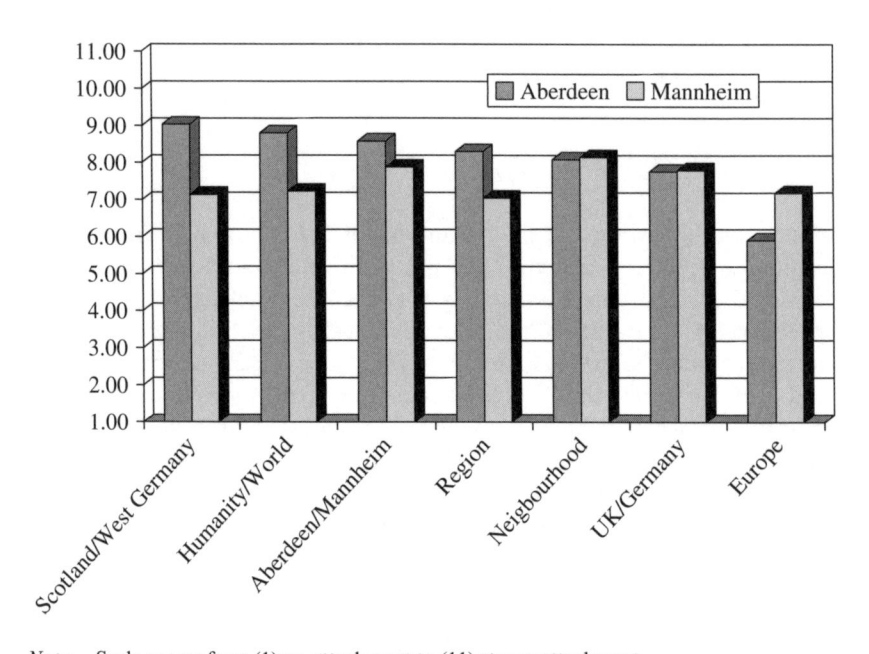

Note: Scale ranges from (1) no attachment to (11) strong attachment.

Figure 3.2 Attachments towards various objects among respondents in Aberdeen and Mannheim (means 1–11)

Euro-scepticism than their continental neighbours, including Germany. For example, European Commission data from 2000 found that 58 per cent of Germans were very/fairly attached to the EU, the UK figure was 37 per cent, and the 2001 UK population survey by Pattie *et al.* (2004: 35) reported that the mean attachment score of UK citizens to the EU was 3.96 (on an eleven-point scale). However, Pattie *et al.* (2004) found that UK citizens with organizational affiliations exhibited greater levels of attachment to the EU than the general population.

3.5.2 Political Engagement

Are there differences in average degrees of interest in European affairs among supporters? Figure 3.3 shows respondents' levels of political interest in Aberdeen and Mannheim in general, and for specific levels of the political system. Although the levels vary in both cities, the patterns are broadly similar: lowest interest in EU[15] and international politics and highest in local and national politics.[16] Given that our samples are drawn from the local associational universe it is not surprising that interest in local (and national) politics is relatively high. To these citizens, local and national

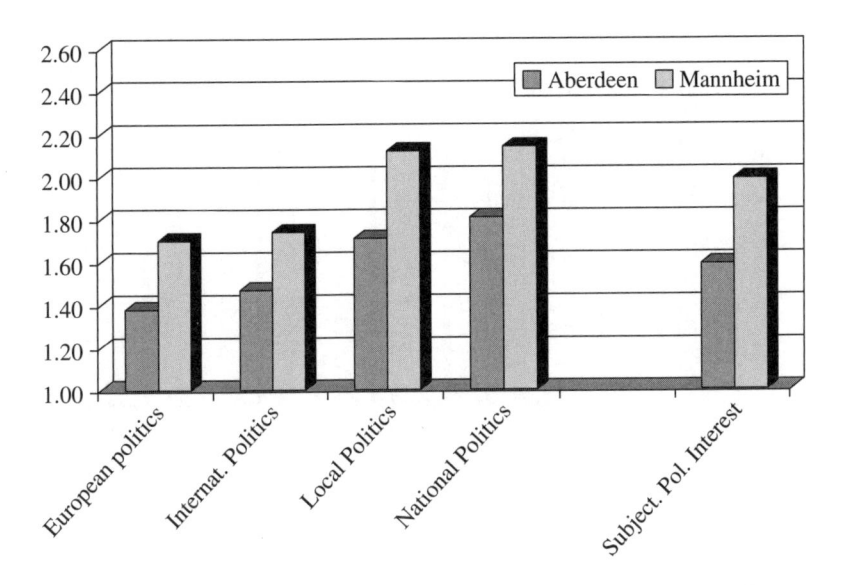

Note: Scale ranges from (1) strongly interested to (4) no interest at all. The scores have been reversed in the graph to facilitate understanding.

Figure 3.3 Interest in politics at various levels among respondents in Aberdeen and Mannheim (means 1–4; reversed scales)

policy making will be more visible and have greater relevance. In Aberdeen, interest in EU politics is very low, ranked below international politics. In fact the UK respondents are much less interested in politics generally than their German counterparts.

3.5.3 Political Confidence

Figure 3.4 shows the average levels of political confidence in various political institutions in Aberdeen and Mannheim. These levels appear to be marginally higher in almost all the institutions in Mannheim, but basically there is not much separating the cities and the patterns are broadly similar. In both locales the highest levels of confidence are shown in institutions of the executive branch (police, the courts, and to a somewhat lesser degree the civil service) and the lowest in clearly political institutions, parties, politicians and the European Union. All other political institutions show average levels of confidence. This pattern is replicated in Eurobarometer 62 (UK Report) (CEC 2004a) and the work of Pattie *et al.* (2004: 38): mean levels of confidence in the police were 6.29, the courts 5.5, the Scottish Parliament 3.67, politicians 3.26 and the EU 3.46 (eleven-point scale).

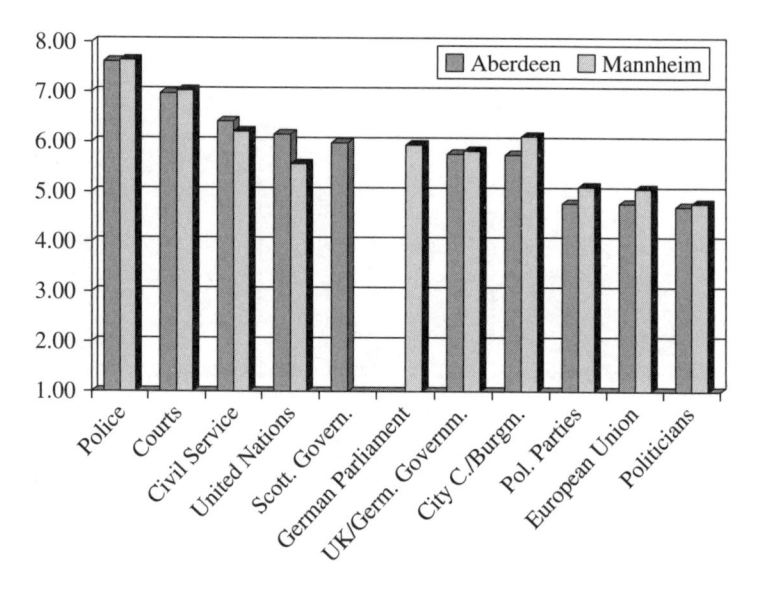

Note: Scale ranges from (1) no confidence to (11) very much confidence.

Figure 3.4 Confidence in political institutions among respondents in Aberdeen and Mannheim (means 1–11)

However, like the data on attachment, UK supporters exhibited higher confidence levels than the general population.

The levels of confidence in the domestic governing institutions in Germany and the UK are distinctive compared to those exhibited in political parties, politicians and the EU. The lowly position of the European Union is once again quite remarkable and is clearly a major cause for concern for European civil society architects. In fact, the results in Figures 3.2, 3.3 and 3.4 do not make particularly comfortable reading for these individuals: attachment, levels of interest and confidence are low. However, there is some comfort in the fact that supporters display higher levels of confidence than the general population. In addition to this, if one takes a more critical stance in the social capital debate, then relatively low levels of confidence in political office holders and parties can be presented as healthy for democracy – citizens should be attentive and critical. Of course, it is important that citizens maintain confidence in fundamental state and political institutions (courts, police, legislatures, the EU and so on).

3.6 A TYPOLOGY OF ATTITUDES TOWARDS EUROPE

The main characteristics of the three orientations towards Europe are summarized in the first part of Table 3.3. On all three descriptive measures it is clear that Mannheimers are more positive Europeans than Aberdonians. The average levels of attachment, interest and confidence in the European Union is higher in Germany. These findings underline the common sense expectation (noted above) that in Britain Euro-scepticism is more prevalent than in Europe generally. Moreover, the three orientations are clearly related to the individual level in a meaningful way (note the highly significant correlations in the second part of Table 3.3). Those who are more attached have higher levels of interest and trust in both cities – and vice versa.

The significant correlations presented in Table 3.3 suggest that we do not necessarily have to use all three indicators to characterize the orientations towards Europe. Since confidence is specified for the European Union as a political institution and attachment and interest refer to Europe in general, we construct a typology based on these last two indicators only. This typology of attachment and interest towards Europe is summarized in Figure 3.5.

The four-fold typology categorizes supporters according to their orientation towards Europe. The most positive respondents, who show both a high level of attachment and a high level of interest, are labelled *Committed*. The least positive – individuals who are neither attached nor interested in what is going on in Europe – are described as *Aloof*. Those that have a high level

Table 3.3 Attitudes towards Europe in Aberdeen and Mannheim (means and standard deviations)

	Aberdeen		Mannheim	
Interested in European politics (4–1)	2.62 (0.849)		2.30 (0.777)	
Feelings of attachment to Europe (1–11)	5.87 (2.972)		7.19 (2.495)	
Level of trust in the European Union (1–11)	4.76 (2.395)		5.06 (2.227)	
Pearson's Correlations	Interest	Attach	Interest	Attach
Feelings of attachment to Europe	−0.304***	–	−0.176***	–
Level of trust in the European Union	−0.264***	0.371***	−0.305***	0.157***

Note: *** significance p < 0.000.

		Interest in European politics	
		high (1–2)	low (3–4)
Attachment to Europe	high (7–11)	Committed	Attached
	low (1–6)	Interested	Aloof

Figure 3.5 A typology of attachments and interest towards Europe

of interest in European politics, but have low attachment are labelled *Interested*, and individuals who are more strongly attached to Europe, but have a low interest in European politics, are referred to as *Attached*.

Table 3.4 shows the distribution of the four types across Aberdeen and Mannheim. It is of little surprise given the evidence presented thus far (Figures 3.2 to 3.4 and Table 3.3) that the *Committed* are much more prevalent in Mannheim and the *Aloof* is the largest group in Aberdeen. In Mannheim, 43 per cent of the respondents can be characterized as *Committed*, while the corresponding figure is less than half in Aberdeen (21 per cent). In contrast, the distribution of the *Aloof* moves in the opposite direction: 36 per cent in Aberdeen and 22 per cent in Mannheim. The *Interested* and the *Attached* are roughly the same size in each city.

Table 3.4 *Distribution of types of European attachment (percentages)*

	Aberdeen	Mannheim
Committed	21	43
Attached	20	17
Interested	24	18
Aloof	36	22
N (100%)	801	1732

Note: The figures for Aberdeen do not total to 100 percent because of rounding.

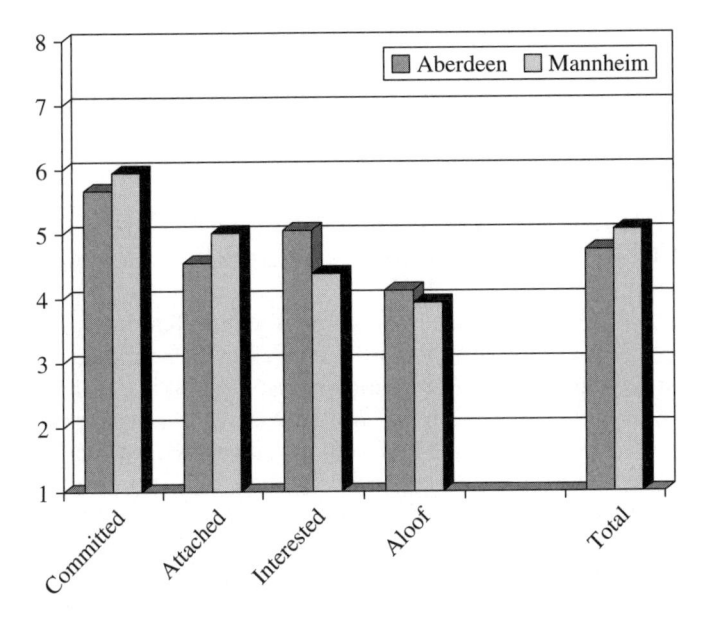

Figure 3.6 *Confidence in the European Union among different types (means)*

Before we turn to assess the impact of associational life on attitudes towards Europe we attempt to validate our typology by examining average levels of confidence in the European Union among the four categories of respondents. Obviously, we expect to find that the *Committed* exhibit greater levels of confidence than those in the *Aloof* category. The clear differences in the distributions of the four types in Aberdeen and Mannheim, however, might disturb this simple pattern. Figure 3.6 shows the mean levels of confidence in the European Union, and these findings corroborate the expectations about the two extreme types. In spite of all differences between Britain and Germany, the mean levels of confidence in the European Union are more or less similar among the *Committed* and *Aloof* in both cities. Differences appear when we look at the mixed categories, which reflect the different ways attachment and interest can be combined. The *Attached* in Mannheim have greater levels of confidence than their Aberdeen counterparts and the *Interested* in their own city. The *Interested* in Aberdeen show higher levels of confidence than their Mannheim peers and the *Attached* in their own city. It is interesting to note that the *Attached* in Mannheim and *Interested* in Aberdeen have confidence levels above the Aberdeen mean and at the German mean. Attachment in Mannheim drives greater levels of confidence, and interest in European politics in Aberdeen delivers on this measure. It shows that different mechanisms operate in discrete political and cultural settings and that there may not be a one-size-fits-all solution to increasing confidence in the European Union (across member states).

3.7 THE IMPACT OF ASSOCIATIONAL LIFE ON ATTITUDES TOWARDS EUROPE

Many social capital approaches stress the Tocquevillian interpretation of voluntary associations as 'schools of democracy'. Participation in these organizations enables citizens to improve their social skills, to develop prosocial values and norms and to get involved in various networks. Each of these factors is considered to be relevant for citizens' engagement and participation in democratic politics. In this section we focus on the possible impact associational activities have on political orientations. Since all our respondents belong to at least one association, we cannot analyse the impacts of associational activities in general. Instead, we focus on the question whether different associations have different consequences for attitudes towards Europe among their supporters.

Below we examine three dimensions of the associational universe that may have an impact on levels of European commitment or aloofness. Table 3.5 shows the distribution of the confidence categories (*Committed* to *Aloof*) across various associational types (for example, sport, culture, politics, religion). Do all associational types have the same impact on attachment towards Europe? Are members of political associations more or less likely to be more committed Europeans than say members of welfare groups? Or are members of religious organizations more or less likely to be more aloof Europeans than say members of new politics groups? In Table 3.6 we assess the impact of organizational size (measured in terms of membership levels). In small associations there are likely to be greater opportunities for face-to-face contact and hence individuals linked to these organizations should exhibit higher levels of social integration than those in large groups. Accordingly, the social capital model would predict that smaller more intimate associations[17] are more likely to generate higher levels of attachment and interest. What impact does organizational size have on attachment and interest? Finally, in Table 3.7, the different involvement patterns of supporters are examined.[18] Citizens that eschew involvement have fewer opportunities to develop political confidence and engagement and are likely to be more aloof than active participants. Thus to what extent do attachment patterns vary among respondents with different patterns of involvement?

3.7.1 Different Types of Associations

Do various associations have a differential impact on attachments towards Europe? In summary, the answer is yes (Table 3.5). There are clear differences in the patterns between Aberdeen and Mannheim. (It is of course no surprise that there are many more committed Europeanists in Mannheim than Aberdeen and considerably fewer aloofists.) In Aberdeen 'family', 'general welfare' and 'politics' groups have the greater levels of commitment and 'religious', 'culture', 'sports' and 'group-specific welfare' are the most aloof. In Mannheim, 'community concerns', 'politics' and 'general welfare' are heavily committed and 'new politics', 'religious' and 'family' are more aloof. It is interesting that in both cities religious groups are amongst the weakest identifiers with the European project and that there is a similar attitudinal division between 'general welfare' and 'group-specific welfare' organizations.

We might have expected that those groups concerned with politics in both cities would be the most committed Europeans. This is the case in Mannheim, but not in Aberdeen. It is also interesting to note that the 'new politics groups' in Mannheim are the most aloof. This is slightly surprising for two main reasons: (1) given the direct political content of much of the activities of these groups, we might expect political interest and attachment to be high; and (2) the European Union has been heavily involved in developing policy in areas such as the environment and human rights, and the Commission has been highly active in harmonizing much policy and regulation across Europe. Thus we might have expected 'new politics groups' to identify more closely with the EU. Of course, it could be the case that the rate of progress is too slow for many 'new politics groups', which would rather see more radical changes as opposed to negotiated and bargained incremental ones. In addition to this, there may be some anti-system

Table 3.5 Distributions of different types among various associations in Aberdeen and Mannheim (row percentages)

Aberdeen	Committed	Attached	Interested	Aloof	N (100%)
Family	43	29	–	29	7
Sports	22	25	16	37	73
Culture	18	15	27	39	33
Community concerns	–	–	50	50	2
Politics	33	–	44	22	9
'New' politics	–	–	–	–	–
General welfare	41	26	15	17	46
Group-specific welfare	18	30	16	36	89
Religion	17	19	23	40	192
Other concerns	18	16	29	37	200
Overall	20	20	23	36	651

Chi-Square: 21.148; df: 8; significance: 0.007 (Kruskal-Wallis Test)

Mannheim	Committed	Attached	Interested	Aloof	N (100%)
Family	34	22	14	31	140
Sports	32	20	18	29	139
Culture	41	24	17	18	122
Community concerns	53	14	20	13	123
Politics	59	14	16	10	49
'New' politics	38	–	25	38	8
General welfare	53	17	15	15	130
Group-specific welfare	36	14	21	29	151
Economic interest	36	14	21	29	48
Religion	32	20	15	33	75
Other concerns	45	18	18	19	573
Overall	43	18	18	22	1558

Chi-Square: 44.335; df: 10; significance: 0.000 (Kruskal-Wallis Test)

Note: The figures do not total to 100 percent because of rounding.

sentiment among 'new politics groups' that would see them distance themselves from all governing institutions.

3.7.2 Different Sizes of Associations

A second associational feature that might impact on orientations towards Europe is size. Do supporters of small and large associations have different attitudes towards Europe? Are these small and more intimate associations

Table 3.6 Distributions of different types among associations of various size in Aberdeen and Mannheim (row percentages)

Aberdeen	Committed	Attached	Interested	Aloof	N (100%)
no members	17	26	25	32	134
small (1–55)	20	24	21	35	149
medium (56–225)	24	14	28	34	148
large (>225)	17	19	22	42	158
overall	20	21	24	36	589

Chi-Square: 3.232; df: 3; significance: 0.357 (Kruskal-Wallis Test)

Mannheim	Committed	Attached	Interested	Aloof	N (100%)
no members	44	14	20	22	94
small (1–55)	47	14	17	22	430
medium (56–225)	43	17	18	23	471
large (>225)	45	18	17	20	347
overall	43	18	18	22	1342

Chi-Square: 1.193; df: 3; significance: 0.755 (Kruskal-Wallis Test)

more cosy sites for the generation of positive European attitudes? Or are larger associations that may be more likely to have wider political contacts and links (possibly even to the EU level) the most optimistic Europeans? If we look at the results in Table 3.6 we see that organizational size has no impact. There is little variation between groups with no members and the largest membership organizations. This is the case in both cities, but it is clearest in Mannheim: 47 per cent of those affiliated to small groups and 45 per cent of large groups are committed; and 22 per cent of small groups and 20 per cent of large groups are aloof.

3.7.3 Different Levels of Associational Engagement

Finally, in Table 3.7 we examine the impact of patterns of associational involvement. Do supporters who spend a lot of time in their organizations have different attitudes towards Europe? Is greater involvement generating greater levels of commitment? The findings here replicate those above on the associational size dimension. There is little variation between the inactive and the super-active in both cities. Once again the variations in Mannheim are narrow, but they are not particularly large in Aberdeen either: 47 per cent of those who participate less than one hour per month in organizations in Mannheim are committed, while the corresponding figure for the super-active (20+ hours) is 46 per cent. In

Table 3.7   Distributions of different types among various levels of associational involvement in Aberdeen and Mannheim (row percentages)

Aberdeen	Committed	Attached	Interested	Aloof	N (100%)
less than 1 hour	17	15	24	43	46
1–4 hours	23	25	21	30	183
5–10 hours	21	19	21	40	224
11–20 hours	20	18	30	32	181
more than 20 hours	21	21	21	37	158
overall	21	20	23	36	792

Chi-Square: 5.606; df: 4; significance: 0.231 (Kruskal-Wallis Test)

Mannheim	Committed	Attached	Interested	Aloof	N (100%)
less than 1 hour	47	16	17	20	159
1–4 hours	44	14	20	22	413
5–10 hours	41	19	17	23	485
11–20 hours	41	17	19	23	366
more than 20 hours	46	19	15	19	298
overall	43	17	18	22	1721

Chi-Square: 4.289; df: 4; significance: 0.368 (Kruskal-Wallis Test)

Aberdeen 17 per cent of the least active and 21 per cent of the most active are committed.

3.8   CONCLUSIONS

In this chapter we have presented empirical information about supporters of voluntary associations in Aberdeen and Mannheim. In spite of the obvious differences between these two cities and the peculiarities of the two data collection procedures, we find remarkable similarities between the respondents in Scotland and Germany. The 'typical supporter, member, activist or volunteer' is about 52–55 years old, married, has a middle-level education and income, and has been active in the groups concerned for about 14 years. These characteristics deviate clearly from the 'typical citizen' in each city. Apparently, being involved in voluntary activities is related to a specific category of the population – irrespective of the specific circumstances and traditions in Aberdeen and Mannheim. The EU faces the same enduring problem of skewed participation as national governments. It will be a significant challenge to widen participation and involvement to groups of citizens that have hitherto been uninvolved.

In a second step, we analysed the main attitudes of supporters towards Europe. We developed a typology of attachment and found that the German respondents were more pro-European than their British counterparts – something that accords with the commonplace notion that the British are more Euro-sceptic than many of their European neighbours. Beyond this we examined the impact of associational type, size and involvement levels. The results were clear. Associational size and levels of involvement were irrelevant. However, associational type mattered. In Aberdeen, family and general welfare groups were the most committed, religious, culture, sports and group-specific welfare were the least. The pattern in Mannheim showed some similarity, but not symmetry – community concerns, general welfare and politics groups being the most enthusiastic and new politics and religious groups having the weakest attachments.

In conclusion, although we concentrated on differences and similarities between supporters, we have not compared the findings for these activists with information about people who are not involved in any voluntary associations in any detailed or systematic way. Nevertheless, the tentative conclusion is that it is the type of group, not the local context, the level of involvement or size, that matters.

NOTES

1. The Commission perceives civil society as including: 'trade unions and employers' organisations ("social partners"); non-governmental organisations; professional associations; charities; grass-roots organisations; organisations that involve citizens in local and municipal life with a particular contribution from churches and religious communities' (CEC 2001; see also OJ C329, 17 November 99: 30).
2. However, Reilly (2004: 140, 145) notes that concerns were voiced in Germany and the UK, 'about the democratic credentials that civil society actors could bring to the practice of governance'. Some German Länder (Baden-Württemberg, Bavaria and Saxony) raised doubts about the 'democratically legitimate representativeness' of non-elected bodies, while UK local government associations were concerned about the possible usurpation of their own 'legitimate democratic mandate'. In short, these bodies argued that it was more important to include local and regional government organizations than many civil society groups.
3. Interestingly, Michalowitz (2004) cites Warleigh's study of non-governmental organizations (NGOs) active at the EU level which found that most groups that were potential civil society agents (as envisaged by the Commission) were wanting in terms of their internal democratic procedures. Warleigh (2001: 635) argued that the 'internal governance' of many NGOs 'is far too elitist to allow supporters a role in shaping policies, campaigns and strategies, even at one remove. Moreover, and more disconcertingly, it appears clear that most NGO supporters do not actually want to undertake such a role' (quoted in Michalowitz, 2004: 155).
4. Hereinafter abbreviated to 'supporters'.

5. This study was developed as part of the international 'Citizenship, Involvement, Democracy' project (see www.mzes.uni-mannheim.de/projekte/cid and Maloney and Rossteutscher (2005) for further information). The financial support for this research was provided by the Anglo-German Foundation for the Study of Industrial Society. Furthermore, we would especially like to thank Sigrid Rossteutscher, Marina Berton and Linda Stevenson for organizing much of the fieldwork and data coding.
6. Sections '3.2 Setting the Contexts' and '3.3 Mapping, the Research and Design and the Sectorial Taxonomy' draw heavily from Maloney et al. (2008).
7. To be included in our samples organizations had to be: (1) independent of government and self-governing (we included organizations that received government patronage – for example, grants, subsidies or other financial support – but decision making and control had to remain internal); (2) Not-profit-distributing and primarily non-business (we included voluntary associations of businesses – for example, Chambers of Commerce, Business Federation); (3) voluntary – they should be sustained by voluntary citizen involvement and voluntary philanthropic contributions: there should be absolutely no compulsion; and (4) visible – for example, having a name and being in existence for at least a few months. Adapted from Kendall and Knapp (1996: 18).
8. The decision on the number of questionnaires mailed to each association was partly driven by group response: if a selected group said they had (or we saw from our organizational survey data that they had) five members then we sent them five questionnaires; the maximum mailed to any group was 25. Where a group agreed to participate in the second stage of our project but did not indicate the number of questionnaires it would like to receive – and our organizational survey data showed that they had more than 25 members – we mailed 25 to it.
9. Clearly we had practical difficulties in calculating an unequivocal n and response rate because while we tried to check as rigorously as possible we could not be categorical that the questionnaires mailed to organizations were distributed by the local organizer (such as Chair, Secretary), or whether this individual distributed some or all of the questionnaires. There was no way around this problem because the groups would not provide us with the names and addresses of their members for confidentiality and anonymity reasons.
10. An additional method – MDS (multi-dimensional scaling) – was used in the case of Mannheim.
11. Clearly, the key question is: Can we use this comparison of different methods of data reduction for the construction of a meaningful taxonomy of voluntary associations? As there is no clear standard guide concerning 'the' proper method, we applied three discrete criteria to select common aspects of the various solutions: (1) stability across methods (used as a starting point for the construction) – only those dimensions or types of concerns were selected that were prevalent across all three analytical steps; (2) unambiguity of cluster or group composition: items such as 'youth' were excluded from the taxonomy, because in some solutions it is part of the 'family' type, while in others it grouped together with certain leisure activities; and (3) equivalence across cities: keeping dimensions or types that emerge in all cities, but permitting the composition of items to vary between cities. The result is a taxonomy of substantively equivalent types from non-identical items.
12. It should be noted that the taxonomy could be challenged because of its sub-optimal use of available cases or the limited number of cases in specific categories. However, we do not perceive the exclusions to be highly problematic. The main aim of this taxonomy is to reduce and/or consolidate an abundance of information and to identify fewer dimensions that structure the civil society domain. The taxonomy is perfectly well-equipped for this task: it provides a wide enough range of organisational concerns.
13. The members, activists and volunteers that returned our questionnaire are called 'respondents' here in order to avoid any confusion about the actual activities, levels of involvement or formal positions of these persons.
14. See the official statistics published by the city of Mannheim on: www.mannheim.de (last access: 20 March 2005).

15. Pattie *et al.*'s (2004: 229) UK population survey also reported the lowest levels of interest in the EU (36 per cent) and the highest in national (58 per cent) and local politics (43 per cent).
16. Notice that the responses to these questions on political interest are scored from '1. very interested' to '4. not interested at all' and so a higher score means a lower level of interest. In Figure 3.3 these scores are reversed in order to facilitate visual inspection of the graphical presentation.
17. The size of the organization is measured here by its exact number of members. In Aberdeen, about 24 per cent of the respondents belonged to associations with no members; the figure in Mannheim was seven per cent. These groups had supporters and volunteeers, they were not groups with no active or involved citizens. For the remaining cases, the associations were categorized in about three equal groups in the two cities: small associations (1–55 members), medium association (56–225 members) and associations with more than 225 members. Apart from the number of organizations with no members, the similarities between the distributions in the two cities are striking (i.e. the borders of 55 and 225 establish a similar cutting-off point in both cities).
18. The level of involvement is measured straightforwardly by asking the respondents to indicate how many hours per month they commit to the association: less than one hour, 1–4 hours, 5–10 hours, 11–20 hours, more than 20 hours. The distributions for Aberdeen and Mannheim are virtually identical, with only slightly more people in Aberdeen spending less than one hour (9 per cent) than in Mannheim (6 per cent).

REFERENCES

Banner, M. (2002) 'Christianity and civil society', in S. Chambers and W. Kymlicka (eds) *Alternative conceptions of civil society*, Princeton, Oxford: Princeton University Press, pp. 113–30.
Barber, B. (1984) *Strong democracy*, Berkeley: University of California Press.
Berton, M., Maloney, W.A., Rossteutscher, S., Stevenson, L. and van Deth, J.W. (2002) Unpublished End of Award Report: *Welfare through organisations: A comparative analysis of British and German associational life*, Anglo-German Foundation for the Study of Industrial Society.
CEC (2001) *European governance: A white paper*, 25 July 2001 COM(2001) 428 final, Brussels: CEC.
CEC, Commission of the European Communities (2004a) *Eurobarometer 62 National Report, United Kingdom*, Brussels: CEC.
CEC (2004b) *Report on European Governance (2003–2004)* (Commission staff working document), 22 September 2004 SEC(2004) 1153, Brussels: CEC.
Erlach, E. von (2005) *Aktivierung oder Apathie? Eine empirische Analyse zu den Zusammenhängen zwischen der Mitgliedschaft in Freiwilligenorganisationen und politischem Engagement in der Schweiz*, Dissertation, Bern: University of Bern.
Hall, P. (2001) 'Sozialkapital in Grossbritannien', in R.D. Putnam (ed.) *Gesellschaft und Gemeinsinn*, Gütersloh: Bertelsmann, pp. 45–113.
Kendall, J. and Knapp, M. (1996) *The voluntary sector in the UK*, Manchester: Manchester University Press.
Kriesi, H. and Baglioni, S. (2001) 'Putting local associations into their context', paper presented at the *ECPR General Conference*, Canterbury, UK, September 2001.
Maloney, W. and Rossteutscher, R. (2005) 'Welfare through organizations', in

S.Rossteutscher (ed.) *Democracy and the role of associations: Political, organizational, and social contexts*, London: Routledge, pp. 89–112.

Maloney, W.A., van Deth, J.W. and Rossteutscher, S. (2008) 'Civic orientations: Does associational type matter?' *Political Studies*, 56(2).

Michalowitz, I. (2004) 'Analysing structured paths of lobbying behaviour: Why discussing the involvement of "Civil Society" does not solve the EU's democratic deficit' *European Integration* 26 (2), 145–70.

Official Journal of the European Communities (1999) 'Opinion of the Economic and Social Committee on "The role and contribution of civil society organisations in the building of Europe"', 17 November, C329/30.

Official Journal of the European Union (2004) 'Council decision of 26 January 2004 establishing a community action programme to promote active European citizenship (civic participation)' 4 February 2004/100/EC.

Pattie, C., Seyd, P. and Whiteley, P. (2004) *Citizenship in Britain: Values, participation and democracy*, Cambridge: Cambridge University Press.

Registrar General for Scotland (2003) *Scotland's Census 2001: Key statistics for council areas and health board areas Scotland*, Edinburgh: General Registrar Office for Scotland.

Reilly, A. (2004) ' "Governance": Agreement and divergence in responses to the EU White Paper' *Regional and Federal Studies* 14 (1), 136–56.

Rossteutscher, S. and van Deth, J.W. (2002) *Associations between associations: The structure of the voluntary association sector*, MZES working paper 56, Mannheim: Mannheim Centre for European Social Research.

Scheuch, E.K. (1993) 'Vereine als Teil der Privatgesellschaft', in H. Best (ed.) *Vereine in Deutschland: Vom Geheimbund zur freien gesellschaftlichen Organization*, Bonn: Informationszentrum Sozialwissenschaften, pp. 143–207.

Sloat, A. (2003) 'The preparation of the governance White Paper' *Politics* 23 (2), 128–36.

Svallfors, S. (1993) 'Policy regimes and attitudes to inequality: A comparison of three European nations', in T.P. Boje and S.E. Olsson Hort (eds) *Scandinavia in a new Europe*, Oslo: Scandinavian University Press, pp. 87–133.

Verba, S., Schlozman, K.L. and Brady, H.E. (1995) *Voice and equality: Civic voluntarism in American politics*, Cambridge Mass: Harvard University Press.

Warleigh, A. (2001) ' "Europeanizing" civil society: NGOs as agents of political socialization', *Journal of Common Market Studies* 39 (4): 619–39.

Wuthnow, R. (1996) *Christianity and civil society*, Valley Forge: Trinity Press.

Zimmer, A. (1996) *Vereine: Basiselemente der Demokratie*, Opladen: Leske and Budrich.

4. The political opportunity structure for civil society organisations in a multilevel context: social movement organisations and the European Union
Marc Hooghe

4.1 INTRODUCTION

In the White Paper on European Governance (Commission of the European Communities 2001) the European Commission argues for a stronger involvement of civil society organisations in the European decision-making process. The Commission considers these associations as important partners in its effort to develop open and transparent governance procedures at the European level. The European Commission wants to achieve this goal by providing more access and participation opportunities for non-governmental organisations (NGOs). It is hoped not only that these opportunities will increase the quality and legitimacy of European decision making, but also that they will contribute to the creation of a truly European civil society. Basically, the European Commission follows a top-down method of reasoning: it is expected that the incentives provided by the political system will result in the flourishing of civil society organisations at the European level. Various authors have questioned whether the European Union is likely to achieve this goal, or whether the intentions in the White Paper should be considered as mere window dressing that will not change the elitist character of European interest mediation practices (Armstrong 2002; Magnette 2003; Tsakatika 2005). Nevertheless, from a theoretical perspective, the top-down perspective used by the Commission is more than plausible. In the field of social movement studies, it is generally expected that opportunities created by the political system will have major consequences for the development of social movement organisations. Since the 1990s, this 'political opportunity structure' approach (or POS) has become one of the dominant approaches in the study of social movements. Thus far, however, the POS approach has never been combined systematically with the study of multilevel political systems. From a theoretical point of view, multilevel systems like the European Union should provide an ideal setting for the development of social movement organisations since they offer a multitude of access points for social movement organisations wishing to influence government policy (Marks and McAdam 1996; Imig and Tarrow 2001b).

In this chapter we want to explore how the theory of political opportunity structures can be applied in a multilevel context. This should allow us not only to assess in a more theoretically informed manner whether the strategy of the White Paper could be applied successfully, but also to provide a unique testing ground for the validity of this theoretical approach itself. To ascertain how social movement organisations react and develop in a multilevel setting, we rely on consideration of civil society at the European level but we also take into consideration historical evidence about the relation between the environmental movement and the creation of a federal system in Belgium and the development of an environmental policy at the UN level.

4.2 THE POLITICAL OPPORTUNITY STRUCTURE APPROACH

Since the development of the political process model (McAdam 1982), a remarkable consensus has emerged among social movement scholars about the importance of characteristics of the political environment for the development and success of social movement organisations (Davis et al. 2005). The opportunities created by the political system are thought to determine to a large extent whether or not social movements will be able to establish themselves as important collective actors in the political decision-making process. The introduction of the concept 'political opportunity structure' can be considered as an important breakthrough in the study of social movements, because it allowed scholars to get rid of the idea that there would be something like a direct and automatic relation between social concerns and the emergence of social movement organisations addressing these concerns. The absence of this relation can be explained partly by invoking various intermediary variables, and the set of opportunities created by the political system is one of the most important of these variables. The introduction of the POS concept basically amounts to a reversal of the causal logic in the study of social movements. Instead of using a bottom-up approach, by assessing how social movement organisations express feelings of discontent among the population, this line of research relies on a top-down approach, studying what kind of political system offers most opportunities for the development of social movement organisations (McAdam, McCarthy and Zald 1996).

A basic problem with this approach, however, is that various scholars developed widely differing definitions of the POS concept, thus rendering it difficult to use in an unequivocal manner in research. While originally the concept was used in a quite narrow political sense, some authors systematically widened its use so that there is a clear danger of it losing any specific meaning. In part of the literature, cultural and social variables can be grouped just as well under this label of a 'political' opportunity structure. To avoid such broad definitions in this paper, we will restrict ourselves to a rather conventional interpretation of the 'political opportunity structure' (POS), limiting ourselves to elements that are inherent to the political system as such.

Despite these shortcomings, it is clear that the concept of a political opportunity structure offers an important tool to study in a systematic manner the relationship between social movement organisations and political structures. The concept allows us to operationalise the claim already made by Sidney Tarrow (1998) that the development of social movement organisations tends to mirror the process of nation and state building, as social movements respond to new opportunities being created by institutional transformations. If this is the case, the ongoing process of Europeanisation should also have major consequences for the structure of social movements in Europe (Imig and Tarrow 2001a). Thinking in terms of a political opportunity structure also allows us to predict the most likely outcomes of structural transformation processes. For example, it has been argued that a weak state structure, where competences and authorities are divided among various government agencies and structures, offers a positive environment for the development of social movement organisations. If the state structure allows for multiple points of entry into the decision-making process, this would render it relatively easy for oppositional actors to become integrated in the political process (Kriesi *et al.* 1992). A federal system like Germany is usually seen therefore as more conducive for the development of a flourishing social movement sector than a strictly centralised system like France. In the 1970s and 1980s, for example, the environmental movement in Germany clearly had more opportunities to influence government policy than it had in France, and this strengthened the appeal of the German green movement (Koopmans 1993).

While the POS concept thus far has been used successfully to compare various countries and to rank their openness to oppositional actors, it is striking to observe that the idea of multilevel governance has never been fully integrated into this approach, despite some attempts to arrive at such a synthesis in the mid-1990s (Tarrow 1995; Marks and McAdam 1996). This lack of a clear connection between both theoretical approaches is remarkable because at first sight multilevel governance offers an ideal testing ground for the POS approach. Multilevel governance is characterised by a loose form of coordination and cooperation between various levels of government, mostly in the absence of a clear and well-defined hierarchical relation between the various levels (Hooghe and Marks 2001). The POS concept predicts clearly that such an open and divided political system should lead to a proliferation of oppositional groups, taking advantage of the availability of multiple points of access to the political decision-making process.

The European Union quite clearly fits this definition: the EU, more than any other political system, can be considered as a weak, extended, multi-level and therefore theoretically open political system (Hix 1999; Hooghe and Marks 2001). Decision making is the result of a complicated interaction process between the European Parliament, the Commission and the Council, while the European Union also has a strong and well-established system of judicial review. All of these decision-making bodies, in principle, are accessible for civil society organisations wishing to influence European decision making. To complicate matters even further, it has been shown that EU decision making can be targeted at various levels simultaneously. While, for example, some interest groups will contact their national Members of the European Parliament, others will lobby their own national government, in an effort to influence its point of view during the Council meetings (Rucht 2001; Beyers 2002). The system of multilevel governance that has emerged as a result of European integration, therefore, should lead to a very conducive environment for civil society organisations that are confronted with a host of new opportunities to influence decision making at a European level.

And yet, the available evidence thus far suggests that the availability of all these opportunities has only led to a very specific response among social movements. First, professional advocacy groups and European federations of national interest groups seem to flourish quite abundantly, and indeed organisations of this kind are closely involved in various European concertation and decision-making procedures (Mazey and Richardson 1993; Marks *et al.* 1996; Greenwood 2003; Skocpol 2004). Often, however, these policy networks are perceived as elitist and closed, and in this regard they can hardly be considered as an asset for the democratic legitimacy of the European Union (Armstrong 2002). Second, national social movement organisations have adapted to the growing influence and impact of European decision making by adopting a European action repertoire, for example, by staging European campaigns or by organising demonstrations before the buildings of the European institutions (Imig and Tarrow 2001c). These changes in the action repertoire, however, do not seem to affect the organisational structure of social movement organisations that remain firmly entrenched in their own nation-state.

Contrary to expectations, therefore, the political opportunity structure provided by the European Union does not seem to have led to the creation of truly European social movements with a mass-membership base (Delanty 1997). This does not imply, of course, that there is not an organised civil society at the European level. It does mean, however, that this 'civil society' is dominated by a very specific kind of social movement organisation, which is the highly professionalised and predominantly economic interest group (Armstrong 2002; Smismans 2003).

The fact that there are very few mass-membership social movement organisations at the European level poses a challenge for the expectations derived from the POS concept. Apparently, there are important variations in the way the social movement sector reacts to changes in the political opportunity structure. An opening up of the political opportunity structure does not automatically lead to a flourishing civil society, as some authors suggest. Despite the fact that the European Union, by itself, offers an open and conducive environment for collective actors to emerge, this clearly should be seen as a necessary but not as a sufficient condition for such a proliferation to occur. Despite the fact that in numerous areas (environment, labour, equal rights, traffic, . . .) there is more than sufficient reason to develop European-wide civil society organisations, apparently other elements play a role too, actually preventing this proliferation from taking place. A naïve assumption would be that there is every reason to develop mass-membership European environmental groups, farmers' associations or labour unions. The fact that in all these policy domains national organisations are already well-established and active, however, seems to inhibit the formation of European-wide social movement organisations. In order to gain access to the European decision-making process, networking with other national social movement organisations seems to be by far a more effective procedure than creating totally new organisational structures.

This finding could still mean two different things. On the one hand, we could assume that the political opportunity structure cannot be combined that easily with a multilevel system of decision making. The fact that social movement organisations are already present at different levels of decision making inevitably also has a bearing on the development of new emerging levels of decision making. On the other hand, this finding might be linked specifically to the nature of European decision-making procedures that are often described as elitist and closed. These European procedures might just stimulate the emergence of a specific kind of organisation, while preventing the creation of mass-membership-based organisations. To ascertain which of these two possibilities is most likely, we will compare the process of Europeanisation with the creation of other multilevel contexts, the federal system in Belgium and environmental policy at the UN level. With this comparison, we can ascertain whether these observations should be linked to multilevel policy settings as such, or rather to specific characteristics of the European Union.

4.3 THE CONCEPT OF A POLITICAL OPPORTUNITY STRUCTURE

In the recent literature on social movements, it is generally assumed that they will enjoy better chances to develop and to gain entrance to the political decision-making process if the political system provides a sufficient number of opportunities for oppositional activities. Tarrow (1996: 54) defines the concept:

> By political opportunity structure, I refer to consistent – but not necessarily formal, permanent, or national – signals to social or political actors which either encourage or discourage them to use their internal resources to form social movements.

Since its original introduction in the social movement literature in the early 1980s, the concept has been very influential, and various authors have developed their own definitions. Not only political, but also cultural, structural, material and organisational elements are seen as belonging to the political opportunity structure (POS). This does not seem the most promising way to arrive at a clear and useful operationalisation, as Gamson and Meyer (1996: 275) rightfully note: 'The concept of political opportunity structure is in trouble, in danger of becoming the sponge that soaks up virtually every aspect of the social movement environment . . . used to explain so much, it may explain nothing at all'.

It seems evident that cultural variables also determine the viability of new social movements (Mansbridge and Morris 2001), but it would be erroneous to include them in the concept of a *political* opportunity structure. Koopmans and Statham (2000), therefore, have argued that instead of lumping together all kinds of cultural and political elements in one POS concept, it makes more sense to distinguish a political and a discursive (or cultural) opportunity structure. Although of course it will not always be possible to separate analytically cultural and political variables, in practice it does make sense to use the concept purely for political variables that have a direct relation with characteristics of the political system.

One of the most comprehensive attempts to arrive at a full operationalisation of the POS concept can be found in the work of the Amsterdam research team that was led by Hanspeter Kriesi (Kriesi *et al.* 1995). They introduced a distinction between formal and informal characteristics of the political system, each of them limiting or enhancing the chances of oppositional actors to develop and gain acceptance in the political decision-making process. Their conceptualisation can also be seen as dynamic, since they not only include the initial structure, but also allow for subsequent feedback effects. This implies that the 'Amsterdam' model comprises four basic elements within the political opportunity structure: formal institutional structure, informal procedures and dominant strategies, the current configuration of power and the strategic response by the authorities (Kriesi *et al.* 1992; Kriesi *et al.* 1995).

One of the most important elements of the opportunity structure, and the one on which we will focus predominantly in this chapter, is the formal institutional structure. This concept mainly refers to the extent that societal actors have formal means at their disposal to influence political decision making. First of all, this applies to the basic liberties, like freedom of association, expression and print. But taken in a larger sense, it also represents the degree to which these actors actually have access, for example, by having a seat on an advisory committee or being able to be heard in parliament. An important component of the formal institutional structure is also the extent of judicial review. If oppositional groups have access to independent courts to fight government decisions, this implies that they can use an additional and completely independent access point to get their opinion reflected in the decision-making process. Certainly in Germany the environmental movement has repeatedly used courts and administrative judicial colleges to oppose government decisions, thus effectively blocking a number of government programmes.

Kriesi *et al.* (1992) also include the very basic characteristics of the state as part of this institutional structure. Their argument is that federal states, where authorities and competences are being shared, provide oppositional actors with more opportunities to influence decision making. For example, a decision taken by one of the Länder in the Federal Republic of Germany can still be debated at the federal level, and it can even be taken to court. In a strong centralised state like France, on the other hand, these multiple points of entry simply do not exist. The argument therefore is that social movement organisations will tend to flourish in an open and weaker state, compared to closed and strong political systems.

The institutional political structure, however, only tells part of the story. In most political systems, elite actors have developed routine responses to contestation by oppositional actors. While in some countries, like Belgium or the Netherlands, consensus building and consensual forms of decision making are predominant, in other countries majoritarian styles of decision making are more strongly prevalent. The expectation is that this style of interaction will simply be continued and will also be extended toward new groups that want to be included in the policy. A form of criticism that could be brought in against this expectation is that this form of political culture is not necessarily a fixed feature of a political system (Hooghe 2005). Groups that are allowed in during the build-up of the regime of concertation and openness will not automatically apply the same openness toward collective actors arriving later on at the scene, since this would dilute their own hold on power. Therefore it is just as likely that we would be witnessing a process of taking up the ladder once one has passed the access point oneself.

A third element is the current configuration of power within the political elite. The expectation here is that some elite actors could have an interest in actually promoting opposition from outside the system in order to further their own interests. For example, during the 1980s the oppositional socialist parties clearly supported the peace movement in various West European countries as part of their oppositional strategy. Being able to rely on such elite allies can self-evidently function as a powerful tool for oppositional actors, as they can obtain crucial information, various forms of facilitation or even material resources from their elite allies. An oppositional group that has to fight its way into the polity all by itself clearly faces a much more uphill struggle.

One of the major criticisms that was expressed against the early formulations of the POS concept was that it was too static. In part of the literature, the POS was seen as a kind of all-determining structure in which very little freedom was left for social movement pioneers and entrepreneurs. If the structure of political opportunities really determines a movement's chances of development and/or survival, it makes little sense to start an oppositional movement in negative circumstances. Agency does not have a place in this kind of structural reasoning. However, one can also turn the relationship around: social movement organisations also shape the way a political system functions. Or as McAdam (1996: 35) expresses it: a political opportunity structure should also be seen as a dependent variable, since we can assume that successful contestation and mobilisation will eventually lead to a redrawing of the map of the political system. Although this kind of influence will be relatively rare, we do have access to various studies documenting this social movement impact (Kriesi and Wisler 1999). The least one could do is to allow for a form of reciprocal influence between the political system and oppositional movements: 'Given that most movement scholars would probably say they study movements because they view them as a powerful force for change in society, our failure to undertake any serious accounting of the effect of past movements on the various dimensions of political opportunities is as puzzling as it is lamentable' (McAdam 1996: 36).

Partly as a response to this form of criticism, Kriesi *et al.* (1992, 1995) also included a feedback loop in their model: the response by the political elite determines the opportunities available to oppositional actors, but to a large extent this response is also determined by the action repertoire adopted by the actor. Despite this addition, the standard use of the POS concept relies on a one-way analysis: it is assumed that more or less fixed features and characteristics of the political system determine the way a social movement organisation will be able to develop and/or to prosper.

The work of Sidney Tarrow (1998) offers one of the strongest critiques of this one-sided view of the interaction between social movements and political institutions. Following the approach adopted by Charles Tilly (1978), Tarrow assumes that movements and political institutions constantly interact with one another, each side adjusting its strategy and the tools it uses to react to the actions of the other side. This means that social movements might be influenced by the political opportunity structure, but that their influence on the political system might be just as important. In the example Tarrow develops, it is clear that the socialist and labour movements fundamentally changed the character of liberal democracy, thus opening up the opportunity structure for all kinds of new demands. Mass-based workers' parties first demanded universal suffrage, and eventually succeeded in obtaining this. This chronology of events implies that the social movement was able to develop and was quite successful, even before the political system offered any opening or incentive for workers' associations or for parties to unite. Tarrow's line of reasoning implies that the interaction between movements and the political system does not adhere to a top-down logic but rather adheres to a model of mutual influencing. Returning to our initial question, the approach developed by Sidney Tarrow implies that merely opening up political opportunities at the European level will not be sufficient to create a truly European civil society.

In order to study the relation between civil society organisations and the political system more in depth we will rely on two historical examples, both involving the environmental movement. One of the reasons we chose to study the environmental movement was that since 1972 the European Community, and later the European Union, had developed into a powerful player in the field of environmental regulation. The environmental movement is therefore often quoted as one of the social movements where a development at the European level would be most likely (Dalton 1994; Bursens 1997). In the subsequent sections, we will briefly review how the environmental movement responded to the federalisation of environmental policy in Belgium, and to the globalisation of environmental policy within the UN system.

4.4 THE ENVIRONMENTAL MOVEMENT IN BELGIUM

The contemporary ecological movement in Belgium developed during the mid-1960s, mostly at a local level (Hooghe 1997). Various groups protested against the planning of new highways, the construction of waste incinerators and other forms of locally unwanted land use. These local groups were typical examples of new social movement organisations adopting a rather unconventional action repertoire, and recruiting mainly young, left-libertarian members (Hellemans and Hooghe 1995). As such, there was very little coordination with the older nature conservation associations that were already active from the early 20th century onward.

After just a few years, the various local groups started to form some kind of coordination in the 'Federation for a Better Environment' (Bond Beter Leefmilieu, BBL), which was established to function as the main umbrella organisation for environmental groups in Belgium. The BBL was founded in 1972 and it soon succeeded in establishing itself as the main organisation within the environmental movement, uniting eventually more than 100 local groups, and functioning as the main political actor within the environmental movement in Belgium. At the time it was founded, BBL was active in the entire country, but it already had separate chapters for Flanders, Brussels and Wallonia. Although the BBL tried very hard to establish itself as an interaction partner with the Belgian government, it gained hardly any entrance. With regard to the political struggle on nuclear energy that was at its heyday in the mid-1970s, the BBL initially succeeded in playing a substantial role, but it was quickly overtaken by more specialised action groups that concentrated their efforts exclusively on the nuclear issue (Steenkiste 1982).

It was already clear by 1972 that the local groups of Flanders and Wallonia did not share the same culture and objectives. It is not easy to pinpoint exactly the differences between the two regions, but one could say that the Flemish environmental groups were much more 'political', linking their local case with a more thorough critique of economic processes in general. The Walloon groups, on the other hand, were more involved with the preservation of natural habitats and they devoted less time to purely political matters (Hellemans and Hooghe 1995).

The differences between the two sections became so outspoken that gradually the regional chapters grew more independent from BBL-Belgium. In

1976, four autonomous regional organisations were set up: for Flanders, Wallonia, and the French- and Dutch-speaking parts of Brussels. For a couple of years, BBL-Belgium still remained in existence, although it hardly fulfilled any function any more, and was certainly not taken seriously by the government or any other political actor. In the end, in 1979, BBL-Belgium was completely dissolved and all that is left now as an umbrella structure for the Belgian environmental movement are these four regional federations. Since 1979 there has been no single organisation left that can speak on behalf of the Belgian environmental movement as a whole.

The most intriguing element in this entire process is that from a political opportunity structure perspective, the breaking up of BBL-Belgium does not make any sense at all. Until 1980, Belgium was a strictly unitary state, with all competences firmly in the hands of one federal government. In 1980, some competences were already decided on at the regional level, but it was not until the constitutional reforms of 1988 and 1993 that the competence for environmental regulation was transferred to the regional level. So between 1976 and 1993 the rather odd situation occurred that the federal minister or secretary of state in charge of environmental policy did not have a major organisation available to negotiate at the federal level. In practice, the Flemish and the Walloon associations sometimes tried to come forward with a joint proposal or a joint point of view, but most often this did not succeed. In fact, the Secretary of State for the Environment, Ms Miet Smet, at some point complained about the fact that she did not have a strong federal pressure group in her field since this would have strengthened her position within the federal government. Because few voices were heard calling for a reinforcement of environmental policy on a federal level, Ms Smet had a hard time convincing her colleagues about the importance of augmenting the budget for environmental policy.

The development of the Belgian environmental movement is self-evidently only a small national example, but nevertheless it can be seen as theoretically relevant. By 1976 the environmental movement had already split up into regional associations, while only in 1993 was authority on environmental policy completely delegated to the regions. The 1976 decision cannot be seen as an anticipation of changes in the political structure. Despite the fact that the federalisation process in Belgium was well under way by then, there were no indications whatsoever that environmental policy too would be involved in this dynamic. This only became apparent in the negotiations leading to the 1988 constitutional reform.

The end result is that the environmental movement was organised in a sub-optimal manner to exert pressure and the main reason for the split-up was the cultural differences between the Dutch- and French-speaking environmental associations that prevented them from reaching agreement on a joint strategy and a joint agenda.

What the example demonstrates is that the political opportunity structure did not have any impact at all on the structure of civil society. The evidence, therefore, suggests that civil society organisations did not simply wait for changes in the political system, but that they rather responded to cultural dynamics, even well before this had become a rational strategy if one was simply interested in maximising one's chances to influence the political agenda. The example suggests that cultural elements, too, might influence the structure of the social movement sector, just as strongly as the political opportunity structure does. Furthermore, it highlights Tarrow's notion that social movements can have an impact on the structure of government as important as the other way around.

4.5 THE GLOBAL ENVIRONMENTAL MOVEMENT

The 1960s were also the era in which a new, globally oriented environmental movement came into existence. The main difference between these new associations and the existing organisations was the scope of issues being addressed. While traditionally environmental groups had involved themselves mostly with local or national affairs, the new organisations were occupied more strongly with global concerns about the environment (Dalton 1994).

One of the earliest and well-known examples of this kind of environmental association is of course Greenpeace, which was established in 1969 as an action group to protest against US nuclear tests in Alaska. As was quite typical in the early days of the new social movements, various motivations were intertwined in this group. On the one hand peace demonstrators wanted to stop any form of nuclear testing, while on the other hand environmentalists were mainly concerned about the consequences of these tests for the environment in Alaska and Canada (Hooghe 1996). Again, from a political opportunity perspective, the establishment of the action group 'Don't Make a Wave', that later became known as Greenpeace, did not make any sense at all. Most of the members were either Canadians or US citizens escaping the Vietnam draft in Canada. Their action repertoire in the first instance was purely confrontational, as they tried to block the US tests with a small fishing boat. This group clearly did not have an interaction partner, since the Canadian government was not involved at all in the nuclear tests, while on the other hand the group did not even try to initiate any official talks with the US government. In fact the moment their fishing boat entered US territorial waters around Alaska, the crew members were arrested by the US Coast Guard.

Two years later, in 1971, another token organisation of the international environmental movement was founded, Friends of the Earth (FoE), adopting an equally radical and confrontational action repertoire. While FoE was founded independently in the UK, the US, France and Sweden, just a few months later these national associations went on to establish an international federation that is still one of the most active international environmental NGOs. Today, the organisation claims to be active in some 70 countries, uniting 5000 local groups, and it enjoys consultative status in numerous international environmental institutions and treaties.

The main problem for these global environmental NGOs, however, was that they had no one to address themselves to. The NGOs did not respond to newly established political structures, but rather the opposite phenomenon occurred. On a global level, no international organisation was actively involved with the environment in the 1960s. In 1949, the United Nations had organised a successful 'United Nations Scientific Conference on the Conservation and Utilisation of Resources' (UNSCCUR), but this conference did not lead to any long-lasting initiatives within the UN system (McCormick 1989: 25–43).

It would take until the end of the 1960s for the UN system to get involved in environmental protection again, eventually leading to the 'Man and Biosphere' research programme, organised by UNESCO in 1971. This too, however, was merely a scientific research programme, without any direct impact on decision making or policy. The Swedish government and various UN officials, however, pushed for a more active role for the UN in combating worldwide pollution. They did so with various goals in mind (Rowland 1973). For the Swedish government, the first priority was to develop an active policy against acid rain that, by that time, had begun to be recognised as a serious problem threatening the vitality of the Swedish forests. Various high-ranking officers within the UN, on the other hand, clearly noticed a growing concern about environmental protection among public opinion in the developed countries. Their ultimate goal was to heighten the legitimacy and the relevance of the UN by addressing this topic on a more global scale.

However, the developing countries in particular were not really convinced about the need to get involved as strongly in environmental protection. Their fear was that imposing environmental norms on industry and trade would hamper their capacity for further economic development. So even within the UN system there was a strong resistance against broadening the scope of involvement. The very ambitious and outspoken UN diplomat Maurice Strong, however, developed an effective counter-strategy

(Strong 1973). To demonstrate that public opinion was highly concerned about the environment, he proposed to establish an NGO forum running parallel to the planned official conference. Strong's intention was to demonstrate that concern about the environment was not just an academic issue, but was indeed a topic that received a significant amount of attention within public opinion and civil society. The organisation of parallel NGO meetings was at that time still a novelty for the UN system, but it has become a kind of habit for various specialised meetings and conferences, reaching an all-time high at the United Nations Conference on Environment and Development held in Rio de Janeiro in 1992.

Strong's plans were eventually approved and he was appointed Secretary-General of the United Nations Conference on the Human Environment (UNCHE, Stockholm, 5–16 June 1972). Eventually, 113 nations and 400 NGOs took part in the conference, which produced an action plan for environmental policy within the UN system. The impact of the Conference was huge. Not only did it mean the start of UNEP (the United Nations Environment Programme), it also served to heighten public awareness about the need for international cooperation with regard to the environment. For example, just a few months later, in October 1972, the European Council decided that the European Community would from now on be involved with environmental protection, despite the fact that the Community had not received any clear mandate for this policy area in the 1957 Treaty of Rome.

Again, we see a complex form of interaction. For Maurice Strong, who was to become the first director of UNEP, the presence of NGOs was meant as a strategic tool to get his pet projects approved by the United Nations General Assembly. The successful NGO forum at Stockholm demonstrated that there were already some policy networks on the environment in place, even long before the UN started to get explicitly involved in environmental protection. Subsequently, however, one of the key strategies of Strong and UNEP in general was to seek a strong NGO involvement in any future international decision making on the environment. For example, UNEP was instrumental in designing the first international agreements both on the protection of the ozone layer and the fight against the greenhouse effect. In both negotiations, and the subsequent monitoring scheme, NGOs were strongly involved.

Looking back at the development of the global environmental movement in the late 1960s and the early 1970s, it is clear that here, too, we do not find any evidence for a top-down logic. The global environmental organisations were founded at a time when public awareness was raised about global environmental degradation, but during this era there were no political institutions available yet to address these problems. The establishment of these structures, mainly within the UN system, followed a logic of mutual influencing, whereby leading bureaucrats explicitly used global NGOs to strengthen their own negotiation positions within the United Nations. Again, the impact of a political opportunity structure did not prove to be overwhelming, as social movement organisations developed their own structures well ahead of the reactions of political institutions.

4.6 CONCLUSION: TOWARD A EUROPEAN CIVIL SOCIETY?

Obviously these are just small examples, within a specific movement, and the examples by themselves cannot be generalised. Yet it is striking that for a number of other organisations and movements exactly the same logic applies. International human rights associations were established well before the international community set up a strong monitoring regime for human rights. Trade unions established world federations long before there was any international agency that could effectively be lobbied by these federations.

What these examples demonstrate is that, to borrow Doug McAdam's expression (1996), the political opportunity structure of a political system can function just as well as a dependent variable. The fact that numerous civil society organisations were organised separately in Flanders and Wallonia made it easier for Belgian political parties to develop a federal system with a large degree of autonomy for the regions. The autonomy of Flanders and Wallonia is taken to reflect that these are indeed two separate cultural communities, both living within the Belgian state. With regard to the environment, it is clear that various UN bodies and treaties were established as a result of effective campaigning by NGOs. The examples also show that cultural and linguistic elements are just as important in shaping the structure of civil society. Social movement organisations do not respond to some instrumental design, set up with the sole purpose of building an effective policy network (Mansbridge and Morris 2001).

Although we rely on just a few historical examples, these observations lead to a number of suggestions for further research, with regard both to the theoretical validity of the POS concept and to the functioning of the European Union.

First, it should be clear that any application of the POS concept should take historical considerations into account. Tarrow (1998) has demonstrated successfully how the nation-building process of the 18th and 19th centuries facilitated the creation of nationwide social movement organisations. It cannot be taken for granted, however, that the same kind of process will occur as a result of the contemporary tendency toward multilevel government. The essential difference is that, in the current process, national social movement organisations are already present, and these organisations have access to a wealth of organisational and structural resources (Martin and Ross 2001). To put it differently: much of the ground is already covered. Rather than to expect that a new mass-membership-based European environmental organisation will arise, it seems more likely that we will witness the coordination at a European level of the action of the already existing national organisations. If one is interested in influencing European decision making, this can be seen as an effective strategy. The impact of an interest group on the European system partly depends on a simultaneous strategy of access to national and European decision makers (Bouwen 2004). This simultaneity can be accomplished most effectively by national organisations coordinating their actions. It would be harder for European-level social movement organisations to gain access to decision makers at the national level. The structure of European interest organisations, with a dominance of umbrella organisations for national groups, therefore corresponds to the structure of European decision making, where authority lies simultaneously at the national levels and at the level of the European institutions.

Introducing the historical dimension implies that changes in the political opportunity structure can lead to various outcomes, depending on exact circumstances. In the past, this often meant the creation of new social movement organisations, addressing themselves to new decision-making procedures. But if various collective actors are already established and present, the newly opened political space might just as well be filled by an expansion of the action repertoire of the established actors. If national social movement organisations and interest groups develop effective strategies to lobby at the European level, there is less need for the establishment of separate and autonomous organisations at the European level. Taking the historical dimension seriously could also mean that the response of the social movement sector will not take the same form in every era. The mass-membership based national social movement is a typical 19th-century form of organisation (Tarrow 1998). Although we often equate this form of organisation with democratic mobilisation as such, it should be remembered that this is a historically determined form of organisation that will not automatically occur in other eras too. In the early 21st century, professional advocacy organisations seem to be more prevalent than mass-membership social movement organisations (Skocpol 2004), and apparently the professionalised European lobby organisations are no exception to this trend.

Second, the importance of a political opportunity structure should also be qualified if we consider the importance of cultural elements. Social movement organisations can also be seen as the result of a cultural dialogue and an expression of shared beliefs and convictions. This sense of community leads to the creation of organisations, even if their scale is suboptimal from a policy point of view. It should be remembered in this respect that social movement organisations are not just an instrumental response to political opportunities, but that they are also the expression of cultural values and of a sense of community.

With regard to the European Union, our suggestions for further research do not look all that promising. The key expectation of EU officials seems to be that, in some way or another, European civil society will eventually develop as a result of European integration. Given the fact that numerous political decisions are being taken at the European level, it would be a rational strategy for NGOs to get organised at the European level, where they can directly influence decision-making processes. The fact that the EU system claims to be quite open for NGOs should make this process even easier.

Yet despite the fact that for more than three decades now the European Union has been a crucial decision maker with regard to environmental matters, and the fact that most of the environmental policy in the member states is actually being shaped by European environmental directives, we find little evidence for the existence of a flourishing environmental movement at the European level. Admittedly, the European Environmental Bureau (EEB) can be considered a very active organisation, as it represents 143 member organisations in 31 European countries. What is equally clear, however, is that these member groups invest just a small part of their working budget in the EEB, concentrating their efforts at the national level. The EEB typically functions as a professional lobby and coordination group, not targeting public opinion as such; it can therefore be considered as a professional advocacy group, an organisational type which tends to dominate European civil society, not as a mass-membership-based social movement organisation.

The fact that a mass-membership-based form of social movement is largely absent at the European level raises again the question of how open European decision-making procedures really are, if we go beyond the rhetoric in the White Paper and other EU documents. A very sceptical conclusion might even go a step further, by questioning the character of the entire European integration process. Although during the 20th century, various movements for European integration were active, it clearly remains an elite-driven process, where the bottom-up dimension is only very weakly developed. In the historical examples we discussed, we saw that organised civil society took the lead, followed by the development of political structures. This is clearly not the case for the European integration process.

Implementing the objectives of the White Paper on Governance by establishing a truly European civil society sector, therefore, might be necessary to strengthen the democratic legitimacy of the European Union, but it will clearly not be an easy process. While the structural and the top-down conditions might be present, the cultural sense of community that is equally crucial to develop a civil society sector seems to be developed to a much lesser extent at the European level.

REFERENCES

Armstrong, K. (2002) 'Rediscovering civil society: The European Union and the White Paper on Governance' *European Law Journal* 8 (1), 102–32.
Beyers, J. (2002) 'Gaining and seeking access: The European adaptation of domestic interest associations' *European Journal of Political Research* 41 (5), 585–612.
Bouwen, P. (2004) 'Exchanging access goods for access: A comparative study of business lobbying in the European Union institutions' *European Journal of Political Research* 43 (3), 337–69.
Bursens, P. (1997) 'Environmental interest representation in Belgium and the EU: Professionalisation and division of labour within a multi-level governance setting' *Environmental Politics* 6 (4), 51–75.
Commission of the European Communities (CEC), *European governance: A white paper*, 25 July 2001 COM(2001) 428 final, Brussels: CEC.
Dalton, R. (1994) *The Green Rainbow: Environmental groups in Western Europe*, New Haven: Yale University Press.
Davis, G., McAdam, D., Richard Scott, W. and Zald, M. (eds) (2005) *Social movements and organization theory*, Cambridge: Cambridge University Press.
Delanty, G. (1997) 'Models of citizenship: Defining European identity and citizenship' *Citizenship Studies* 1 (3), 285–303.
Gamson, W. and Meyer, D. (1996) 'Framing political opportunity', in D. McAdam, J.D. McCarthy and M.N. Zald (eds) *Comparative perspectives on social movements*, Cambridge: Cambridge University Press, pp. 275–90.
Greenwood, J. (2003) *Interest representation in the European Union*, Basingstoke: Macmillan.
Hellemans, S. and Hooghe, M. (eds) (1995) *Van Mei '68 tot Hand in Hand: Nieuwe sociale bewegingen in België*, Leuven: Garant.
Hix, S. (1999) *The political system of the European Union*, Basingstoke: Palgrave.
Hooghe, L. and Marks, G. (2001) *Multi-level governance and European integration*, Boulder: Rowman and Littlefield.
Hooghe, M. (1996) *Met vlag en spandoek: Hedendaagse actiegroepen*, Brussels: Globe.
Hooghe, M. (1997) *Nieuwkomers op het middenveld: Nieuwe sociale bewegingen als actoren in het Belgisch politiek system*, PhD Political Science, Free University of Brussels.
Hooghe, M. (2005) 'Ethnic organisations and social movement theory: The political opportunity structure for ethnic mobilisation in Flanders (Belgium)' *Journal of Ethnic and Migration Studies* 31 (5), 975–90.

Imig, D. and Tarrow, S. (eds) (2001a) *Contentious Europeans: Protest and politics in an emerging polity*, Lanham: Rowman and Littlefield.
Imig, D. and Tarrow, S. (2001b) 'Studying contention in an emerging polity', in D. Imig and S. Tarrow (eds) *Contentious Europeans: Protest and politics in an emerging polity*, Lanham: Rowman and Littlefield, pp. 3–26.
Imig, D. and Tarrow, S. (2001c) 'Mapping the Europeanization of contention: Evidence from a quantitative data analysis', in D. Imig and S. Tarrow (eds) *Contentious Europeans: Protest and politics in an emerging polity*, Lanham: Rowman and Littlefield, pp. 27–49.
Koopmans, R. (1993) 'The dynamics of protest waves: West Germany, 1965 to 1989' *American Sociological Review* 58 (5), 637–58.
Koopmans, R. and Statham, P. (eds) (2000) *Challenging immigration and ethnic relations politics*, Oxford: Oxford University Press.
Kriesi, H. Koopmans, R., Duyvendak, J.W. and Giugni, M.G. (1992) 'New social movements and political opportunities in Western Europe' *European Journal of Political Research* 22 (2), 219–44.
Kriesi, H., Koopmans, R., Duyvendak, J.W. and Giugni, M. (1995) *New social movements in Western Europe: A comparative analysis*, London: UCL Press.
Kriesi, H. and Wisler, D. (1999) 'The impact of social movements on political institutions: A comparison of the introduction of direct legislation in Switzerland and the United States', in M. Giugni, D. McAdam and C. Tilly (eds) *How social movements matter*, Minneapolis: University of Minnesota Press, pp. 42–65.
Magnette, P. (2003) 'European governance and civic participation: Beyond elitist citizenship?' *Political Studies* 51 (1), 144–60.
Mansbridge, J. and Morris, A. (eds) (2001) *Oppositional consciousness: The subjective roots of social protest*, Chicago: University of Chicago Press.
Marks, G. and McAdam, D. (1996) 'Social movements and the changing structure of political opportunity in the European community' *West European Politics* 19 (2), 249–78.
Marks, G., Nielsen, F., Ray, L. and Salk, J. (1996) 'Competencies, cracks, and conflicts: Regional mobilization in the European Union' *Comparative Political Studies* 29 (2), 164–92.
Martin, A. and Ross, G. (2001) 'Trade union organizing at the European level: The dilemma of borrowed resources', in D. Imig and S. Tarrow (eds) *Contentious Europeans: Protest and politics in an emerging polity*, Lanham: Rowman and Littlefield, pp. 53–76.
Mazey, S. and Richardson J. (eds) (1993) *Lobbying in the European Community*, Oxford: Oxford University Press.
McAdam, D. (1982) *Political process and the development of black insurgency*, Chicago: University of Chicago Press.
McAdam, D. (1996) 'Conceptual origins, current problems, future directions', in D. McAdam, J.D. McCarthy and M.N. Zald (eds) *Comparative perspectives on social movements*, Cambridge: Cambridge University Press, pp. 23–40.
McAdam, D., McCarthy, J.D. and Zald, M.N. (eds) (1996) *Comparative perspectives on social movements: Political opportunities, mobilizing structures and cultural framings*, Cambridge: Cambridge University Press.
McCormick, J. (1989) *Reclaiming paradise: The global environmental movement*, Bloomington: Indiana University Press.
Rowland, W. (1973) *The plot to save the world: The life and times of the Stockholm Conference on the Human Environment*, Toronto: Clarke and Irwin.

Rucht, D. (2001) 'Lobbying or protest? Strategies to change EU environmental politics', in D. Imig and S. Tarrow (eds) *Contentious Europeans: Protest and politics in an emerging polity*, Lanham: Rowman and Littlefield, pp. 125–42.

Skocpol, T. (2004) 'Voice and inequality: The transformation of American civic democracy' *Perspectives on Politics* 2 (1), 3–20.

Smismans, S. (2003) 'European civil society: Shaped by discourses and institutional interests' *European Law Journal* 9 (4), 473–95.

Steenkiste, G. (1982) 'Actief en passief van de milieubeweging' *De Nieuwe Maand* 25 (6), 365–75.

Strong, M. (1973) 'One year after Stockholm: An ecological approach to management' *Foreign Affairs* 51 (4), 690–707.

Tarrow, S. (1995) 'The Europeanization of conflict: Reflections from a social movement perspective' *West European Politics* 18 (2), 223–51.

Tarrow, S. (1996) 'States and opportunities: The political structuring of social movements' in D. McAdam, J.D. McCarthy and M.N. Zald (eds) *Comparative perspectives on social movements*, Cambridge: Cambridge University Press, pp. 41–61.

Tarrow, S. (1998) *Power in movement: Social movements, collective action and politics*, Cambridge: Cambridge University Press.

Tilly, C. (1978) *From mobilization to revolution*, Reading: Addison-Wesley.

Tsakatika, M. (2005) 'Claims to legitimacy: The European Commission between continuity and change' *Journal of Common Market Studies* 43 (1), 193–220.

5. Bringing the citizens closer to the EU? The role of civil society in Wales in the European Convention
Deborah Cook

5.1 INTRODUCTION

The Convention on the Future of Europe[1] was billed as the opportunity to decide upon Europe's direction, to make efficient and comprehensible both the European Union's (EU) structures and its processes to the public, thereby ensuring its legitimacy (see d'Estaing, quoted in European Convention, 2002a: 13). Civil society was to be a key mechanism in relaying views both to and from the Convention. Indeed the Convention's very success depended 'upon its ability to be receptive to the concerns and expectations expressed by society – through among other channels – the different national debates and the European Civic Forum' (Aznar, quoted in European Convention, 2002a: 4). The French and Dutch 'nos' to the constitutional treaty that the Convention helped to shape challenge the Convention's and civil society's success in relaying such views. Thus, research is needed to confirm what civil society's role actually was in the Convention process and to explore the factors shaping this role.

Research has been conducted primarily at the European level of analysis on civil society's role in the Convention (for example, Lombardo 2003; Borragán, 2004), although a major project has been conducted at the national and local level (see Will *et al.*, 2005). Civil society research at the sub-national or regional level is also important because of the proximity of this level to the general public and the number of regions with legislative power in the EU,[2] and to explore the presence and shape of multi-level governance (MLG) in this specific instance. Research at and below the Member State level is particularly pivotal given the need to broaden out the Convention debate:

> There is danger that the Convention is only in touch with/listened to by NGOs at the European level. This is very important, but I think that we have to decentralise and have contacts with NGOs at the national level. (Translation

of Convention Vice President Dehaene, quoted in European Convention, 2002b: 7)

This chapter draws upon research conducted in Wales to give some insight into the role of civil society below the level of Member State in the Convention and in EU MLG. Wales, a region on Europe's periphery, has recently gained executive devolution,[3] with civil society intended to be a key beneficiary and participant in the devolved institution's work (Royles, 2004: 101). Thus, research on Wales provides a unique regional perspective, and additionally offers a potentially facilitative policy environment for civil society.

The chapter draws upon semi-structured interviews with civil society organisations and policy makers,[4] documents, newspapers and academic literature to explore the phenomenon. First, the concept of MLG must be outlined to enable discussion of whether MLG occurred and its shape during the Convention. Second, to analyse EU–civil society dynamics, the concept of civil society, the approach used and the background into civil society in Wales and EU policy making, must be detailed. Third, general Convention–civil society relations will be discussed to highlight the structural constraints and opportunities presented to civil society by the Convention. A review of Convention activity in Wales follows, to explore how the Welsh context may have shaped civil society's involvement. In relation to this context, the findings of civil society organisations (CSOs) in Wales's Convention participation will be outlined, demonstrating that, despite the presence of CSOs participating in some MLG, the role of civil society in Wales was limited in the Convention, due to a number of structural and actor specific factors. This suggests that the Convention failed to reconnect with its citizens through civil society at the regional level of Wales.

5.2 MULTI-LEVEL GOVERNANCE AND THE RESEARCH AREA

MLG emerged from observations on EU structural fund programmes (Bache and Flinders, 2004: 2), where nation states do not dominate policy making, and decision-making competencies are shared by actors below, above and outside the nation state. In turn, in MLG different territorial levels are understood to be interconnected and can interact directly, bypassing the Member State (for example, the Assembly can interact with the European Commission). Policy making is diffuse and shared among a range of actors (Hooghe and Marks, 2001). As such, it is possible that sub-national actors, in this case CSOs, can partake directly in MLG in relation to EU policy making. Moreover, although MLG studies assume the involvement of sub-national actors, they tend to concentrate on sub-national authorities overlooking non-governmental actors (George 2004: 122f; for an exception see Constantelos, 2004). MLG studies typically focus on matters of low politics, and research into areas of high politics such as the Convention will help explore MLG's broader applicability to EU policy making (Jordan 2001: 12). Finally, in line with sentiments expressed by Zimmer and Freise (Chapter 2) this chapter fills a research void (until recently), 'investigating the horizontal as well as the vertical dimension of European multi-level governance', by exploring the Convention, an issue with implications across policy sectors and addressing the vertical dimensions of different territorial levels. The legitimacy of MLG arrangements is also touched upon. This chapter aims to shed light on the existence and nature of MLG through the case of Wales and civil society organisations.

5.3 BACKGROUND

5.3.1 Civil Society, Wales and European Union Policy Making

The definition of civil society is by no means settled. Currently there is a consensus of sorts, particularly in empirical studies, which Anheier (2004: 20) evokes – that civil society is not state nor economic, and usually not familial. This chapter will use this conception of civil society, whilst admitting that in practice all of these boundaries overlap, and will explore civil society through part of its infrastructure (Zimmer and Freise Chapter 2) – civil society organisations (CSOs). The chapter broadly utilises Zimmer and Freise's civil society approach by looking at the extent to which civil society can bring citizens closer to the EU via CSOs' Convention involvement. Aspects of the third sector and social capital approaches are also employed. The former is evident with the focus on CSOs as actors within the policy process and the latter through the emphasis on the input side of policy making and the involvement of members in their organisation's Convention activities. With this in mind, does civil society in Wales usually engage in EU policy making?

Prior to devolution, civil society in Wales was said to be weak, lacking the political institutions arguably needed to sustain it (Drakeford, 2006). It was hoped that devolution would help cultivate a civic culture and buoy up civil society (Day, Dunkerley and Thompson 2000: 25). There is some evidence of civil society engagement in EU policy making post-devolution, with the Assembly involving civil society as partners in the implementation of EU structural funds programmes and monitoring committees (Royles 2003). Moreover, the Assembly has included some of civil society in crosscutting European issues through forums such as an enlargement working group and the Wales European Forum (where public, private and voluntary sectors meet on European issues). Thus, the Assembly made efforts to include civil society organisations, albeit a small section of largely Waleswide and professionalised groups, in EU policy issues, and as a result, CSOs have been engaged in EU policy making. Moreover, research suggests that the Assembly is the key political institution through which civil society groups in Wales participate in EU policy making (Cook 2006), despite its limited legal role.[5] This finding also indicates that civil society in Wales largely participates in EU MLG arrangements through the sub-national authority rather than directly with the EU or via the Member State. This potential co-ordinating function of institutions in MLG arrangements is remarked upon by Peters and Pierre (2004: 78f). This argument makes it important to study the role of the Assembly within the Convention as a potential vehicle for the participation of civil society in Wales. However, much of the Assembly's role depends on the EU policy at hand. Thus, the scope for civil society and for its Welsh political institutions in the Convention must be identified.

5.3.2 The Convention and Civil Society

With the Nice Intergovernmental Conference 2000 failing to reform a cumbersome EU, the Laeken Council of 2001 convened a Convention. This Convention would, over the course of a year, consider the future role of the EU and reforms, but the outcome of a constitutional treaty was by no means certain (Regan *et al.* 2003: 15). The Convention was unique with its broad mandate, long duration, composition and process. It was comprised of supra-national and national representatives/actors as Conventioneers, and 13 Observers. A Presidium (including the Presidency of three) gave impetus to the Convention.

President d'Estaing stipulated that the Convention would work through three phases: the listening phase (ended in June 2002), the study phase (finished in December 2002) and the reflection phase (from January–June 2003) (European Convention 2002a: 20; Miller, 2003: 7). In the listening phase, the Convention explored people's expectations of the EU. For the study phase, the Presidium created six working groups (expanding into eleven) for the Conventioneers to explore in depth the Laeken declaration's topics. The final reflection stage concentrated on institutional concerns and the Presidium suggested draft texts, which the Convention debated and proposed amendments to.

Where did civil society fit into all of this? The Laeken declaration accorded civil society with its first ever formal role in treaty reform, through the Convention. Civil society's contributions were intended to 'serve as input into the debate' (European Council 2001: 5). Civil society was envisaged as a vehicle for citizen participation, bringing citizens' views to the Convention's attention, stimulating debate and later on for translating the Convention's work to the citizens (European Economic and Social Committee 2002a: 2).

Civil society could contribute through the following avenues:

- Internet forum
- Civil society contact groups
- Convention observers – social partners, European Economic and Social Committee and Committee of the Regions
- Civil society plenaries – 24 and 25 June 2002
- National debates
- Conventioneers
- In practice also Futurum (a message-posting website).

The formal participation of civil society occurred at the end of the listening phase in June 2002, through the two-day plenaries. Beforehand, eight thematic civil society contact groups were created and these contact groups decided upon the plenary speakers, which arguably resulted in a bias towards expert, well resourced, European-wide[6] groups speaking (Lombardo 2003: 27):

> It was a gathering of the Commission's payroll of funded lobby groups, the usual suspects saying the usual things. Naturally these represented 'Euro' viewpoints rather than varied national voices. (Scott 2002: 2)

The Internet forum was another outlet open to any CSO to articulate its opinions. However, most of the participating groups were European, and marginal sectors like asylum were under-represented (Lombardo 2003). The forum came to be viewed as a 'comedy' (Magnette 2003: 32) and a 'black hole' (Interview, European civil society organisation 2004) as: a) no feedback was given to contributors, b) advertisement was questionable and c) the vast numbers of contributions made it unlikely that they would all be heard (Scott 2002: 2; Lombardo 2003). Futurum was a message-posting website, where anybody could post their thoughts on the EU, which similarly made it hard to monitor and feed into the debate.

The Observers and the Conventioneers were intended to act as intermediaries, stimulating the national debate and conveying civil society's views to the Convention. Notably the European Economic and Social Committee (2002b: 1) was a pivotal 'bridge between the Convention and civil society'. It carried out eight information and dialogue sessions with civil society, but once more, these meetings were only 'open to *European* civil society', (European Economic and Social Committee 2002c: 1, italics added). National Economic and Social Councils instead were meant to engage national and grassroots civil society. The UK does not have an Economic and Social Committee, thus closing off a further potential avenue for the British CSOs.

The real lobbying occurred outside the formal channels 'in the usual way of personal contacts and the effect of NGO campaigns' (Beger 2004: 8) and occurred as 'business as usual' (Shaw, Hoffman and Bausili 2003: 17). The civil society contact group, a collection of European CSOs, argued that CSOs had to be proactive to influence the Convention. This same group viewed the Convention experience and its outcome as largely positive (Beger 2004: 8). Nonetheless, there was a dissonance between the social and largely substantive concerns of civil society and the Convention's focus on institutional issues (Lombardo 2003: 28; Shaw 2003: 65), thereby questioning civil society's actual room for influence.

At the national level, civil society debate was lacking (Shaw, Hoffman and Bausili 2003: 17). In the UK there was limited press coverage, a Eurosceptic climate and the Euro dominated the national debate (Keohane 2002). Cook's (2006) analysis of the Forum (in February 2004) found that 34 out of 1164 submissions came from identifiably UK-based organisations, demonstrating some activity (the Forum has since changed). The Foreign and Commonwealth Office did have an on-line forum with Convention information and the opportunity to send views to the Minister for Europe. Miller (2003: 13), however, found that the 'British government has not organised as many open discussions as some Member States'.

Thus the formal structural opportunities in the European Convention open to civil society in Wales, at the supra-national and also partly at the national level, appeared to be few and far between, and far from conducive to top-down MLG. The stress on European civil society is moreover found in the European Commission's and the European and Economic Social Committee's discourse of civil society, and this may also have acted as a barrier to the engagement of CSOs in Wales. The Convention placed an emphasis on CSOs which could input into the Convention, in other words, those with expertise and EU knowledge, inadvertently leading to a focus on Brussels-based, supra-national organisations, curtailing the scope of MLG in relation to non-state sub-national actors. This Brussels bias was sustained with the Convention deliberating entirely in Brussels. Implicit obstacles to civil society participation included the focus on institutional issues and the need for Internet access and for CSOs to be proactive. This situation was exacerbated given that even European civil society was listened to formally only once, and, with so many other actors, CSOs influence could only be limited. Equally, a lack of Convention engagement is likely given the importance of language in engaging civil society (Hoffman 2003), with authors finding the Convention's language to be Euro-speak and legalistic (Magnette 2003: 32).

5.4 CONTEXT: WALES AND THE CONVENTION

With this general picture in mind, what civil society activity was there in Wales on the Convention and did the Assembly generate much of this? The Assembly's role in the Convention was limited, with the regions having six Committee of the Regions Convention observers, and 'all insiders know it is of little significance' (Jones 2002: 7). Regional issues and public authorities were included instead in the Convention arrangements for civil societies in the plenaries and the forum. Moreover, only one Convention representative came from Wales – Peter Hain – as an influential representative of the UK government (dubbed the 'shadow President' (Magnette 2004: 217). Thus, from the outset the Assembly had no formal role in the Convention. Equally, with regional interests lumped together with civil society in the forum, regions would probably be competing for attention, not transmitting CSO's ideas.

As a result, the Assembly was reliant on its intermediaries (such as RegLeg – Regions with Legislative Power) and the UK government. This means the Assembly had little autonomy in the Convention, making it unlikely that it would convey competing civil society claims.[7] Indeed, the Welsh Assembly Government, perhaps in response to its limited formal position, focused on specifically regional concerns, the place of regional governments in the EU architecture and the policy process, and on subsidiarity: 'Naturally we are interested in changes in the big picture, but we have a special interest in subsidiarity' (First Minister quoted in National Assembly for Wales 2002a: 1). The Welsh Assembly Government's most significant contribution was its role in shaping a paper presented by the UK government to a plenary on regions in 2003 (see European Convention 2003).

Part of the explanation for the limited activity of the National Assembly for Wales at the start of the Convention may also be found in its perception of the Convention, as well as other more pressing concerns (Cook 2006). Thus the Assembly's limited autonomy, other salient issues,[8] its perception of the Convention, and Convention activities and focus seem to further curtail the opportunity for civil society input from Wales via the Assembly: 'I think the constitutional debate was largely about setting in place the structural building blocks which would allow civic society to contribute . . . there wouldn't be very much that civic society could say in respect of more powers for regions' (Interview, Assembly Member (AM), 2003). Did civil society agree with this perception and did the Assembly for Wales consult civil society on the issue?

The Assembly's European and External Affairs Committee invited responses on the White Paper on European Governance from 17 organisations (comprising large, Wales-wide farming, business and public sector bodies), which fed into the Welsh Assembly Government's Convention approach. The Committee received only five responses (from the Welsh Local Government Association, Wales Council for Voluntary Action (WCVA) and three quangos). The responses (see National Assembly for Wales 2002b) generally focused on the organisations' experiences of EU issues and called for further structures to involve civil society in EU policy making, protection of subsidiarity and simplification of the EU; they also recognised the importance of the Wales European Centre. These views give some credence to the idea that CSOs would merely reiterate the Welsh Assembly Government's Convention's regional concerns, but some different issues were present.

The Wales European Forum (WEF) was convened on 'European Governance' and the Convention was discussed in relation to arrangements for Welsh representation. Similarly, the civil society and media groups present were large Wales-wide organisations. Thus, the Assembly carried out some consultation on the governance debate, which translated into their Convention work. However, this consultation was not completely open, and neither was civil society completely interested in or able to respond on broad EU issues, as the number of respondents to the written consultation demonstrates.

CSOs could have also attended a number of other events in Wales and the UK, organised variously by the European Parliamentarians, the Welsh Office MPs and the European Commission Office in Wales as well as civil society organisations (such as the UK's Institute for Citizenship). This demonstrates the facilitation and occurrence of some MLG across different territorial levels by political institutions and CSOs. A number of events were held after the Convention's listening stage, when civil society's formal input occurred, arguably limiting their impact. Moreover, many events were not purely Convention focused, encompassing a more general debate on the future of Europe or on the Euro. The Cardiff conference held by the Green and European Free Alliance (EFA) group in July 2002 was conducted with civil society in mind. Attending organisations were mainly

Wales-wide offshoots of UK parent groups and covered a range of social interests including: women, international issues, trade unions, disability, the environment and ethnic minority groups. Their concerns were again wider than the role of the regions, including for example the abolishment of the Euratom treaty, workers' rights, subsidiarity, openness and the need for civil society to have a role in the process.

Similarly, the Welsh Assembly Government sponsored a WCVA-run Welsh 'Colloquium on civil society and governance' in December 2002. Organised 'to ensure synergy with key development in the EU surrounding the "Convention on the Future of Europe"' (WCVA 2002: 1), it seemed to be more orientated towards the governance debate. Nonetheless, the participation of fifteen grassroots organisations from Wales in the Colloquium represents a broadening out of the debate. With this limited context for involvement, could the media spur on the participation of civil society in Wales?

The media can also create further opportunities for collective action because it shapes frames in the public sphere (Grimm 2004). A brief overview of the analysis of four Welsh newspapers[9] will help shed light on how the Convention was portrayed and whether it encouraged civil society participation and created cultural opportunities. In terms of the articles spread over time, there are two discernible clusters which are identifiable with two issues: first, in October 2002 Peter Hain becoming Secretary of State for Wales and second in May/June 2003 with the debate over a UK Constitution referendum and Peter Hain becoming Leader of the House of Commons (see Figure 5.1).

The content of the articles showed that the largest coverage was on Peter Hain becoming Secretary of State for Wales while continuing his role in the Convention, rather than on the Convention itself. The Euro and the actions

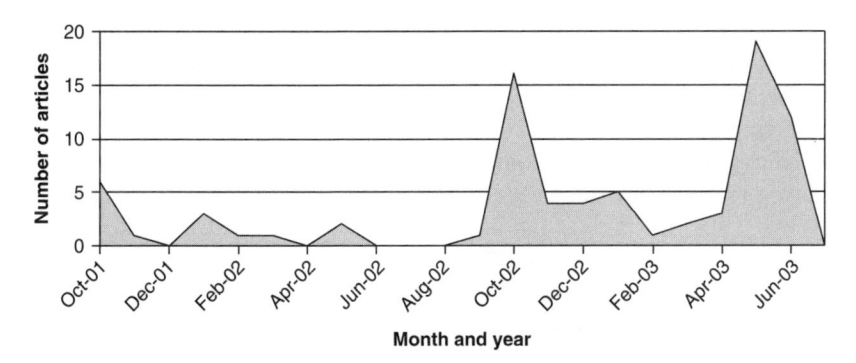

Figure 5.1 Chronological spread of Welsh newspaper coverage of the Convention on the future of Europe, October 2001–July 2003

of British and Welsh representatives on the Convention also received substantial coverage. Moreover, regional rights and institutional issues were given more attention than the Convention's discussion of the EU's policies and values, where more civil society concerns might have been expected. This was not favourable for facilitating the Convention participation of civil society in Wales.

Activity in Wales on the Convention does not seem to have offered much scope for civil society participation. Indeed, civil society involvement appears to emerge through tangential one-off events, although some civil society groups did organise and facilitate the debate. There is some evidence of institutional and civil society actors engaging with different territorial levels on this topic, demonstrating some MLG. However, political structures and media sources in Wales do not offer the prospect of facilitating a widespread debate. This stands in comparison to the Catalan Convention that brought together over 300 politicians, academics, political parties and civil society 'to discuss the future of Europe' (McLeod 2002: 4). The Scottish Parliament also arranged a one-day Convention and the Scottish Executive ran a website and carried out written consultation and seminars with civil society (see Scottish Executive 2002 and Scottish Parliament 2002: Annex A). Nonetheless, what was the actual experience and the role of civil society groups in Wales in the Convention?

5.5 CIVIL SOCIETY ACTIVITY

Seventeen CSOs in Wales were interviewed about their Convention involvement. The CSOs had two routes for participation: a) via external events and activities and b) through European, international, British or Welsh networks and parent bodies. The latter route is important, as European civil society groups were charged with aiding the national debate. It is essential to note that much of the CSOs' participation has been traced following interviews; the extent of participation may therefore be underreported.

Nine groups had some contact with the Convention, with six of these having external involvement outside of their civil society partners or networks. Three CSOs were more proactive, of which one CSO had discussions with AMs, European Commission officials and the Secretary of State for Wales. The women's group also had contact with AMs and the Conventioneer MPs. Finally, another CSO actually sent in a submission to the Internet Forum. Two less proactive CSOs both attended the Green/EFA event and one of these also attended the WEF. The final CSO staff member had some informal contact with the European Commission office in Wales on this topic. Thus, on the Convention civil society activity was not solely gathered around the Assembly, and this indicates the presence of some MLG, perhaps in response to the Assembly's limited role.

One of these proactive CSOs viewed the Assembly as accessible because of the WEF consultation: 'it was probably a bit more open in fairness, at least they [the Assembly] did make an attempt to consult'. Similarly the women's group found access to MP Conventioneers relatively easy by attending a public meeting of the European and External Affairs Committee. However, there was some divergence over the accessibility of the European-level structures, as one CSO discovered: 'for us to feed directly into Europe was very difficult' because they were not a European group, illustrating the barrier that the EU's discourse of civil society presents. Nonetheless, the Forum user perceived access via the Forum as straightforward:

> It was just so easy to make a submission to the Convention, and the Convention really laid over backwards, fell over backwards to encourage people to make a submission (Interview, civil society group 2004).

This suggests that despite the negative political and media context for civil society in Wales to contribute, if organisations were aware of the Convention, then structures did not prevent collective action (although they may have limited participation) and instead obstacles may have been elsewhere. The external participating CSOs' concerns encompassed claims like gender equality and recognition for regional civil society in EU policy making. These therefore differed from the Assembly's focus.

Seven CSOs participated via parent groups or other civil society groups, and five of these received information from their partners. Involvement varied from one British parent group requiring its committee in Wales to discuss the issue, to one CSO attending an event organised by another civil society group. Only one CSO was proactive in contacting its European networks on this issue and in organising a related event.

Thus, it appears that some British or European arms of Welsh groups did make an effort to inform their subsidiaries. Responses reflected the idea that Welsh, British and even European parent bodies or networks should, and would, deal with a European event like the Convention, thereby effectively contracting out high-level EU policy issues, curtailing the scope of MLG. Accordingly, groups felt that as long as some participation was occurring, even if it did bypass their regional or local level, this was more important than their group contributing:

> We would probably tend to say that we would trust our partners to actually make our voice heard at that particular level (Interview, religious group 2003).

This finding confirms the notion of Zimmer and Freise (Chapter 2) that the arrangement of organisations across different territorial levels affects CSOs' opportunity structures in MLG.

CSOs' Convention participation was concentrated among one or two group members. Two groups did make an effort to consult their committees, and an additional two CSOs spread information on how to participate (through an event or email actions) to their members. This constricted the role that civil society in Wales could play in connecting citizens with the EU through the Convention.

All of these participating groups, except one, were engaged in EU policy making outside of the Convention. The one that was not usually involved did have very marginal involvement, with staff attending the Green/EFA event in Cardiff, thereby indicating that the Convention did not reach out to those not usually engaged in EU issues.

How do these groups compare with the non-involved in terms of resources and size, did they want to participate, and what would have been their concerns? A fairly straightforward reason for non-involvement, which was also cited by some of the involved groups (showing the precarious nature of their actual participation), was that they were not aware of the Convention. Indeed five of the interviewees had no prior awareness of the Convention. Many of these groups had found out about it through the media and had a rather shaky knowledge of it:

> But much of the information we have got hasn't risen above the tabloid level of Britain in Europe, and Britain out of Europe (Interview, trade union 2004).

As many more organisations were aware of the Convention than participated, it is evident that being slightly aware did not result in internalising the Convention's work to their own organisation's activities.

Aside from a lack of awareness, non-participating CSOs brought up similar obstacles to action, namely the concern that CSOs wouldn't make much difference, a lack of previous experience and the broad nature of the Convention, which was outside their organisation's core remit:

> I think you would like to see such and such and you know you've got as much chance as a snowflake in the equator (Interview, community/heritage group 2004).

> I don't think I have the experience and the language to have had a valid input (Interview, environment group 2003).

Groups also cited resources, whether of personnel, money and time, as a reason for not getting involved. Moreover, two groups which were normally involved in EU policy making did not contribute – one because the Convention was not its core business and for the other because they didn't feel they could make a difference.

Among those groups not involved, six CSOs would have liked to participate. This suggests that more could have been done to engage civil society fully. However, CSOs again seemed to acquiesce to the notion that the topic may have bypassed them and should be dealt with higher up in their organisation. Indeed, twelve out of the total seventeen interviewed CSOs had British or European partners which were involved in the Convention:

> If the [European and international branches of the organisation] had any input into it then really whatever we would have said would have just been repeating it . . . if you have too much consultation then I think you can't see the woods from the trees and you know if people are merely repeating the points that other people made more succinctly then all you are doing is clogging up the system (Interview, environmental group 2003).

A couple of groups generally concurred with the Welsh Assembly Government's Convention concerns: namely, they wanted the role of the regions in EU policy making improved. However, many of the other non-involved groups were concerned with specific clauses or policy areas pertinent to their interests, suggesting the need for further civil society involvement.

In demographic terms, the non-involved CSOs comprised all of the local and regional groups interviewed, most of the groups outside of South Wales (where the National Assembly for Wales is based) and all except one of the 'Welsh' groups (that is, without a UK or European parent body). In terms of mobilisation structures, staffing was important as all the involved CSOs bar three had staff, and those without staff either had other resources (entrepreneurial or expertise), or lack of staff had severely constricted their involvement.

Similar obstacles were encountered by the involved organisations that limited the scope of their participation. Internal material concerns such as time and resources (people and financial) were present. External structural concerns included questioning how groups in Wales could have an influence, a lack of awareness of events or Convention activities and recognition of the limited role of the Assembly as opposed to the UK government in the EU. The perceived barriers towards regional civil society groups in the EU were also mentioned. The perception of the Convention itself, together with how the media and the government presented it, and, more broadly, conceptions of 'Europe' in the UK, were commonly mentioned as barriers to participation for civil society generally.

5.6 CONCLUSION

The Convention, despite articulating the need for civil society involvement to create a successful constitution, did not re-engage civil society on the ground. The Convention did however represent a broadening out of the process of treaty reform previously unseen in the EU. The formal opportunities granted to civil society in the Convention came early on in the Convention process and seemed to be dominated by Brussels-based European NGOs which had expertise and wherewithal, indicating that in this particular instance the already active CSOs remained the engaged CSOs. The national civil society debate, to be organised by the Member States and Conventioneers, appeared to be similarly lacking. In Wales itself, the National Assembly for Wales had little formal role and the Welsh Assembly Government concentrated its efforts on regional institutional issues through the UK-devolved administration EU machinery, late in the Convention. Nonetheless, some previous consultation had been carried out on the White Paper on European Governance, which fed into their Convention discussion. This meant that, overall, formal opportunities for civil society to input through the Assembly were limited. There was also a range of Convention-related events in which civil society in Wales could have participated. The brief analysis of some Welsh newspapers further serves to demonstrate the uninviting cultural atmosphere in relation to civil society, with coverage peaking towards the later stages of the Convention and a focus on regional rights and institutional issues rather than civil society issues.

The views and activities of the interviewed CSOs demonstrate that participation by these groups was largely indirect and one-off. However, it does appear that the political context and institutions did not entirely constrain their actions. Instead participation seems to be also linked to an interplay of group-specific, supply-side factors such as levels of awareness, mobilisation and communication structures with European and British partners. Notwithstanding, one CSO did encounter barriers at the supra-national European level in the form of the EU's institutional discourse on civil society. The lack of awareness about the special Convention mechanisms, together with a sizeable number of groups which would have liked to participate, suggests that more could have been done to engage civil society groups in Wales in the Convention. This chapter directs attention to CSOs' organisational structures and the influence of their cultures in determining where it was appropriate to engage in EU issues. Perhaps unsurprisingly, given the limited EU mandate of the National Assembly for Wales, many of these groups preferred to delegate MLG and EU issues to their upper echelons. Without such local and broad participation by civil society in the

EU's constitution-making process, the legitimacy of the constitutional outcome was compromised.

In terms of MLG, the Convention activities of a few CSOs did span different governance levels and they liaised directly with EU institutions or EU Convention mechanisms or Conventioneers, demonstrating the presence of some MLG in the arena of high politics. However, neither the EU's institutional discourse on civil society nor the Convention structures were entirely conducive to top-down MLG, serving to question the legitimacy of MLG arrangements. The activities of the sub-national authority, together with some CSOs acquiescing that the Convention be dealt with higher up in their organisation, similarly seem to point to the continued prominence of the Member State and above in this instance of EU high politics, bypassing local citizens.

NOTES

1. Hereafter referred to as the Convention.
2. A submission by a Euro group Regions with Legislative Power in 2001 was signed by 52 European regions, testifying to the considerable number of such regions in Europe.
3. Welsh devolution was based on a corporate model, with executive power (to make secondary legislation in certain areas) invested in the whole of the National Assembly for Wales as defined by the Government Wales Act (1998). However a de facto separation between the Assembly and its cabinet occurred with the creation of a Welsh Assembly Government in 2001. When this chapter makes reference to the National Assembly for Wales or the Assembly, this therefore refers to both the Welsh Assembly Government and the wider Assembly deliberative body. The corporate status of the Assembly was being debated at the time of writing, with the Government of Wales bill in the UK parliament (now the Government of Wales Act 2006).
4. Seventeen interviews with Welsh CSOs, together with eighteen interviews of policy makers in the Wales–EU policy process, were conducted from November 2003 to September 2004. CSOs were identified through both snowball and stratified sampling to interview a range of groups which varied in size, function, resources, sector, geographical remit and Convention participation. This sample is not representative of civil society in Wales at large but is meant to provide a snapshot of civil society participation and to explore civil society perceptions.
5. The EU, despite affecting many of the Assembly's competencies, is a reserved matter for the UK government. Nevertheless, the Assembly must abide by EC obligations and has the power to implement EC policies (Government of Wales Act 1998 section 106.1) and create subordinate legislation to carry out that legislation when European orders have been designated to it under section 2 (2) of the European Community Act of 1972. Moreover, the Assembly is permitted to have EU representation in Brussels and to have a Standing European Committee. The UK government does involve the Assembly Cabinet (Welsh Assembly Government) in EU policy decisions that affect devolved areas and Wales, as laid down in the Memorandum of Understanding and individual Concordats (these are codes of good practice, not legally binding rules).
6. By European-wide or European groups is meant organisations that have membership in one or more European countries and/or are umbrella groups at the European level.
7. As Meyer (2003: 23f) points out, a strong degree of high integration in other institutional contexts not only decreases an institution's (in this case the Assembly's) potential for

independent thinking from the higher institution (the UK government), but also reduces civil society's ability to press competing claims to that institution, as it can be less open to alternative views.
8. There were two other key issues which occupied the Welsh Assembly Government at this time. There was the debate over the future of the Wales European Centre (which represented the interests of member Welsh organisations in Brussels), following the Welsh Assembly Government's decision to leave in May 2002. In addition, the Assembly was engaged in the debate on European Governance, during the first few months of the Convention.
9. Four Welsh newspapers – *The Western Mail, South Wales Echo, South Wales Evening Post* and *Wales on Sunday* on the database Lexis Nexis were searched for the key words 'European Convention', 'future of Europe', 'draft constitution' and 'draft treaty'. After excluding non-relevant articles, 81 articles were identified within the time frame. The time frame of October 2001 to July 2003 gives insight into the debate both preceding and following the Convention (although it is recognised that the future of Europe debate had been started with the Nice Treaty of 2000). It is conceded that these papers only comprise a small proportion of newspaper readership in Wales. Nonetheless, they give some insight into the framing of the Welsh debate.

REFERENCES

Anheier, H.K. (2004) *Civil society: Measurement, evaluation, policy*, London: Earthscan.

Bache, I. and Flinders, M. (2004) 'Themes and issues in multi-level governance', in I. Bache and M. Flinders (eds) *Multi-level governance*, Oxford: Oxford University Press.

Beger, N. (2004) 'Participatory democracy: Organised civil society and the 'new' dialogue', paper presented at: *Towards a European Constitution: from the Convention to the IGC and beyond*, Federal Trust Conference, London, 1–2 July 2004.

Borragán, N.P.S. (2004) 'A constitution for Europe: What role for organised interests?' paper presented at: *Towards a European Constitution: from the Convention to the IGC and beyond*, Federal Trust Conference, London, 1–2 July 2004.

Constantelos, J. (2004) 'The Europeanisation of interest group politics in Italy: Business associations in Rome and the regions' *Journal of European Public Policy* 11 (6), 1020–40.

Cook, D. (2006) *Civil society in Wales and European Union policy-making: The case of the European Convention. A contextual analysis of opportunity, behaviour and democratic effects*, unpublished PhD thesis, University of Glamorgan.

Day, G., Dunkerley, D. and Thompson, A. (2000) 'Evaluating the "new politics": civil society and the National Assembly for Wales' *Public Policy and Administration* 15 (2), 25–37.

Drakeford, M. (2006) ' "Infiltration or incorporation": The voluntary sector and civil society in post-devolution Wales' in G. Day, D. Dunkerley and A. Thompson (eds) *Civil society: Policy, politics, space*, Cardiff: University of Wales Press.

European Convention (2002a) *The Secretariat: Speeches delivered at the inaugural meeting of the Convention on 28 February 2002*, CONV 4/02, Brussels: The European Convention.

European Convention (2002b) *Plenary Session with civil society, 24 June 2002*, Brussels, 1–53.

European Convention (2003), *The Secretariat: Contribution by Peter Hain, member of the Convention – Europe and the Regions*, CONV 526/03, Brussels: The European Convention, http://register.consilium.eu.int/pdf/en/03/cv00/cv00526en03.pdf.
European Council (2001) 'Declaration on the future of the European Union' in *Annex I to Conclusions of the presidency*, Laeken, 14 and 15 December 2001, pp. 1–5.
European Economic and Social Committee (2002a) *European Convention/EESC: Mr Jean Luc Dehaene takes stock at the half way stage of the Convention's work*, Press release No. 79/2002, Brussels: EESC.
European Economic and Social Committee (2002b) *ESC members stress their specific value to the European Convention*, Press Release No. 12/2002, Brussels: EESC.
European Economic and Social Committee (2002c) *European Convention: Jean-Luc Dehaene welcomes the European ESC's initiatives for organised European civil society*, Press Release No. 23/2002, Brussels: EESC.
George, S. (2004) 'Multi-level governance and the European Union', in I. Bache and M. Flinders (eds) *Multi-level governance*, Oxford: Oxford University Press, pp. 107–26.
Grimm, D. (2004) 'Treaty or constitution? The legal basis of the European Union after Maastricht', in E.O. Eriksen, J.E. Fossum and A.J. Menéndez (eds) *Developing a Constitution for Europe*, London: Routledge, pp. 69–87.
Hoffman, L. (2003) 'The Convention on the Future of Europe: Thoughts on the Convention model', in J. Shaw, P. Magnette, L. Hoffman and A. Verges (eds) *The Convention on the Future of Europe: Working towards an EU constitution*, London: The Federal Trust for Education and Research, pp. 73–94.
Hooghe, L. and Marks, G. (2001) *Multi-level governance and European integration*, Oxford: Rowman and Littlefield.
Jones, H.C. (2002) 'Europe's crossroads' *Agenda* (Spring), 1–8.
Jordan, A. (2001) 'The European Union: An evolving system of multi-level governance . . . or government?' *Policy and Politics* 29 (2), 193–208.
Keohane, D. (2002) *EPIN briefing note: The UK and the Convention: The centre for European Reform* www.epin.org/papers/NatDebandPositions/08_Kehoane_UKdebate.pdf, last access: 13 September 2004.
Lombardo, E. (2003) *The participation of civil society in the debate on the future of Europe: Rhetorical or action frames in the discourse of the Convention?*, working paper, Zaragoza: University of Zaragoza.
Magnette, P. (2003) 'Will the EU be more legitimate after the Convention?' in J. Shaw, P. Magnette, L. Hoffman and A. Verges (eds) *The Convention on the Future of Europe: Working towards an EU constitution*, London: The Federal Trust for Education and Research, pp. 21–41.
Magnette, P. (2004) 'When does deliberation matter? Constitutional rhetoric in the Convention on the Future of Europe', in C. Closa and J.E. Fossum (eds) *Deliberative Constitutional Politics in the EU*. ARENA Report No. 5/04, Oslo, Zaragoza: ARENA – University of Zaragoza, pp. 205–239.
McLeod, A. (2002) *Regional parliaments and the Convention*, The Federal Trust for Education and Research: Constitutional Online Papers 05/02, www.fedtrust.co.uk/default.asp?pageid=267&mpageid=67&msubid=277&groupid=6, last access: 19 November 2007.
Meyer, D.S. (2003) 'Political opportunity and nested institutions' *Social Movement Studies* 2 (1), 17–35.

Miller, V. (2003) *The Convention on the Future of Europe: The deliberating phase* House of Commons Library Research Papers 03/16, London: House of Commons Library.

National Assembly for Wales (2002a) *Regions must play their part in the future of Europe says first minister*, Press Release 17 October 2002, Cardiff: NAW.

National Assembly for Wales (2002b) *European and External Affairs Committee: White paper on governance – written submissions* Paper EUR 01-02, Cardiff: NAW.

Peters, B.G. and Pierre, J. (2004) 'Multi-level governance and democracy: A Faustian bargain', in I. Bache and M. Flinders (eds) *Multi-level governance*, Oxford: Oxford University Press, pp. 75–89.

Regan, E., Mcleod, A., Miller, V. and Williams, B. (2003) *The proposed treaty establishing a constitution for Europe*, Inter Parliamentary Research Network Briefing 03/01, 7 November 2003, www.scottish parliament.uk/business/research/briefings-03/iprn03-01.pdf, last access: 19 November 2007.

Royles, E. (2003) 'Objective one', in J. Osmond and J.B. Jones (eds) *Birth of Welsh democracy: The first term of the National Assembly for Wales*, Cardiff: Institute for Welsh Affairs/Welsh Governance Centre, pp. 131–48.

Royles, E. (2004) 'Civil society and objective one' *Contemporary Wales* 16 (1), 101–21.

Scott, J. (2002) 'The culture of constitution-making? 'Listening' at the Convention on the future of Europe' *German Law Journal*, 3 (9), 1–7.

Scottish Executive (2002) *Consultation responses* last access: 12 December 2003.

Scottish Parliament (2002) *European Committee: Report on the future of Europe*, SP Paper 705, Edinburgh: Scottish Parliament.

Shaw, J. (2003) 'Process, responsibility and inclusion in the EU constitutionalism' *European Law Journal* 9 (1), 45–68.

Shaw, J., Hoffman, L. and Bausili, V. (2003) 'Introduction', in J. Shaw *et al.* (eds) *The Convention on the Future of Europe: Working towards an EU constitution*, London: The Federal Trust for Education and Research, pp. 9–20.

Wales Council for Voluntary Action (2002) *Welsh colloquium on civil society and governance: The Office of Eluned Morgan MEP, European Parliament, Brussels* www.wcva.org.uk/images_client/ACF4E89.rtf, last access: 16 March 2005.

Will, C., Crowhurst, I., Larsson, O., Kendall, J., Olsson, L.-E. and Nordfeldt, M. (2005) *The challenges of translation*: *The Convention and debates on the future of Europe from the perspective of European third sectors*, Third Sector European Policy Working Paper 12, www.ise.ac.uk/collections/TSEP/Open AccessDocuments/12TSEP.pdf, last access: 19 November 2007.

6. Europeanisation as empowerment of civil society: all smoke and mirrors?

**Cristina Elena Parau and
Jerry Wittmeier Bains**

6.1 INTRODUCTION

Despite an explosion of research into the field of Europeanisation in recent years, the outcomes and processes that constitute it remain empirically underexplored, particularly in the context of the newly acceded EU Member States of Central and Eastern Europe (CEE). This chapter endeavours partly to to fill this gap by exploring Europeanisation through a 'bottom-up' lens, asking which domestic actors get empowered and how they utilise the opportunities and avoid the constraints created by the EU at the domestic level. These questions are examined through three cases studies of a series of domestic controversies over public accountability and input legitimacy. The case studies are drawn from (at the time of writing): a current Member State, the UK; a new Member State (a leading EU accession candidate), the Czech Republic, and a poorly performing EU accession candidate, Romania (now a Member State). The cases studied are genetically modified organisms (GMO) legislation in the Czech Republic; the South East London combined heat and power incinerator in the United Kingdom;[1] and the Transylvanian motorway in Romania. These case studies will shed light on how domestic civil society and government utilise the EU and its new opportunities in political contests aimed at influencing domestic policy making, and ultimately altering domestic power relations.

Public accountability is understood in this chapter to be a series of political proceedings whereby the general public seeks to double-check the representativeness of democratic government against such criteria as transparency of decision making; public access to information in the possession of government; the adequacy of the government's consultation of the public; and the public's participation in the myriad workaday decisions which government takes between infrequently occurring elections.

6.2 THE APPROACH OF THIS CHAPTER

Most Europeanisation research to date follows a distinctly 'top-down' perspective, which purports to explain the impact of the EU on the domestic arena in terms of the linear causal effect of certain theorised EU 'mechanisms'. The dominance of the top-down paradigm has been questioned in recent years for its heavy reliance on a dependent–independent variable research design, and for its neglect of the complexity and non-linearity of multi-level governance in the EU (Featherstone 2003; Olsen 2002). Such linearity often proves incapable of isolating the EU from other causes which may be producing the same effect independently, reinforcingly or countervailingly (Anderson 2003: 49). Examples of such supervening causes include globalisation and the new public management (Goetz 2001a). The 'top-down' approach has several limitations and has been exported to the study of Eastern Europe. Here the scope for top-down Europeanisation has been assumed to be much larger than in the old EU Member States, because of the highly asymmetrical power relations theorised to exist between the EU and the accession candidates (Grabbe 2001). The 'accession conditionality' imposed by the EU on the candidates has been theorised to be the key Europeanisation mechanism. A significant 'misfit' between EU and domestic institutions creates 'adaptational pressure' in the Europeanisation process and the Communist legacy of CEE countries is generally assumed to generate further stresses in this area (Grabbe 2001, 2003; Lippert *et al.* 2001). When combined with accession conditionality, this would transform every aspect of CEE governance. This view has also been challenged recently because of the widespread expectation that the EU's attempts to transform the CEE countries would have a very limited success (Goetz 2001b). Indeed, several scholars claimed that the EU's efforts to Europeanise administrative capacity in CEE were also not particularly successful. Accession conditionality has not produced clearly identifiable effects, leaving room for reinterpretation of the conditions by the accession countries – particularly where the EU *acquis* has been 'thin'. The Commission's 'fuzzy commands' have often seen changes in favour of domestic agendas rather than pursuing EU objectives. Thus, EU conditionality has not proved to be a linear cause, but a 'tool bag of differentiated and shifting instruments including prescriptive norms, institutional formats and preferences', which domestic actors have been able to interpret and deploy for their own purposes (Hughes *et al.* 2004: 3).

This state of affairs calls for research that treats the EU and accession conditionality not as *the* independent variable, but as a complex and multi-level process characterised by 'the interaction between multi-level actors, perceptions, interests, different rewards and sanctions, temporal factors,

[and] institutional and policy compliance' (Hughes *et al.* 2004: 3). More attention needs to be paid to domestic actors and institutions, and how they strategise conditionality 'from the bottom up' (Goetz 2005: 480). To address these problems, the research discussed in this chapter has followed a bottom-up design. The term 'bottom-up' has been employed for some time, often rather loosely (Giuliani 2001); recently however, it has been recognised as a fully distinct approach to Europeanisation research (Dyson and Goetz 2003: 13). Bottom-up Europeanisation, in other words, is not a theory but a research design:

> that . . . start[s] from the analysis of the system of interaction (actors, resources, problems, style, and collective problem-solving rules) at the *domestic* level and . . . raise[s] the question whether the EU affects this system of interaction and if so in what way (as a resource, as a reformulation of the problem, as a new set of collective problem-solving rules, as a constraint on what is feasible, as an alteration to the opportunity structure, as a new frame of reference, etc.). (Franchino and Radaelli 2004: 948 original italics)

As a research design, it differs from a top-down approach in the way it conceptualises the EU and Europeanisation as well as in its empirical focus. The EU is only one 'element in domestic political manoeuvres and in legitimising domestic reforms' (Dyson and Goetz, 2003: 13). Thus, bottom-up approaches put the focus on domestic actors and the way they utilise the EU in domestic political conflicts – aspects largely neglected by top-down perspectives (Dyson and Goetz 2003: 13; Jacquot and Woll 2003; Franchino and Radaelli 2004). This chapter address two main questions: 1) Which domestic actors utilise the opportunities and avoid the constraints created by the EU at the domestic level? And 2) What effect does this have on domestic power relations?

For the purposes of this chapter, empowerment is defined relative to domestic government: that is, civil society will have been seen to be empowered by the EU if without it civil society would not have prevailed upon the government to change a given decision, and if the latter would not have changed that decision without EU involvement (Lukes 1974). In other words, if the interests of the civil society that are challenging the substance and/or procedure of government decisions and are reflected in outcomes – interests that the government would have been likely to disregard – then civil society can be seen as having been empowered over the government.

Before addressing the question of who gets empowered, we briefly review the literature on the effect of the EU on domestic power relations. The empirical evidence related to bottom-up causation (presented below) will be contextualised and clarified by a discussion of the range of effects that the EU may have in the domestic arena. What do we know about the effect of the EU on domestic power relations? The case studies below focus only on two domestic actors, civil society and the Executive (both central and local), and generate three hypotheses from the literature based on the Executive Empowerment thesis, the Diffusion thesis, and the Network Governance thesis.

The Executive Empowerment thesis (Moravcsik 1994) claims that the EU augments the political resources domestic central executives possess, leading to a further centralisation of power at the expense of other domestic actors. Participation in international institutions like the EU redistributes power at the domestic level in a way that systematically benefits national executives. The EU is *par excellence* a power resource for national Executives, as decisions that affect many policy domains are made in Brussels, and the decisional process there is very often too costly for most domestic actors to participate in. These factors enhance the Executive's relative capacity for action by isolating it from the pressures of domestic and trans-national interests (Wolf 1999: 234). Their autonomy is thus enhanced (Featherstone 2003: 9).

The main rival of the Executive Empowerment thesis is the Diffusion thesis. It claims that participation in the EU diffuses power from the Executive to domestic civil society and sub-national governments (Risse *et al.* 2001: 11). The EU provides new resources and opportunities to these actors, especially to: EU supranational organs, which empower them to bypass domestic constraints (Risse *et al.* 2001: 11); pan-European networks, which empower them to participate indirectly in EU decisional processes and influence EU policy independently of the domestic Executive (Börzel 2003); EU funding, which enhances their resources and action capacity; and EU legislation, which enables their direct participation in domestic decisional processes. Such resources are particularly important when the State is hostile to civil society actors (Cowles Green 2001) – as one may expect in post-Communist countries. Domestic Executives thus find themselves constrained by 'alliances among sub-national and supranational actors' (Moravcsik 1994: 3).

Indeed, the Executive Empowerment and Diffusion theses both assume an adversarial relationship between the State and civil society. By contrast, the Network Governance thesis posits that the EU does not empower one actor over another; rather it transforms domestic governance, leading to co-operative relationships between State and non-State actors (Kohler-Koch 1999). Participation in the EU creates constraints and opportunities for all domestic actors and does not indiscriminately empower one specific set of actors over another, but rather increases their mutual interdependence (Kohler-Koch 1999). The co-operative network mode of governance, having emerged and become dominant in Brussels, has trickled down to EU

Member States, where it is replacing other modes of governance (for example, corporatist or statist) (Kohler-Koch and Eising 1999: 7). The case studies presented below reveal evidence of some, but not all, of these theorised effects of Europeanisation. The main point, however, remains that these effects are produced from the bottom up by the actions of domestic actors, and are not merely produced by abstract 'EU mechanisms'.

6.3 EVIDENCE OF THE CASE STUDIES

6.3.1 The Case of Legislation on Genetically Modified Organisms in the Czech Republic[2]

Biotechnological research has been on-going in the Czech Republic since the 1970s. By 1996 the first foreign biotech firms had entered the Republic and conducted the first field trials of genetically modified organisms (GMOs). Until 2000 no regulation of GM practices existed; however, in 1997 civil society opposition to GM emerged, catalysed by the opening of a Greenpeace office in Prague. Following the Czech Republic's application to become a member of the EU, *acquis* conditionality required it to set up an institutional framework for implementing that part of the *acquis* that regulates GM products and practices. The Environment Ministry was charged with this task. The Ministry chose as its expert advisory committee in matters of transgenosis the Czech Commission for Genetically Modified Organisms and Products (CCGMOP), which had been formed by scientists in that field in 1986. Several members of CCGMOP also joined a group of academic biologists involved in biotechnological research who, citing a climate of 'fear and manipulation' allegedly created by Greenpeace, founded and became the first directors of Biotrin, a pro-GM non-governmental organisation (NGO), to countervail opposition to GM. The two organisations, Biotrin and CCGMOP, one private and the other public, became entwined through interlocking directorates.

Biotrin opposed EU regulation of Czech biotechnology and was the strongest advocate in favour of transgenosis in the Czech Republic. Its directors were proactive and effective at generating pro-GM publicity. The head of Biotrin argued that the EU directives regulating GMOs were 'irrational' and were the creature of partisan interests that indirectly supported the emotional fears of an ignorant public. Biotrin argued that the precautionary principle was 'vague' and designed to disavow scientific facts, and was an import barrier to boot (Stöckelová 2003: 9).

In their capacity as advisers to the Environment Ministry through CCGMOP, the Biotrin directors played a major role in drafting Act

153/2000 of the Czech Parliament on the Use of Genetically Modified Organisms and Products, that transposed into Czech law the transgenic *acquis* – EU Directives 90/219/EEC and 90/220/EEC (Stöckelová 2003: 7). The results, both legal and practical, were in no way contrary to expectation. The Czech GM law of 2000 excluded the precautionary principle, a keystone of EU environmental policy (European Commission 2000). The law imposed some surprisingly low constraints regarding failures to register new transgenic organisms, an important aspect of the regulatory scheme, which led to widespread non-compliance to the registration procedure by Czech biotech researchers. Biotrin assured a minimalist transposition of the Directives, greatly reducing the 'undesirable' impact (from the industry's viewpoint) of the EU's regulatory scheme (Stöckelová 2003: 9f).

Through their experience with this transposition, Biotrin (through the CCGMOP) succeeded in forging a long-term relationship with the Environment Ministry. The 2000 Act became controversial in Parliament and had to undergo modification by the Environment Ministry to remedy some of the in-built defects. Ironically, the interlocking directors of Biotrin and CCGMOP also drafted the modifications. By implementing these modifications, Biotrin abandoned its strategy of outright hostility to the EU Directives and replaced it with a strategy of minimal compromise and co-operation to maintain its influence within the Environment Ministry.

The new strategy proved successful, allowing Biotrin's directors to 'capture' the Czech Ministry of the Environment. This allowed them to act in ways that minimised public participation in GM regulatory decision making, as mandated by the EU Directives – a class of decisions in which the capturing private parties had an interest. The capture was evidenced by the policy outcomes reflected in the legislative drafts and in the subsequent public consultation practices of the Environment Ministry. The EU Directives had included public accountability procedures, including mandates to make information available to the public and to consult civil society when authorising GMO trials and products. The interlocked directors of Biotrin and CCGMOP adamantly opposed these provisions: one of Biotrin's directors, for example, opined that the participation of civil society in the procedures for authorising GM practices was 'a nonsense' (Stöckelová 2003: 9). Biotrin members labelled their political opponents 'irrational, ignorant, pseudo-religious and fundamentalist', and insisted that the public, incapable of acquiring substantial knowledge of genetics, had to be 'correctly' educated about GMOs by scientists (Stöckelová 2003: 10). Biotrin opposed the participation of the Czech public in administrative procedures as mandated by EU law, and took whatever steps it could to prevent any substantial participation from occurring.

The EU Directives were remoulded by Biotrin not only in relation to transposition, but also, even after the transposed law was amended years later, in its implementation by the competent Czech ministerial agency. This was possible through the Biotrin's directors' continuing influence within the Ministry and its administrative practice. The net result was to reduce 'public participation' to little more than a hollow formality, as the Ministry neutered the Directives' public participatory provisions. The few members of the general public who took part in consultations on GMOs were not permitted to attend the proceedings or to bring any of their expertise to bear on the issues being debated. The Ministry marginalised expert opposition to the biotech industry. When Greenpeace attempted in 2002 to participate in the proceedings authorising field trials of Monsanto's Bt-corn by submitting comments and objections, its input was neither included in the transcription of the minutes of the proceedings nor published on the Ministry's website – unlike the comments of pro-GM lobbyists. The minutes of at least one of the consultations were drawn up by two civil servants of the Environment Ministry with the participation of a member of CCGMOP, and approved by the chairman of CCGMOP (Stöckelová 2003: 15). In acting thus, the CCGMOP went far beyond its delegated competence, from an expert-advisory capacity to one supervising the work of administration. Indeed, CCGMOP played the crucial role in all Ministry decisions to approve field trials or commercial uses of GMOs. All of these facts indicate that Biotrin had 'captured' the Czech government agency responsible for regulating the industry's activities, and was using the capture to shape ministerial proceedings in their own interests.

Given that the public participatory provisions in the EU Directives are actually intended to enhance public participation and increase input legitimacy of the Member States' decisions about GM regulation, the Czech case illustrates how domestic factors outside the control of the EU can constrain the proper implementation of the Directive. Directives may be redirected by domestic actors to serve the interests of only a faction of civil society. Indeed, the Czech case illustrates how one narrow faction of civil society, the biotech industry, competing for input into government decisions, prevailed over all other civil society interests. This was achieved through straightforward agency capture, and was possible because EU directions tend to be fuzzy, allowing for significant leeway on crucial matters such as agency staffing. Neither the EU supranational organs nor EU legislation exerts any control over the staffing of the Member States' domestic organs charged with implementing EU legislation. When a domestic government agency charged with implementing EU law is 'captured' by certain civil society interests, these actors are well positioned to restrict the meaningful involvement of specific (opposing) interests. The implementation (if not the transposition) of the *acquis* may actually limit the accountability of government agencies. The captured government organs are likely to implement procedures in ways that serve the dominant interests. The EU does not have the power to prevent this from happening, given its lack of competence to influence personnel policy and ministerial appointments by Member States' domestic governments.

In the Czech case, agency capture by industry was also greatly facilitated by the lack of any mobilisation or general development of civil society. This inhibited the policy input of the least-developed factions of domestic civil society, suggesting (somewhat ironically) that established actors are likely to be further empowered by the EU. The GMO Directives presume a developed civil society at the domestic level, but if certain civil society interests lack basic action capacity (such as media savvy, funding, technical expertise, access to an independent judiciary), EU legal provisions for participatory democracy and governmental accountability are insufficient. The EU can do no more than provide opportunities. Who gets empowered ultimately depends on the actors' capacity to make use of these opportunities. Few Czech civil society organisations had the capacity to enter into a dialogue with either the government or the industry on the regulation of GMOs, or to express autonomous views on any of the issues arising from GM or its regulation. Even Greenpeace, the only organised Czech opposition to GMOs, only had one person working on transgenic issues, and was unable to mobilise other members of the public to countervail the biotech industry. Thus Czech civil society was generally too weak to exploit the opportunities created by accession to the EU.

6.3.2 The South East London Combined Heat and Power Incinerator in the UK[3]

In 1986, the South East London Waste Disposal Group, a joint committee of the Councils of the London Boroughs of Lewisham, Greenwich and Southwark, agreed to build a waste incinerator for the disposal of household wastes – the South East London Combined Heat and Power (SELCHP) incinerator. The incinerator was to be sited in Deptford, an impoverished part of the Borough of Lewisham composed of a largely immigrant population. In 1988, the Waste Disposal Group agreed to include certain private interests, the winners of a competitive tendering process, in order to spread the high costs of building and operating the incinerator. The SELCHP Consortium was formed, which also included the Councils as shareholders. In the same year the EU Directive 85/337 on Environmental Impact Assessments (EIA) was transposed into UK regulations. As part of the building permit process, the Directive required developers to conduct

Environmental Impact Assessments in order to assess the environmental impact and propose ways to minimise it. SELCHP became one of the first large-scale projects in the UK to fall under these regulations. The Lewisham Planning Department, which served all three Boroughs in the capacity of a permit-granting authority, was required to submit an environmental statement, a summary of the EIA, to stakeholders in the project. By statute, all stakeholders had 21 days to comment on and/or challenge the permit application, or to request further information. The new law obliged the Planning Department to take account of stakeholders' input into its decisions on permit applications. At the same time, however, Lewisham Council itself held a stake in the development consortium applying for the permit to build the incinerator. Thus the Borough of Lewisham was both a Consortium shareholder and the planning authority.

When opposition emerged it was very weak. During the statutory 21 days for public comment, the Planning Department received only seven letters of complaint from individuals and two petitions in opposition signed by 25 and 57 residents respectively. The complaints concerned the impact on their health of an incinerator operating nearby, as well as a lack of transparency in the decision-making process. They also contested the brevity of the public consultation period. Indeed, the Planning Department met the requirement to notify stakeholders in absolutely minimal form: the affected community was consulted as narrowly as possible, that is, in yards rather than miles.

The Waste Disposal Group responded to challengers by organising a few public meetings. These were attended by around a hundred people. As a result of the meetings, the Group agreed to fund an independent review of the EIA, which would re-check the accuracy of the environmental statement, 'translate' the technical data into 'plain English' and recommend improvements to the incinerator design to abate some of its impacts. As a result of this review, £10 million was spent on a redesign. The Group, moreover, suggested that residents in opposition set up an Incinerator Monitoring Group to 'monitor' the operation of the incinerator.

EU Directive 85/337 furnished the general public from the top-down with an accountability tool – the EIA procedure and the public consultation it mandates. It thus created an opportunity for the residents of Deptford to air their opposition to the SELCHP incinerator in a public forum, and then, perhaps, to influence the final shape of the project. However, the Deptford public proved too weak to challenge the project significantly. They were largely ignorant of their right to hold governments accountable in the first place. Most residents were recent immigrants who were little aware of ecological issues and were unlikely to appreciate the environmental as well as health risks posed by nearby incineration. The

Waste Disposal Group and the Lewisham Planning Department are likely to have understood these elementary points when in 1986 they decided, consulting nobody, where to site the incinerator. They settled on Deptford as a neighbourhood where resistance was least likely to arise, or was least likely to succeed if it emerged. Indeed, the minutes of one Lewisham Planning Department meeting, in which the incinerator permit application was discussed, recorded how one officer remarked on the unlikelihood of any public inquiry. Placing infrastructure such as an incinerator in a poor, immigrant and/or working-class neighbourhood, where the residents would probably lack the human resources and economic power to mobilise effectively, would still meet the requirements of any accountability proceedings, including those mandated by EU law. Holding a government to account requires mobilisation and expertise, which in turn require money, which the public or organised civil society must draw from its own private purse. We do not know whether the private interests that later became involved in the Consortium played any role in the decision over where to site the incinerator. However, the local Councils appear to have planned in advance the filtering-out of policy input from any civil society interests other than the waste disposal industry, by cherry-picking a public that had been previously identified as too weak to resist.

Further evidence that Deptforders lacked the civic means to make effective use of the EIA accountability tool transpired in the aftermath of the public consultation. Lewisham Council and the Consortium reacted to the rather feeble resistance with a co-optation strategy to persuade them of the incinerator's safety. They paid to take the protest leaders on junkets abroad to visit similar incinerators already operating in urban districts in Europe. According to Joan Ruddock, the Member of Parliament for Lewisham and Deptford:

> Initially there was a lot of concern from the local residents and so the Council undertook steps to convince them that the incinerator would be safe. So for example they took them to Switzerland to see a state-of-the-art incinerator and the leadership of the tenants association came back convinced that it was okay. They saw that in Switzerland the plant was in a city centre area, and therefore they felt that if it was okay for the Swiss, it was going to be okay for the Brits. So their concerns about emissions were quickly removed through an exercise undertaken by the Council. This was not in any sense either accountability or consultation, because the very body that had to take the decision, which was the planning authority for the decision, was also wishing to gain public support, and therefore their consultation went beyond consultation to persuasion.

The MP's account highlights the civic weakness of the residents, whose resistance was overpowered by a commonplace public relations strategy on the part of Lewisham Council and the Consortium. The residents' associations also lacked the expertise to understand the technicalities of incineration, or the capacity to mobilise the expertise of others to challenge the Council's technical representations. If these residents' associations had enjoyed the support and facilitation of ecological groups like Greenpeace, which can mobilise expertise, then the outcome of the consultation might have been different.

The Waste Disposal Group and the Consortium funded junkets aimed at persuading the locals. The Councils also had more information than the residents about the intended uses of the incinerator, and exploited this by falsely promising locals that the plant would provide them cheaper electricity and heat. In reality the by-produced electricity was to be sold to the national power grid and the heat exhausted. The Councils' success was greatly eased by the inexperience of the affected public, as shown above.

Second, the Councils, charged with implementing EU law, chose to meet these EU requirements minimally. For example, Lewisham Council chose to consult as few of the residents of Deptford as possible. (On the other hand, one of the Lewisham Planning Officers did claim one year previously that the zone was so narrow because Lewisham had had little experience of the EIA procedure.) The Southwark and Greenwich Councils decided against consulting any of their citizens at all, although the incinerator would also impact on residents of these boroughs. Furthermore, the Councils did not extend the time for consultation beyond the legal minimal requirement of 21 days, despite complaints from locals that they were not able to grasp such complex matters in such a short time. Furthermore, the Councils could have revisited their original decision to build an incinerator in a densely populated urban setting. However, they chose to ignore the complaints of the Deptford residents (expressed in their letters of protest) that they had never been consulted about this original decision. They released no information about this initial decision when requested by the residential associations, despite the fact that the EIA law required domestic governments to divulge information they possess about projects under review.

In the SELCHP case, as in the Czech GM case, the EU merely provided domestic civil society and the public with an opportunity which they could in theory exploit if they had the social capital to do so. The Deptforders, however, lacked technical expertise and professional protest organisers. The lack of such basic capacity allowed the Councils to win amidst the very EU-designed procedure aimed at holding domestic governments accountable. On the other hand, it can be argued that the Waste Disposal Group's behaviour proved that it had acted in good faith to comply with accountability requirements. Indeed, the Councils and the Consortium paid an outside expert to review the EIA report and paid £10 million for a design that would ensure greater dispersal of air emissions. Although this appears to be a significant investment, it can also be viewed as a strategy to forestall a review by an expert less predisposed to the Consortium's interests than one handpicked by Lewisham Council. The SELCHP case illustrates how domestic governments can easily act as a civil society gatekeeper by: complying minimally with EU procedures; choosing a social context where public opposition is least likely to emerge; and strategically deploying their resources to constrain the use of EU opportunities by an isolated public. This undermines the input legitimacy envisioned in the relevant directives. The power resources of domestic governments are potent enough to trump the intentions of the EU for wider civil society policy input, especially where civil society lacks the social capital to resist.

6.3.3 The Case of the Transylvanian Motorway in Romania

In December 2003, the Romanian government, only a year before closing negotiations with the EU, signed a contract with the American firm Bechtel committing the Romanian State to engage external credit of more than €2.5 billion to finance the building of a motorway through Transylvania. The contract negotiations were never subject to a public call for tenders required by the Romanian law that had partially transposed the public procurement *acquis*, and the solemn undertakings of the Romanian government before the European Commission to abide by the untransposed EU law of public procurement prior to accession. Instead, the government in 2003 adopted a special executive instrument (Emergency Ordinance 60/2003) exempting the contract with Bechtel from certain provisions of this law and of these undertakings. When news of the expensive contract – the largest ever in Romania's history – broke in January 2004, the Commission reacted strongly, especially as the Bechtel-built motorway was to render redundant Romania's section of Corridor IV of the Trans-European Network, running south of Transylvania – the building of which the EU had previously committed itself to funding. Consequently, in February 2004 the Commission began an investigation into the contract, focusing particularly on the peculiar public tendering conditions set up by the Emergency Ordinance. For reasons to do with the Bechtel contract, but also with corruption in general and unregulated international adoptions, several Members of the European Parliament demanded that the EU suspend its accession negotiations with Romania.

The Commission then widened its inquiry to include Romanian conformity with the EU's accession conditions and with its Single Market rules. As the contract had already been signed, the Commission could do nothing to undo it, and it feared that suspending negotiations would cause too much damage to the EU's strategy of enlargement. However, it proceeded by other means to constrain the Romanian government, interdicting any EU financial support for the motorway:

> [S]ince there was no public tendering, the European Commission . . . will not be able to provide any financial support for this project. Furthermore, the European Commission will not be in a position to support any funding by the European Investment Bank for Reconstruction and Development for the construction of the highway (European Commission 2004).

The Commission also insisted that the Romanian government ensured that the motorway would comply with EU environmental legislation, in particular the Directive on Environmental Impact Assessments (European Commission 2004). The Romanian Prime Minister, Social Democrat Adrian Nastase, backed by American officials, stood firm in his commitment to the Transylvanian motorway in the face of severe criticism from Brussels. He issued a formal statement in defence of the decision to exempt Bechtel from the law of public procurement, claiming that the motorway was necessary to prepare Romania for membership of the Atlantic Alliance as well as the EU. The Official Justification to Parliament by the Prime Minister declared:

> Romania belongs *de facto* in the family of European countries, and is committed to integration into the European and Euro-Atlantic structures. In this context modernisation of the system of motorways and national roads is an extremely important condition imposed by international bodies, which has to be met, given the necessity of integrating Romania into the Euro-Atlantic structures . . . The project of building a motorway between Bucharest and Budapest will constitute a first step toward physically connecting our country to the space dominated by NATO and the European Union (Romanian Government 2004).

In thus confounding EU and Atlantic integration, the Romanian government was able to interpret EU accession conditionality in such a way as served its own interests in a domestic political contest, the outcome of which (either way) was unlikely to affect accession as such. On a separate occasion the Prime Minister argued that the motorway was 'essential' to his government's closing negotiations with the EU on Justice and Home Affairs. The motorway was inaugurated on 15 June 2004, and is expected to be completed by 2012.

The Commission's interventions did much to bolster Romanian civil society, which strove to hold its government to account by deploying the Commission's criticisms and authority on top of accession conditionality (European Commission 2004). Indeed, opposition to the project from civil society and opposition political parties erupted simultaneously with

Brussels' censures (in February 2004). Some of the most prominent public policy think tanks in Romania – The Romanian Academic Society and 'The Romanian Think Tank' – attacked the government for the arbitrary and opaque manner in which it had allowed such an expensive contract, especially in the context that: the EU had committed funds for a parallel motorway; Romania's existing road infrastructure was seriously decayed and in need of expensive investments; and the Romanian government was running a tight state budget with many other priorities competing for the scarce financial resources.

Fourteen environmental NGOs submitted letters of protest to the Romanian government, to the European Commission Delegation and to the government's creditors, demanding that the government halt the project immediately and account for its decision. However, the protestors lacked the basic capacity to challenge the project on sound environmental grounds. They had insufficient technical (counter-)expertise to analyse the technicalities of large-scale transportation investment; neither did they have the ability to mobilise such expertise; nor to carry out their own Environmental Impact Assessment; or to work out in the necessary detail an alternative plan (author's interview with Cyclo-Tourism Club Napoca 2004). In addition to this, the opposition was divided over several issues. Some argued that there might be environmental and economic benefits in such a motorway, compared with one built merely to Romanian standards:

> If the motorway is to have environmentally friendly tunnels and bridges, it might disrupt fewer natural habitats than any national motorway . . . which seldom have environmentally friendly tunnels. Besides, if use of the motorway is tolled, and if the toll internalises the environmental cost of transportation, the overall impact may be [relatively] positive' (author's interview with Cyclo-Tourism Club Napoca 2004).

Whatever weaknesses the opposition might be blamed for, the Romanian government further undermined its position by withholding, either deliberately or out of sheer disorganisation, some basic information about the motorway plan. The protestors were shut out of access to the vital information needed to organise a credible campaign:

> We demanded, in accordance with law 544/2001 on Access to Information, information such as the exact route, but were told that such information is not known . . . and that the route in any detail is not known, so we cannot tell whether the motorway will pass through or near nature reserves. Nor could we find out other particulars related to design, for example the number, type and location of tunnels, bridges and noise baffles; or the figures for estimated traffic' (author's interview with Cyclo-Tourism Club Napoca 2004).

Environmental civil society's access was thwarted further by the Environment Ministry's introduction – a year before the Bechtel controversy – of an Order mandating the charging of fees for producing environmental information. This was in spite of both the Romanian Act on Access to Information that had transposed the Directive on Access to Information and the Aarhus Convention on Public Access to Environmental Information, to which Romania was a party, which stated that such information should be produced free of charge. As a result, 'All environmental information, including economic information, is "filtered" in the sense that if you want information you have to pay, and you have to pay so much that you lose your appetite for asking for any more information' (author's interview with Cyclo-Tourism Club Napoca 2004). Romanian NGOs' financial weakness and the Ministry's Order significantly constrained their capacity, disempowered them from carrying out some of the basic functions necessary for accountability proceedings and for input into public policy. In the case of the Transylvanian motorway, '[t]he EIA Report just for one segment of the motorway contains 1500 pages. This would cost millions or tens of millions [of Romanian *lei*] if you paid [the fees] in accordance with the [Ministerial] Order' (author's interview with Cyclo-Tourism Club Napoca 2004). (It is true that the Ministry may have imposed this Order due to its own budgetary constraints, a point that was unable to be checked; in any event, the transaction cost of accountability and legitimacy is a topic that merits further investigation.)

As in the previous two cases, the evidence here shows that, although accession to the EU created unprecedented opportunities for Romanian civil society – access to new organs of government, conditionality, legislation and authority – that may in theory be deployed when attempting to influence public policy, these resources were on their own insufficient to empower them. Their adversary, the Nastase government, used its domestic power and EU resources (as shown by their justificatory discourses) to get around both EU and domestic civil society constraints. The promise of membership of the EU for establishing a better footing for the input legitimacy of public policy of post-Communist countries of CEE remains as yet unfulfilled.

6.4 CONCLUSION

The case studies have shown that the EU creates opportunities and constraints for domestic actors not only in the old EU Member States but also in the accession countries of Central and Eastern Europe in the pre-membership phase. EU-mandated public participatory procedures have the potential to empower domestic civil society, but whether empowerment follows and which section of civil society is empowered depends on domestic factors outside of the EU's control. Domestic governments, with their centrality in the domestic political arena, wield a wide panoply of resources, and are well positioned to counteract the empowerment of civil society through EU tools like the Environmental Impact Assessment. It appears that Executive Empowerment is actually the most common EU effect observed on the ground notwithstanding the intentions of Brussels.

On the other hand, EU effects are also subject to the ability of certain factions of civil society, like industry, to capture government agencies and stultify the implementation of EU-transposed law for their civil society opponents. On the last point, both the Czech and the UK cases, and to a lesser extent the Romanian, revealed that business is by far the most highly organised faction of civil society. This should come as no surprise, as a high degree of organisation and managerial expertise are prerequisites for maintaining profitability in a highly competitive environment. The managerial skills honed in this environment, when transferred to the political arena, help business to prevail over more diffuse civil society interests. Lastly, which civil society factions are empowered to influence public policy depends on their capacity to make use of EU-created opportunities. These findings seem to hold true regardless of whether the civil society in question is organised or not. This suggests that diffusion is also happening, but that one must take care to distinguish between the different factions of civil society, whose empowerment by the EU is highly differential. In all case studies, the existence of EU opportunities and constraints did not radically change the relations between government and civil society but merely reinforced the existing power differential. The fact that case studies drawn from different time periods and different countries show a similar pattern reinforces the belief that this phenomenon might not be the exception, but possibly the norm. This is a hypothesis in need of further investigation.

NOTES

1. The South East London Combined Heat and Power incinerator in the United Kingdom arose from the 'Public Accountability in Contemporary European Contexts' Project, funded by the European Commission under its Fifth Framework Programme, and the case reports submitted as part of it.
2. This case study is based on Stöckelová (2003).
3. This case study is based on Parau and Joss (2003).

REFERENCES

Anderson, J.J. (2003) 'Europeanization in context: Concept and theory', in K. Dyson and K.H. Goetz (eds) *Germany, Europe and the politics of constraint*, Oxford: Oxford University Press.

Börzel, Tanja A. (2003) *Environmental leaders and laggards in Europe: Why there is (not) a southern problem*, Aldershot: Ashgate.

Cowles Green, M. (2001) 'The transatlantic business dialogue and domestic business–government relationships', in M.C. Green, J.A. Caporaso and T. Risse (eds) *Transforming Europe: Europeanization and domestic change*, Ithaca: Cornell University Press.

Dyson, K. and Goetz, K.H. (2003) 'Living with Europe: Power, constraint, and contestation', in K. Dyson and K.H. Goetz (eds) *Germany, Europe and the politics of constraint*, Oxford: Oxford University Press for the British Academy.

European Commission (2000) *Communication from the Commission on the precautionary principle*, Brussels, 2 January 2000 COM(2000) 1 final, http://ec.europa.eu/dgs/health-consumer/library/pub/pub07-en.pdf, last access: 2 March 2003.

European Commission (2004) *Letter to Terra Mileniul III*, ENLARG B3(2004)102078, 27 May 2004.

Featherstone, K. (2003) 'Introduction: In the name of "Europe"', in K. Featherstone and C.M. Radaelli (eds) *The politics of Europeanization*, Oxford: Oxford University Press.

Franchino, F. and Radaelli, C.M. (2004) 'Analysing political change in Italy' *Journal of European Public Policy* 11 (6), 941–53.

Giuliani, M. (2001) 'Europeanization in Italy: A bottom-up process?', in K. Featherstone and G. Kazamias (eds) *Europeanization and the southern periphery*, London: Frank Cass.

Goetz, K.H. (2001a) 'European integration and national executives: A cause in search of an effect', in K.H. Goetz and S. Hix (eds) *Europeanised politics? European integration and national political systems*, London: Frank Cass.

Goetz, K.H. (2001b) 'Making sense of post-Communist central administration: Modernization, Europeanization or Latinization?' *Journal of European Public Policy* 8 (6), 1032–51.

Goetz, K.H. (2005) 'The new member states and the EU: The challenge of adapting to Europe', in S. Bulmer and C. Lequesne (eds) *Member states and the European Union*, Oxford: Oxford University Press.

Grabbe, H. (2001) 'How does Europeanization affect CEE governance? Conditionality, diffusion and diversity' *Journal of European Public Policy* 8 (6), 1013–31.

Grabbe, H. (2003) 'Europeanization goes east: Power and uncertainty in the EU accession process', in K. Featherstone and C.M. Radaelli (eds) *The politics of Europeanization*, Oxford: Oxford University Press.

Hughes, J., Sasse, G. and Gordon, C. (2004) *Europeanization and regionalization in the EU's enlargement to Central and Eastern Europe: The myth of conditionality*, New York: Palgrave Macmillan.

Jacquot, S. and Woll, C. (2003) 'Usage of European integration: Europeanisation from a sociological perspective' *European Integration Online Papers* 7 (12).

Kohler-Koch, B. (1999) 'The evolution and transformation of European governance', in B. Kohler-Koch and R. Eising (eds) *The transformation of governance in the European Union*, London: Routledge.

Kohler-Koch, B. and Eising, R. (1999) 'Introduction: Network governance in the European Union', in B. Kohler-Koch and R. Eising (eds) *The transformation of governance in the European Union*, New York: Routledge.

Lippert, B., Umbach, G. and Wessels, W. (2001) 'Europeanization of CEE executives: EU membership negotiations as a shaping power' *Journal of European Public Policy* 8 (6), 980–1012.

Lukes, S. (1974) *Power: A radical view*, London: Macmillan.

Moravcsik, A. (1994) 'Why the European Union strengthens the state: Domestic politics and international cooperation', paper presented at *The Annual Meeting of the American Political Science Association*, New York, 1–4 September 1994, Center for European Studies, Harvard University.

Olsen, J.P. (2002) 'The many faces of Europeanization' *Journal of Common Market Studies* 40 (5), 921–952.

Parau, C. and Joss, S. (2003) 'The South-East London combined heat and power incinerator (SELCHP)', research paper prepared for: *The Public Accountability in Contemporary European Contexts*, London: Centre for the Study of Democracy.

Risse, T., Cowles Green, M. and Caporaso, J. (2001) 'Europeanization and domestic change: Introduction', in M. Cowles Green, J. Caporaso and T. Risse (eds) *Transforming Europe: Europeanization and domestic change*, Ithaca and London: Cornell University Press.

Romanian Government (2004) *Reasons for emergency ordinance 120/2003*, Bucharest: Romanian Parliament, Chamber of Deputies.

Stöckelová, T. (2003) 'Politics of GMO in the Czech Republic: A case study in public accountability', research paper prepared for: *The Public Accountability in Contemporary European Context*, Prague: Centre for Theoretical Study.

Wolf, K.D. (1999) 'Defending state autonomy', in B. Kohler-Koch and R. Eising (eds) *The transformation of governance in the European Union*, New York: Routledge.

7. Citizenship, welfare and the opportunities for political mobilisation: migrants and unemployed compared
Didier Chabanet and Marco Giugni

7.1 INTRODUCTION

Migrants and the unemployed form the core constituency of two political or issue fields that are central to current debates and policy making in Western Europe: immigration and ethnic relations politics (migrants) as well as employment politics (unemployed). Furthermore, these are two underprivileged minority groups, subject to social and political exclusion, which are poorly equipped in terms of internal resources and mobilising structures that may facilitate collective action. As a result, they share a similar condition insofar as they face a number of obstacles for their mobilisation and therefore have difficulties entering the public domain. Such obstacles, however, are probably higher for the unemployed, given the specific collective action problem faced by them (Bagguley 1992; Faniel 2003; Fillieule 1993; Galland and Louis 1981; Maurer 2001; Richards 2002; Royall 1997). Therefore, we may expect the political mobilisation of the unemployed to be less likely than that of migrants.

This chapter aims to explain cross-national variations in the political mobilisation of migrants and unemployed people following a revised political opportunity approach. We argue that the mobilisation of such underprivileged minority groups is constrained by the political opportunity structures provided by the institutional context of the country in which they act. However, contrary to traditional opportunity theories, we suggest that their mobilisation also depends on a set of opportunities specific to the political or issue field most directly addressed by their claims. We propose to look for these specific opportunities in the institutional approaches to immigration and unemployment.

Following a neo-institutional framework, we maintain that such opportunities stem largely from the ways in which a given political or issue field is collectively defined. Specifically, we aim to show how dominant conceptions of citizenship and of the welfare state channel the mobilisation of migrants and unemployed people, as well as, more generally, the political claim making by collective actors in these two issue fields. In doing so, we draw from recent work on immigration politics that makes the distinction between institutional and discursive opportunities, in order to show how the discursive context in which claim making takes place can either encourage or discourage claim making by minority groups. In other words, political opportunities have both an institutional and a discursive side. From an institutional point of view, they are options for collective action that provide actors with different chances and pose different risks from one context to another (Koopmans 2004). From a discursive point of view, they are options for collective action that provide actors with varying visibility, resonance and legitimacy from one context to another (Koopmans *et al.* 2005). We conceptualise the latter aspect in terms of discursive contexts in which migrants and the unemployed find themselves. Thus, we propose a theoretical framework for explaining claim making by migrants and unemployed, shown in Figure 7.1, which stresses three main factors: (1) the general political opportunity structures, (2) the specific political opportunity structures and (3) the discursive context of claim making.

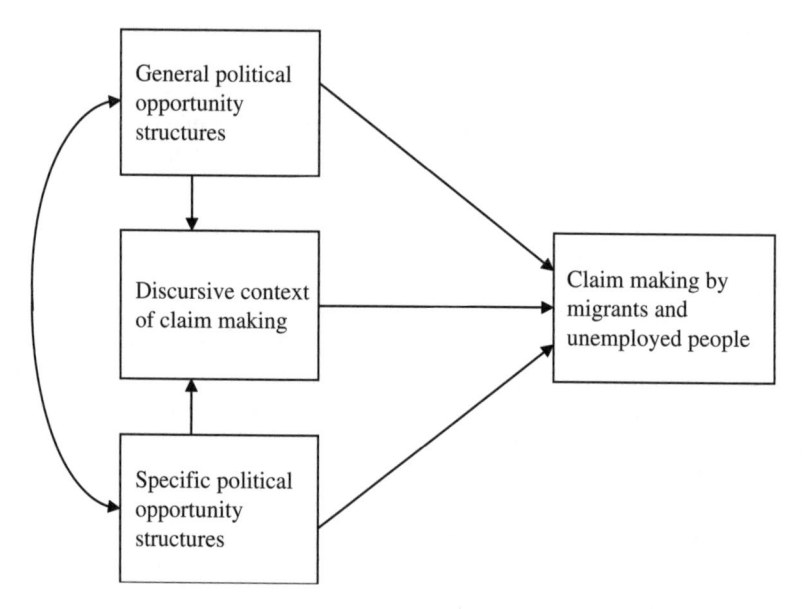

Figure 7.1 A theoretical framework for the analysis of claim making by migrants and unemployed people

We compare four European countries which vary in their institutional approaches to both immigration and unemployment: Britain, France, Germany and Switzerland. The choice of these countries is both theoretically and pragmatically driven. From a theoretical point of view, we have four countries characterised by different political opportunity structures, generally as well as specific to the migration and employment fields. Pragmatically, these are the countries for which we have systematic empirical data on claim making in the two political fields stemming from two comparative projects recently conducted.

7.2 THE POLITICAL OPPORTUNITY APPROACH

Work on social movements and contentious politics has shown through a range of empirical research the impact of political opportunity structures on political mobilisation (see Kriesi 2004; McAdam 1996 and Tarrow 1998 for reviews). Political opportunities are, in the apt formulation of one of its major proponents, 'consistent but not necessarily formal, permanent, or national signals to social or political actors which either encourage or discourage them to use their internal resources to form social movements' (Tarrow 1996: 54). More specifically, they refer to all those aspects of the political system that affect the possibilities that challenging groups have to mobilise effectively. Koopmans (2004: 65) considers them as 'options for collective action, with chances and risks attached to them, which depend on factors outside the mobilising group'.

In an attempt to summarise the various aspects of political opportunity structures, McAdam (1996: 27) has identified four main dimensions that have been used by various authors to explain the emergence of social movements, their development over time, their levels of mobilisation, their forms of action and their outcomes: (1) the relative openness or closure of the institutionalised political system; (2) the stability or instability of that broad set of elite alignments that typically undergird a polity; (3) the presence or absence of elite allies; and (4) the state's capacity and propensity for repression.

The most comprehensive comparative analysis of the impact of political opportunity structures on the mobilisation of social movements in Western Europe was by Kriesi *et al.* (1995). They explained cross-national variations in the levels, forms and outcomes of social movements depending on the degree of openness or closedness of the political institutions, by the degree of inclusiveness of the prevailing strategies of the authorities towards the challengers, and by the configuration of power in the governmental and parliamentary arenas. To simplify a more complex picture, Kriesi *et al.* (1995)

have shown that social movements display a high level of mobilisation and above all a more moderate action repertoire in Switzerland, a country characterised by very open political opportunity structures, while they mobilise less and are more radical in France, where opportunities for mobilisation are less favourable. Germany and the Netherlands are intermediate cases in this respect.

In this approach, political opportunity structures are of a very general nature and imply a pattern of influence that concerns all kinds of challenging groups in a given political context. In other words, political opportunity structures represent a general setting which is assumed to affect all movements in a similar fashion and to a similar extent, as if they could be defined irrespective of the characteristics of specific issue fields and collective actors. However, as was stressed elsewhere (Berclaz and Giugni 2005; Koopmans *et al.* 2005), this conceptualisation of political opportunity structures, in spite of the advances it has brought to the field, is limited in several respects. We suggest that political institutions do not affect all social groups to the same extent. If we take for example groups of immigrants, we see that access to the political system is not the same as for other groups of organised citizens. Immigrants often lack basic citizenship rights allowing them to exert some leverage on these institutions in order to mobilise. Therefore, the institutions that affect their mobilisation are to be found elsewhere, for example in the citizenship rights that facilitate or prevent them from being part of the national community. Similarly, the unemployed, another disadvantaged group, are probably affected more by the specific legislation pertaining to the welfare state than by the general characteristics of the political institutions. Thus, the rights deriving from the social security system will probably have a greater impact on their mobilisation, while they probably play no role whatsoever for other groups and movements. More generally, we would like to suggest that for movements formed by people with full (social and/or political) citizenship rights, the general political opportunity structure has a greater impact than for movements formed by socially and politically excluded groups.

7.3 CITIZENSHIP AND CLAIM MAKING IN THE MIGRATION POLITICAL FIELD

In a recent study on the relationship between political-institutional approaches to immigration and the political conflicts mobilised by collective actors in the public domain on these issues in five European countries, the authors show that prevailing conceptions of the nation and citizenship, as well as their institutionalisation in political practices and policies, shape in significant ways political claim making in the field of immigration and ethnic relations (Koopmans *et al.* 2005; see also Giugni and Passy 2004, 2006; Koopmans and Statham 1999a, 2000). In this perspective, such configurations or models of citizenship play a crucial role in defining and structuring the socially and politically contested field of immigration and ethnic relations. They form a political opportunity structure for the mobilisation of collective actors. These opportunities enlarge or constrain the manoeuvrability of collective actors that mobilise on issues pertaining to migration and channel their intervention into the public domain.

Citizenship models are conceptualised through the combination of two dimensions (one relating to the equality of individual access and the other relating to cultural difference and group rights). The combination of these two dimensions yields four models or configurations of citizenship.

1. Assimilationism combines an ethnic definition of citizenship and a monist view of cultural obligations. Here the state pushes toward assimilation into the norms and values of the national community on an ethno-cultural basis and tends to exclude from this community those who are 'not entitled' to share its norms, values and symbols.
2. Multiculturalism combines a civic conception of citizenship and a pluralistic approach to cultural obligations. Here the children of immigrants in the host country are in principle granted citizenship regardless of their ethnic origin, and minorities' right to ethnic difference is recognised.
3. Republicanism combines a civic conception of citizenship and a monist view of cultural obligations. Here it is relatively easy to obtain citizenship rights, but the price for that is the ceding of ethnic-based identities in favour of accepting the republican ideal of the state.
4. Segregationism combines an ethnic conception of citizenship with a pluralistic view of cultural obligations. This model is probably less common than the other three, at least in Europe, but it exists both theoretically and empirically.[1]

The specific opportunities defined by the prevailing configurations of citizenship work on two levels. First, the institutional level. Citizenship rights define a set of institutional opportunities determining the conditions that impinge upon the costs of different forms of mobilisation and their chances of success (Koopmans 1995; Tilly 1978). However, the mobilisation of collective actors in a given political field does not depend solely on a more or less favourable institutional context. It also stems from certain cultural and discursive conditions. The recent literature on social movements has dealt with these aspects by looking at the role of collective action frames and, more generally, 'the signifying work or meaning construction engaged in by social-movement activists and participants and other parties (e.g. antagonists, elites, media, counter-movements) relevant to the interests of social movements and the challenges they mount' (Snow 2004: 384; see further Benford and Snow 2000). These framing processes can also be conceptualised in terms of opportunities, as producing a set of discursive opportunities. These, in turn, determine which collective identities and substantive demands have a high likelihood of gaining visibility in the mass media, thus resonating with the claims of other collective actors, and achieving legitimacy in the public discourse (Koopmans *et al.* 2005). This is the second level on which the specific political opportunity structures work. However, we consider this aspect as a separate factor characterising the discursive context in which claim making takes place.

7.4 WELFARE STATE AND CLAIM MAKING IN THE EMPLOYMENT POLITICAL FIELD

If the idea that the actors, interests and collective identities involved in the migration political field depend on opportunity structures that are specific to this field is correct, we may expect other political fields to be influenced by certain endogenous characteristics of the institutional and discursive context. We draw from the work in this area and look at the relationship between conceptions of the welfare state and the structuring of public debates in the field of unemployment. We argue that the prevailing view of the welfare state specific to a given country impinges in significant ways upon the 'contentious politics of unemployment', that is, public debates and collective mobilisations pertaining to unemployment. In this neo-institutionalist perspective, dominant conceptions of the welfare state define a political opportunity structure that enlarges or constrains the options for action by collective actors. In other words, our main argument is that the modalities of the intervention of collective actors in the field of unemployment, including the mobilisation of the unemployed, depend on a mix of specific opportunities which derive from the prevailing welfare state regime.

Comparative works on welfare states offer us several typologies that show the differences in the underlying logics of unemployment insurance and social aid regimes. Among the most well-known typologies is that proposed by Esping-Andersen (1990) to distinguish between three welfare state regimes: the liberal or residual regime, the Bismarckian or insurance-based regime, and the universalist or social-democratic regime. Similarly, but more specifically focused on unemployment, Gallie and Paugam

(2000) distinguish between four unemployment-providence regimes: the sub-protecting regime, which provides the unemployed with a protection below the substance level; the liberal/minimal regime, which offers a higher level of protection, but does not cover all the unemployed and in which the level of compensation is weak; the employment-centred regime, which offers a much higher level of protection, but in which the coverage remains incomplete because of the eligibility principles for compensation; and the universalist regime, which is characterised by the breadth of the coverage, a much higher compensation level and more developed active measures.

More recently, Berclaz *et al.* (2004) proposed a typology of conceptions of the welfare state resulting from the combination of two analytical dimensions (the formal criteria of eligibility to social rights and the obligations relating to eligibility) which parallels the typology of Koopmans *et al.* (2005) of citizenship models insofar as both focus on the rights and duties attached to access to a given institution in the broader sense. The combination of these two dimensions generates a four-fold typology of conceptions of the welfare state which can be considered as different political opportunity structures for the mobilisation of the unemployed (and, more generally, for claim making in the field of employment politics): minimalism combines restrictive eligibility criteria and heavy obligations attached to the benefit of social provisions; corporatism also has restrictive eligibility criteria, but less constraints as to the obligations required to benefit from social provisions; universalism couples permissive eligibility criteria with light obligations for eligibility; finally, surveillance is characterised by permissive eligibility criteria, but at the same time heavy obligations for the unemployed in order for them to have the right to social provisions.

Such dominant conceptions of the welfare state define a political opportunity structure for claim making by collective actors in this field, including the mobilisation of the unemployed. Again, such opportunities are both institutional and discursive. For example, changes in the law that regulate unemployment insurance may have an impact on the situation of the unemployed and provide them with new options or motivations to organise and mobilise politically. But above all, cultural notions of social providence and dominant conceptions of the welfare state determine: which demands concerning unemployment and the unemployed are considered as reasonable or acceptable; which constructions of the reality of unemployment are considered as realistic; and which claims and collective actors involved in this field are considered as legitimate within the political system. The question is all the more important when we look at deprived groups, such as the unemployed, as they have difficulties redefining the cultural frames within which the unemployment issue has been socially and politically construed. Such a redefinition is important in order to gain access to the public domain and have their own demands acknowledged as legitimate. As argued above, this aspect is treated separately in our consideration of the discursive context of claim making.

7.5 DATA RETRIEVAL

We test our hypotheses through primary data collected in two comparative research projects: the MERCI project (Mobilisation on Ethnic Relations, Citizenship, and Immigration)[2] and the UNEMPOL project (The Contentious Politics of Unemployment in Europe).[3] The data stem from a content analysis of one national newspaper in each country (*The Guardian* for Britain, *Le Monde* for France, the *Frankfurter Rundschau* for Germany and the *Neue Zürcher Zeitung* for Switzerland) aiming to retrieve reports of political claim making in the migration and unemployment issue fields (that is, all interventions by collective actors in the public domain on issues pertaining to immigration and unemployment). These are all independent newspapers with a nationwide scope of coverage and readership. All of them are broadsheet newspapers with a reputation for consistent and detailed coverage of the field of migration and ethnic relations. From these newspapers, the main news sections of every Monday, Wednesday and Friday issue were sampled and coded.[4] The period covered by the data is 1990–1998 for the migration political field and 1995–2002 for the unemployment political field.

Following the method of political claims analysis (Koopmans and Statham 1999b), which allows us to analyse systematically the relationship between mobilisation and its political-institutional context, the unit of analysis is the single political claim, broadly defined as a strategic intervention, either verbal or non-verbal, in the public space made by a given actor on behalf of a group or collectivity and which bears on the interests or rights of other groups or collectivities. In other words, a claim is the expression of a political opinion by verbal or physical action in the public domain. If it is verbal, a claim usually consists of a statement, an opinion, a demand, a criticism, a policy suggestion and so on, addressed to the public in general or to a specific actor. A political claim can take three main forms: (1) political decision (law, governmental guideline, implementation measure and so on), (2) verbal statement (public speech, press conference, parliamentary intervention and so on); and (3) protest action (demonstration, occupation, violent action and so on). All claims taking one of these forms were coded, provided that they fell into the migration or unemployment issue fields. For each claim retrieved we coded a number of relevant variables. The most important were: the location in time and place of the claim, the actor who made the claim and its policy position relating to the issue at stake, the form of the claim, the thematic focus of the claim, the target of the claim, and the object of the claim (that is, the constituency group).

7.6 OPERATIONALISATION

7.6.1 Political Opportunity Structures

General opportunity structure will be operationalised indirectly, using the typology of the general structural settings for political mobilisation proposed by Kriesi *et al.* (1995: 37). Based on a systematic analysis of the formal institutional structures and the dominant strategy of authorities towards challengers, they characterised the four countries considered in our study as follows. Britain is a case of informal inclusion, characterised by a strong state (hence a closed opportunity structure on the formal side) and inclusive dominant strategy (hence an open opportunity structure on the informal side).[5] France best represents the situation of selective exclusion (strong state and exclusive dominant strategy). Germany is an intermediate case insofar as it presents an intermediate degree of formal openness together with an exclusive dominant strategy. Finally, Switzerland is the best example of integration (weak state and inclusive dominant strategy). The hypotheses derived from these differences in the general structural settings for political mobilisations are discussed below.

To measure specific opportunity structures in the immigration political field, we refer to the procedure followed by Koopmans *et al.* (2005), who gathered systematic information on a series of indicators for each of their two dimensions of citizenship models (the formal criteria and the cultural obligations). A score between zero and one was assigned on each indicator, according to whether it moved in the direction of an ethnic or civic conception of citizenship (formal dimension), or a pluralist or monist view of the cultural obligations (cultural dimension).[6] The results of this operationalisation of the specific opportunity structures for the mobilisation of migrants are shown in Table 7.1. The first line of the table refers to the individual equality dimension of citizenship models, the second to the cultural difference dimension, and the third shows the average score taking into account both dimensions. The four countries in this study are clearly distinguished in terms of their prevailing configuration of citizenship. Britain and France clearly are closer to the civic pole of the individual-equality

Table 7.1 Overall summary scores for the two dimensions of citizenship

	Britain	France	Germany	Switzerland
Individual equality dimension	0.71	0.67	−0.19	−0.58
Cultural difference dimension	0.31	−0.59	−0.20	−0.85
Average score	0.51	0.04	−0.20	−0.72

Note: Results are expressed on a scale ranging from −1 to +1. On the individual equality dimension, code −1 corresponds to the ethnic pole and code +1 to the civic pole. On the cultural difference dimension, code −1 corresponds to the monist pole and code +1 to the pluralist pole. Average scores are computed by adding the scores on the two dimensions and then dividing by 2.

dimension. Germany and especially Switzerland are more ethnic-based. On the cultural-difference dimension, Britain is more pluralist than Germany and especially Switzerland, which have a more monist view. France more or less stands in between. If we combine the scores for the two dimensions, we can see that Britain corresponds to the multicultural model of citizenship, France to the universalist model, and Germany and Switzerland to the assimilationist model.[7]

Unfortunately, we do not have at our disposal equivalent data for the employment political field. In the absence of primary data, for the time being we must resort to existing characterisations of welfare states, such as the typologies of Esping-Andersen (1990), Gallie and Paugam (2000), or Berclaz *et al.* (2004). Our four countries differentiate only partly according to Esping-Andersen's typology. Specifically, Britain belongs to the liberal or residual model, while the other three countries (France, Germany and Switzerland) are all examples of the Bismarckian or insurance-based model. Similarly, our countries can only in part be separated on the basis of Gallie and Paugam's criteria. Specifically, Britain is a liberal/minimal regime (as in Esping-Andersen's typology), while France and Germany fall into the category of the employment-centred regime. Switzerland is not considered in their study. Finally, following the typology proposed by Berclaz *et al.* (2004), Britain can be characterised by a minimalist conception of the welfare state (restrictive eligibility criteria and strong constraints in terms of obligations required to benefit from social provisions; France and Germany follow a corporatist conception (restrictive eligibility criteria and relatively little constraint in terms of obligations required to benefit from social provisions); and Switzerland is also an example of a corporatist conception, but probably closer to a minimalist conception.

Table 7.2   Average discursive positions towards migrants by issue field (1990–1998)

	Britain	France	Germany	Switzerland
Immigration, asylum and alien politics	0.28	0.22	0.21	0.04
Minority integration politics	0.56	0.25	0.35	0.53
Immigration and ethnic relations politics (all fields)	0.43	0.38	0.27	0.21

Note: Results are expressed on a scale ranging from −1 to +1. Code −1 corresponds to anti-minority, racist and xenophobic claims. Code 0 corresponds to neutral, ambivalent and technocratic claims. Code +1 corresponds to pro-minority, anti-racist and anti-extreme-right claims.

7.6.2   Discursive Contexts

To operationalise discursive contexts in both the immigration and employment political fields we can again use the data retrieved in the MERCI and UNEMPOL projects. In both projects we have a raw but nevertheless useful measure of the policy position of claims with regard to the constituency groups which are the ultimate object of the claims: migrants and unemployed people. In other words, we have a general indicator of the discursive position of actors in the two political fields. This indicator was computed as follows: all claims that imply an improvement of the rights and position of the constituency group or an enlargement of its benefits and opportunities received code 1; claims that imply a decrease of the duties of the constituency have also been coded 1; all claims that imply a deterioration of the rights and position of the constituency group or a restriction of their benefits and opportunities were coded −1; claims that imply a increase of the duties of the constituency were coded −1; all neutral, ambivalent, or technocratic claims have received a code 0.[8]

Table 7.2 shows the average discursive positions in immigration and ethnic relations politics in the four countries for each of the two main issue fields (immigration politics and integration politics) and for the entire political field. It is important to stress that we are more interested in the comparison across countries, that is, in the position of the four countries relative to each other, rather than in the absolute values. Such a position changes depending on the issue field (immigration or integration). However, if we look at the entire political field, we see that the general discursive context is clearly most favourable in Britain, as this country has a higher score, followed by France. Germany and, especially, Switzerland present a more hostile context in this respect.

Table 7.3 Average discursive positions towards unemployed people by issue field (1995–2002)

	Britain	France	Germany	Switzerland
Economic dimension	0.48	0.62	0.34	0.49
Social dimension	0.48	0.66	0.30	0.47
Unemployment politics (all fields)	0.48	0.64	0.33	0.48

Note: Results are expressed on a scale ranging from −1 to +1. Code −1 corresponds to claims that imply a deterioration of the rights and position of the constituency group or a restriction of their benefits and opportunities. Code 0 corresponds to neutral, ambivalent and technocratic claims. Code +1 corresponds to claims that imply an improvement of the rights and position of the constituency group or an enlargement of its benefits and opportunities.

Table 7.3 shows the average discursive positions in employment politics in the four countries, for the two main dimensions relating to the debates on unemployment (economic and social[9]) and for the entire political field. Again, the ranking of countries changes depending on the issue field (economic dimension or social dimension). Here cross-issue differences are minimal and the ranking of countries remains virtually the same on both dimensions. Most importantly, we see that, for the entire political field, France presents the most favourable discursive context, followed by Britain and Switzerland, with Germany appearing to be the most hostile context.

7.7 HYPOTHESES

Based on the comparative assessment of the general political opportunity structures, specific political opportunity structures and discursive contexts made above, we can now make predictions about the mobilisation of migrants and unemployed people or, more precisely, their presence in the public domain. Table 7.4 summarises the predictions about the extent of claim making by migrants in the four countries of our study. We make predictions separately for each of the three explanatory factors and then an overall assessment combining the three factors following a cumulative logic. First, concerning the general political opportunity structures, according to the typology of Kriesi *et al.* (1995), the most favourable opportunities for social movement mobilisation among our four countries are to be found in Switzerland. We therefore expect the extent of claim making by migrants to be higher in that country. Britain and France, in contrast, offer a more closed opportunity structure, which should limit migrants' mobilisation. Germany is an intermediate case in this respect. Second, the pre-

Table 7.4 Predictions about the extent of claim making by migrants

	Britain	France	Germany	Switzerland
General political opportunity structures	low	low	intermediate	high
Specific political opportunity structures	high	intermediate	low	low
Discursive context	high	high	intermediate	low
Overall	high	intermediate	intermediate-low	low

Note: If we apply the logic followed to derive the overall prediction for Britain and Switzerland, we would have concluded that in Germany we expect an intermediate level. However we characterise the latter case as intermediate-low in order to discriminate it from the case of France.

dictions for the specific political opportunity structures that we can derive from the scores for the two dimensions of citizenship (see Table 7.1) are very different. Here we expect the highest level of mobilisation in Britain (multicultural model of citizenship), the lowest in Germany and Switzerland (assimilationist model), and France at an intermediate level (republican model). Third, as far as the discursive context is concerned, based on the average discursive positions shown earlier (see Table 7.2), we hypothesise a high level of mobilisation in Britain and France, a low level in Switzerland, and an intermediate level in Germany. Finally, the combination of the three explanatory factors (aggregating the hypotheses for each factor) yields the following overall prediction about the mobilisation of migrants in the four countries: a high level of mobilisation in Britain, an intermediate level in France, an intermediate-low level in Germany, and a low level in Switzerland.

Table 7.5 summarises the predictions regarding the extent of claim making by the unemployed in the four countries. Again, we make separate predictions for each of the three explanatory factors and then an overall assessment combining the three factors following the cumulative logic. First, the predictions for the general opportunities are obviously the same as in the case of migrants: the highest level of mobilisation in Switzerland, the lowest in Britain and France, and an intermediate level in Germany. Second, concerning the specific opportunities, based on existing typologies of the welfare states, we expect a low level in Britain (residual model) and an intermediate level in France and Germany (insurance-based model). Switzerland also follows the insurance model and is often classified together with the other continental states such as France and Germany. However, a first cursory comparison of the French and Swiss welfare systems suggests that

Table 7.5 *Predictions about the extent of claim making by unemployed people*

	Britain	France	Germany	Switzerland
General political opportunity structures	low	low	intermediate	high
Specific political opportunity structures	low	intermediate	intermediate	low
Discursive context	intermediate	high	low	intermediate
Overall	low	intermediate	intermediate-low	intermediate

Note: Again, if we apply the logic followed to derive the overall prediction for Britain, we would expect Germany to have intermediate level. Here too, the latter case is depicted as intermediate-low in order to distinguish between Germany and, this time, France and Switzerland.

Switzerland is more restrictive in this respect. Therefore, we predict a low level of mobilisation for the unemployed in this country. Third, based on the average discursive positions shown earlier (see Table 7.3), we hypothesise that the discursive context will generate the highest level of mobilisation in France, the lowest in Germany, with Britain and Switzerland occupying an intermediate level. Finally, the combination of the three explanatory factors yields the following overall predictions about the mobilisation of unemployed people in the four countries: a low level of mobilisation in Britain, an intermediate level in France, an intermediate-low level in Germany, and an intermediate level in Switzerland.

7.8 FINDINGS

7.8.1 Migrant Mobilisation

The presentation of findings can be quite brief and straightforward, as we focus on a single aspect of claim making by migrants and unemployed, namely their level of mobilisation. Table 7.6 shows the share of migrant actors in claim making in immigration and ethnic relations politics (hence, excluding all claims that do not pertain to this political field, such as homeland-oriented claims). The table distinguishes between three broad issue fields (immigration politics, integration politics and anti-racist politics), in addition to an overall assessment of migrant mobilisation for the entire political field.

Table 7.6 *Share of migrant actors in claim making in immigration and ethnic relations politics by issue field (1990–1998) (%)*

	Britain	France	Germany	Switzerland
Immigration politics	10.2	11.3	5.0	2.7
Integration politics	30.8	19.6	12.5	10.8
Anti-racist politics	15.8	6.9	9.9	10.4
Immigration and ethnic relations politics (all fields)	19.7	11.2	7.3	5.9
N	1313	2388	6432	1365

The most important result concerns the entire field (last row). We expected the share of migrant claims to be highest in Britain, intermediate in France, intermediate-low in Germany, and lowest in Switzerland (see Table 7.4). These predictions are almost perfectly confirmed by our data. Britain is by and large the country in which migrants mobilise the most (19.7 per cent). At the opposite end, the mobilisation is the lowest in Switzerland (5.9 per cent). The other two countries are intermediate cases, but the level of mobilisation is higher in France (11.2 per cent) than in Germany (7.3 per cent).

If we look at the issues fields, we see that our predictions fit best the field of integration politics. This, in our view, strengthens our argument about the impact of configurations of citizenship on migrant mobilisation, insofar as integration politics most directly affects the life conditions of migrants in the host society. The other two issue fields, in contrast, present differing results. To be sure, in all four countries, migrants are more active on issues pertaining to integration politics relative to immigration politics. However, the difference between Britain and France virtually disappears when we look at issues relating to immigration politics. In addition, claims concerning anti-racist politics are more important in Germany and Switzerland than in France, although they remain lower than in Britain. In spite of these variations, the findings largely confirm our hypotheses about the combined impact of general opportunity structures, specific opportunity structures and discursive contexts.

7.8.2 Unemployed Mobilisation

Table 7.7 shows the share of unemployed actors' claim making in employment politics. Again, we make a distinction between issue fields. Specifically, the data show the mobilisation of unemployed people addressing socio-economic issues related to labour market and welfare systems, re-entry into the labour market and a residual category of other issues (which includes

Table 7.7 Share of unemployed actors in claim making in employment politics by issue field (1995–2002) (%)

	Britain	France	Germany	Switzerland
Socio-economic issues relating to the labour market	0.2	1.1	0.2	0.1
Welfare systems and social benefits	–	8.2	0.4	1.7
Individual (re-)insertion into the labour market	–	1.1	–	0.4
Other issues	–	15.4	22.0	4.7
Unemployment politics (all fields)	0.1	3.7	0.8	0.4
N	750	791	3851	2019

protest activities by unemployed people that do not pertain to the employment political field). Once again, the most striking result concerns the entire field: the low level of mobilisation observed in all four countries. The unemployed have a low presence in the public domain. This is a result of several factors, including their lack of organisation, and demonstrates that the unemployed face many obstacles to political mobilisation (Faniel 2003). There are, however, also cross-national variations. We expected the share of unemployed claims to be lowest in Britain and more or less the same in the other three countries, perhaps with a higher level in France and Switzerland (see Table 7.5). Unlike in the case of migrants, our predictions are confirmed only in part. As expected, the share of claims is lowest in Britain (0.1 per cent), which presents the most unfavourable opportunity structures and also a relatively unfavourable discursive context. However, France displays a higher presence of the unemployed than expected (3.7 per cent), as compared to both Germany (0.8 per cent) and Switzerland (0.4 per cent). Furthermore, contrary to our predictions, unemployed mobilisation is higher in Germany than in Switzerland.

The gap between our hypotheses and the empirical findings can be explained in three ways. First, cross-national variations might simply be biased by the very small samples, as we are dealing with a few claims made by the unemployed in four countries. This holds especially for the differences between Britain, France and Switzerland. Second, on a theoretical level, our explanatory model might suffer from a specification problem. In other words, the variations observed might be explained by some other factors, most notably by the different unemployment rates in the four countries.

A third possible explanation deserves further elaboration because it is in line with our main argument. We suggest that, unlike other social movements, the mobilisation of minority groups such as migrants and unemployed people are only to a limited extent influenced by the general political opportunity structures, while they are much more sensible of the specific political opportunity structures. Both movements are composed of marginalised people who often lack basic citizenship rights, politically, socially, or both. As a result, political institutions are less important to them and have a minor impact on their political behaviour.

If we take a second look at our predictions about the mobilisation of unemployed people without taking into account the general political opportunity structures (see Table 7.5), we arrive at the following predictions: an intermediate-low level of mobilisation in Britain, intermediate-high in France, intermediate-low in Germany and intermediate-low in Switzerland. Thus, we expect the unemployed to have a higher presence in the public domain in France than in the other three countries. This is exactly what the findings indicate (see Table 7.7). Furthermore, the same argument holds for migrants. If we advance the hypotheses concerning their mobilisation only on the basis of specific political opportunity structures and discursive contexts, we arrive at the following predictions: a high level of mobilisation in Britain, intermediate-high in France, intermediate-low in Germany and low in Switzerland. Again, these expectations are confirmed by the findings. Thus, it seems that the political mobilisation of minority groups such as migrants and unemployed people is more affected by specific opportunity structures and discursive contexts than by the general opportunity structures stressed by political opportunity theorists.

7.9 CONCLUSION

In this chapter we aimed to account for cross-national variations in the political mobilisation of migrants and unemployed people following a revised political opportunity approach. We have tried to show that the mobilisation of these minority groups largely depends on context-sensitive factors, for example, the general political opportunity structures of a country, the specific political opportunity structures of the policy or issue field, and the discursive context of claim making are all important. Using original data on claim making on immigration, ethnic relations and unemployment politics, we have shown that the level of mobilisation of these two underprivileged minority groups varies in important ways from one country to the other according to the institutional and discursive settings in which they are located.

The findings confirm our hypotheses most strongly in the case of the mobilisation of migrants, while the results for the unemployed are less clear-cut. Several factors explain the differences. First, the immigration political field is a more contentious area compared to unemployment, which can be seen as more consensual. This makes the policy positions of collective actors closer to each other and therefore less likely to produce a varying discursive context for the mobilisation of the unemployed. Second, the higher obstacles to the mobilisation of the unemployed, as compared to migrants, make their mobilisation more difficult regardless of contextual factors. As a result, cross-national variations are somewhat flattened and become less visible. Finally, the mobilisation of the unemployed is probably influenced, at least in part, by the economic conditions and, most notably, labour market conditions. With these qualifications, our hypotheses remain robust and are largely supported by the empirical evidence at our disposal.

More generally, the analysis points to the need for more accurate definition drawing in the political opportunity structure field. More precisely, while in its original formulation the concept represents a general setting which is assumed to affect all movements in a similar fashion and to a similar extent, the evidence presented here suggests that the mobilisation of migrants and the unemployed also depends on a set of opportunities specific to an area or issue. We have further suggested that such specific opportunities stem from the institutional approaches to immigration and unemployment. In this perspective, claim making by collective actors in the immigration and ethnic relations political area is influenced in important ways by the configurations or models of citizenship, while in the unemployment political field it depends on the prevailing conception of the welfare state. In both cases, these specific opportunities enlarge or constrain the margin of manoeuvre for the action of collective actors and channel their interventions in the public domain.

NOTES

1. Historical examples of this model, which has sometimes translated into segregationist practices, are the millet system of the Ottoman Empire (organised along religious rather than ethnic lines) and, more recently, South Africa under apartheid.
2. The MERCI project includes five countries: Germany and Britain (study conducted by Ruud Koopmans, Wissenschaftszentrum Berlin für Sozialforschung and Paul Statham, University of Leeds), France and Switzerland (Marco Giugni, University of Geneva and Florence Passy, University of Lausanne), and the Netherlands (Thom Duyvené de Wit, University of Amsterdam). See Koopmans et al. (2005) for a summary of the main results of the study.
3. The UNEMPOL project includes six countries: Britain (study supervised by Paul Statham, University of Leeds), Switzerland (Marco Giugni, University of Geneva), France (Didier Chabanet, University of Lyon), Italy (Donatella della Porta, European University Institute, Florence), Germany (Christian Lahusen, University of Bamberg) and Sweden

(Anna Linders, University of Cincinnati and University of Karlstad). The project is financed by the European commission and the Swiss Federal Office for Education and Science through the 5th Framework program of research of the European Union). See Giugni and Statham (2002) as well as the project's web site for further information (http://ics.leeds.ac.uk/eurpolcom/unempol/index.cfm, last access: 19 November 2007).
4. See Koopmans et al. (2005: Appendix) for a discussion of the coding of political claims data and its robustness. See further Koopmans and Rucht (2002) and Koopmans and Statham (1999b) for a more general discussion of the protest event analysis and the political claims analysis methods respectively, in particular with regard to potential biases, as well as Olzak (1989) for an overview of the use of event data in the study of collective action.
5. Britain was not part of their study, but the authors included it in their typology for illustrative purposes.
6. The indicators on the formal dimension refer to the acquisition of nationality, social and residence rights political rights and anti-discrimination measures. The indicators on the cultural dimension refer to the school system, the military system, the public media system, religious practices, political practices, labour market practices and citizenship practices. The assessment of the various indicators reflects the situation in 2002. Our indicators for the cultural dimension focus on the question of the recognition of Islam. We opted for this specific aspect for two main reasons. First, it was very problematic to have a more general assessment for all types of ethnic or religious groups. Second, Islam today is at the centre of public discourses and policy measures with respect to the politics of ethnic difference. Scores were assigned on a five-point scale (0, 0.25, 0.50, 0.75, 1). On the formal dimension the value 0 was assigned to those indicators with the maximum degree of ethnic-based conception of citizenship, the value 1 to those indicators with the maximum degree of civic-based conception of citizenship, and the intermediate values accordingly in between. Similarly, on the cultural dimension, the value 0 was assigned to those indicators with the maximum degree of pluralist view of cultural obligations, the value 1 to those indicators with the maximum degree of a monist view of cultural obligations, and the intermediate values accordingly in between. See Koopmans et al. (2005) for more details.
7. It should be stressed that Germany in recent years has moved in the direction of expanding the rights of immigrants, for example by substantially liberalising naturalisation provisions.
8. Both verbal and non-verbal claims were taken into account to determine their position. Claims that could not be classified according to this aspect are excluded from the analyses.
9. The economic dimension includes all claims addressing socio-economic issues relating to the situation of the labour market. The social dimension refers to claims addressing welfare systems and social benefits, individual re-insertion into the labor market, and issues relating to the constituency of unemployed people. For practical reasons, we also included in the social dimensions claims addressing other issues (including claims by unemployed people on issues other than unemployment).

REFERENCES

Bagguley, P. (1992) 'Protest, acquiescence and the unemployed: A comparative analysis of the 1930s and 1980s' *British Journal of Sociology* 43 (3), 443–61.
Benford, R.D. and Snow, D.A. (2000) 'Framing processes and social movements: An overview and assessment' *Annual Review of Sociology* 26 (1), 611–39.
Berclaz, M., Füglister, K. and Giugni, M. (2004) 'Etats-providence, opportunités politiques et mobilisation des chômeurs: Une approche néo-institutionnaliste' *Revue Suisse de Sociologie* 30 (3), 421–40.

Berclaz, J. and Giugni, M. (2005) 'Specifying the concept of political opportunity structures' in M. Kousis and C. Tilly (eds) *Economic and political contention in comparative perspective*, Boulder, CO: Paradigm Publishers.

Esping-Andersen, G. (1990) *The three worlds of welfare capitalism*, Princeton, NJ: Princeton University Press.

Faniel, J. (2003) 'Belgian unemployed and the obstacles to collective action', paper presented at the *Second ECPR Conference*, Section on 'Social Movements, Contentious Politics, and Social Exclusion', Marburg (Germany), 18–21 September.

Fillieule, O. (1993) 'Conscience politique, persuasion et mobilisation des engagements: L'exemple du syndicat des chômeurs, 1983–1989' in O. Fillieule (ed.) *Sociologie de la protestation*, Paris: L'Harmattan.

Galland, O. and Louis, M.V. (1981) 'Chômage et action collective' *Sociologie du Travail* (23), 173–191.

Gallie, D. and Paugam, S. (2000) *Welfare regimes and the experience of unemployment in Europe*, Oxford: Oxford University Press.

Giugni, M. and Passy, F. (2004) 'Migrant mobilisation between political institutions and citizenship regimes: A comparison of France and Switzerland' *European Journal of Political Research* 43 (1), 51–82.

Giugni, M. and Passy, F. (2006) *La citoyenneté en débat*, Paris: L'Harmattan.

Giugni, M. and Statham, P. (2002) *The contentious politics of unemployment in Europe: Political claim-making, policy deliberation and exclusion from the labor market: a research outline*, European Political Communication Working Paper Series 2/02 Leeds: University of Leeds.

Koopmans, R. (1995) *Democracy from below: New social movements and the political system in West Germany*, Boulder, CO: Westview Press.

Koopmans, R. (2004) 'Political. Opportunity. Structure. Some splitting to balance the lumping' in J. Goodwin and J.M. Jasper (eds) *Rethinking social movements*, Lanham, MD: Rowman and Littlefield.

Koopmans, R. and Rucht, D. (2002) 'Protest event analysis' in B. Klandermans and S. Staggenborg (eds) *Methods of social movement research*, Minneapolis: University of Minnesota Press.

Koopmans, R. and Statham, P. (1999a) 'Challenging the liberal nation-state? Postnationalism, and the collective claims making of migrants and ethnic minorities in Britain and Germany' *American Journal of Sociology* 105 (3), 652–96.

Koopmans, R. and Statham, P. (1999b) 'Political claims analysis: Integrating protest event and political discourse approaches' *Mobilisation* 4 (2), 203–21.

Koopmans, R. and Statham, P. (2000) 'Migration and ethnic relations as a field of political contention: An opportunity structure approach' in R. Koopmans and P. Statham (eds) *Challenging immigration and ethnic relations politics: Comparative European perspectives*, Oxford: Oxford University Press.

Koopmans, R., Statham, P., Giugni, M. and Passy, F. (2005) *Contested citizenship*, Minneapolis: University of Minnesota Press.

Kriesi, H. (2004) 'Political context and opportunity' in D.A. Snow, S. Soule and H. Kriesi (eds) *Blackwell companion to social movements*, Oxford: Blackwell.

Kriesi, H., Koopmans, R., Duyvendak, J.W. and Giugni, M. (1995) *New social movements in Western Europe*, Minneapolis: University of Minnesota Press.

Maurer, S. (2001) *Les chômeurs en action (décembre 1997 – mars 1998)*, Paris: L'Harmattan.

McAdam, D. (1996) 'Conceptual origins, current problems, future directions' in D. McAdam, J.D. McCarthy and M.N. Zald (eds) *Comparative perspectives on social movements*, Cambridge: Cambridge University Press.

Olzak, S. (1989) 'Analysis of events in the study of collective action' *Annual Review of Sociology* (15), 119–41.

Richards, A. (2002) *Mobilising the powerless: Collective protest action of the unemployed in the interwar period* Working Paper 175, Madrid: Juan March Institute.

Royall, F. (1997) 'Problems of collective action for associations of the unemployed in France and in Ireland' in R. Edmonson (ed.) *The political context of collective action*, London: Routledge.

Snow, D.A. (2004) 'Framing processes, ideology, and discursive fields' in D.A. Snow, S. Soule and H. Kriesi (eds) *Blackwell companion to social movements*, Oxford: Blackwell.

Tarrow, S. (1996) 'States and opportunities: The political structuring of social movements' in D. McAdam, J.D. McCarthy and M.N. Zald (eds) *Comparative perspectives on social movements*, Cambridge: Cambridge University Press.

Tarrow, S. (1998) *Power in movement*, Cambridge: Cambridge University Press.

Tilly, E. (1978) *From mobilisation to revolution*, Reading, MA: Addison-Wesley.

PART III

Top-down: interest mediation and decision making

8. Addressing the 'communication gap': the difficult connection of European and domestic political spaces
Cécile Leconte

> Those who hold power in a national system may be willing to give it up if they think that its loss is inevitable or that in the long run they will lose more by hanging on to it than by abandoning it. But they rarely like such a prospect and they have a strong tendency to search for arguments to show that there is no need for them to do anything of the kind (Marquand 1979: 56).

8.1 INTRODUCTION

Initially applied to questions of interest representation, civil society participation and policy making (Hooghe and Marks 2001), the multi-level governance metaphor is now increasingly being used to study political representation in the European Union. The research agenda of EU students working on questions of legitimacy and democracy now often includes the question whether a multi-level system of political representation, based on a multi-level party system (which would include infranational, national and European party systems) has emerged in the European Union (Greven and Pauly 2000; Steunenberg and Thomassen 2002). The development of a multi-level system of political representation that would better link citizens' preferences in the domestic political arenas to EU politics (especially to EU politics in the European Parliament) is deemed essential in order to tackle the so-called 'democratic deficit' of the EU. To put it another way, democratic legitimacy in the EU implies that there is some kind of linkage or flow of communication between the political space of EU citizens at the level of mass politics and the 'EU political space'.[1]

Most studies show that until now interactions between these two spaces have been at best limited (Bartolini 2001; Mair 2000; Thomassen 2002). As far as channels of communication from the national towards the European level are concerned, voters in the national arenas certainly have a direct access to political representation at the European level through European elections. Nonetheless, their ability to use this new electoral arena to circumvent the constraints of the domestic party systems is seriously hampered by national political parties, which 'serve as the principal gatekeepers within this European electoral arena and hence seek to monopolize access and to dominate the agenda' (Mair 2000: 38). It is thus difficult for citizens to use this new level of political representation in order to change the dimensions of political conflict, to bring new issues on to the agenda or to strengthen representation, at the EU level, of parties that are marginalised at the domestic level. Consequently, according to Peter Mair, the emergence of a new layer of political representation at the EU level has not yet opened up a new opportunity structure[2] for citizens to express contestation or a desire for change (Mair 2000: 38). As far as communication flows from the EU level towards the national level are concerned, the emergence of an embryonic European party system appears to have had only a limited impact on the national level of political representation. Since they are more a collection of national delegations than real transnational parties (Thomassen 2002), Euro parties have not proven to be serious challengers to their national counterparts in the European electoral arena, nor have they been able to build direct links with citizens in the national arenas. One of the main consequences of this is a discrepancy or 'communication gap' (Scharpf 1999) between, on the one hand, national party leaderships which are 'Europeanised' in the sense that they increasingly interact with sister parties, Euro parties and Euro groups at the EU level (Ladrech 1999) and, on the other hand, widely 'non-Europeanised' mass politics and public spheres at domestic level (Hix and Goetz 2000: 23).

Addressing the problem of this disjuncture is all the more important since it negatively affects the quality of democratic life in the EU by exacerbating the already growing erosion of the links between political elites and citizens (Scharpf 1999; Mair 2000: 49; Raunio 2002b), and between party leaderships and 'rank and file' members (Johansson 2002; Raunio 2002b).

In the existing literature on the EU, at least three theories offer some explanations for this disjuncture: liberal intergovernmentalism, consociative theories[3] of European integration and the literature on the Europeanisation of domestic political systems. While there are many differences between these theories, they share one core assumption: the disjuncture between 'Europeanised' political elites and 'non-Europeanised' mass politics is likely to persist because national party leaderships cause it.

One of the central claims of liberal intergovernmentalism is that Europeanisation strengthens national executives (and thus governing political parties) at the expense of civil societies[4] and citizenries (Moravsick 1993). Certainly, when dealing with their European counterparts at the EU level, governing party elites are not completely shielded from societal pressures. In issues which imply distributional conflicts, they have to take into account the demands of powerful interest groups (for example, big producers) in the domestic arenas. Here they act as the 'agents' of the 'principals', that is, in this case influential constituencies whose electoral support they have to secure. However, the ability of citizens as a whole to control elites' activity at the EU level is hampered by two factors.

First, the degree of control over elites' behaviour varies greatly according to two parameters: the coherence and organisational strength of societal groups and the nature of the issues at stake. 'Agency slack' (Moravsick 1993: 494) emerges in sectors where the distributional dimension is absent (or where gains and losses are difficult to assess) and where societal or civic mobilisations are weak (for instance, foreign policy or the reforms of EU institutions). In these sectors, governing party elites have a much larger room for manoeuvre.

Second, the very characteristics of decision making at the EU level strengthen the control of governing parties over domestic affairs (Moravsick 1993: 507). To begin with, decision making in the Council of Ministers, where transparency is limited, insulates national representatives from possible pressures emanating from domestic arenas. In these arenas member states' representatives feel free to negotiate and make linkages which escape national oversight (Moravsick 1993: 505). Governing party elites refer to the European Union either to legitimise their policy initiatives in the national arena or to avoid the electoral costs of unpopular policies by blaming 'Brussels' for them (Moravsick 1993: 516).

Indeed, when acting at the EU level, elites enjoy a vantage position between two widely disconnected arenas (the European and the national arenas). They benefit from this disconnection because when acting in one arena, they can refer to objective or alleged constraints in the other arena in order to push through their preferences – applying a strategy described by Putnam (1988) as a 'two-level game'. Moreover, they can use the resources gained at the EU level (in terms of privileged access to supranational decision making, networks and information) to reinforce their position at the domestic level.[5] According to liberal intergovernmentalism, governing party elites remain the sole beneficiaries of this 'two-level game' because citizens, as well as civil society actors, are supposedly unable either to organise on a transnational basis or to project themselves directly towards the supranational level.

Contrary to liberal intergovernmentalism, consociative theories of European integration[6] (Taylor 1990; Chryssochoou 1994; Gabel 1998) and the Europeanisation literature (Hix and Goetz 2000; Mair 2000; Bartolini 1999, 2001) argue that Europeanisation could (theoretically) challenge the power of political elites at the domestic level. However, they contend that, until now, elites have managed to protect themselves from these potential impacts. Indeed, while acknowledging the ability of interest groups to organise on a transnational basis (a fact which liberal intergovernmentalism denies), this thesis, like the liberal intergovernmentalism theory, contends that the 'two-level game' metaphor still applies in the sphere of political representation. According to both theories, the development of a full-blown multi-level system of political representation in the EU could have two consequences. First, it could lead to the emergence, in the European electoral arena, of 'challengers' (that is, Euro parties) which would question national political parties' somewhat undemocratic claim to be the only representatives of national constituencies. Second, it could foster a reorganisation of domestic party systems around new, Europeanised cleavage structures, for instance around the pro-/anti-integration divide (a scenario already discernible in the intra-party divisions which EU issues crystallise in some national political parties).[7] By doing so, it would expose the relative inadequacy of the cleavage structures on which contemporary domestic party systems are based. Eventually, thus, Europeanisation could give substance to the perception of an increasing irrelevance of national political parties, by questioning their very *raison d'être*. To avoid such dramatic consequences, national party elites engage in diverse strategies in order to break the development of vertical links between the EU and the national levels and the emergence of horizontal, that is, transnational political allegiances.[8]

For consociative theories, national representatives tend to block those institutional reforms that would increase the democratic legitimacy of the EU because they would also foster the development of transnational political links between national constituencies. This would blur the borders between domestic political arenas on which their power ultimately rests. A good example of this is the clinging of member states' representatives to the national veto, a highly symbolic institution which allows executives to reproduce logics of national pillarisation, by indulging in a rhetoric centred on the notion of the 'national interest'. Consociational theories argue that any significant progress in political integration exacerbates political elites' desire to reaffirm their control over national constituencies (Taylor 1990: 177). This is why, according to consociative accounts of European integration, 'regional integration can increase anti-democratic tendencies among elites' (Taylor 1990: 177; see also Chryssochoou 1994: 3).

Most works on the Europeanisation of domestic political systems share similar assumptions. According to Peter Mair for instance, national party elites have managed to insulate political competition at the domestic level from the possibly disturbing impacts of Europeanisation. He argues that, until now, 'Europe' has had only a limited impact on domestic party systems because European integration has not led to a reorganisation of the dimensions of political conflict around a pro-/anti-European divide (Mair 2000: 35). In order to avoid such a challenge, elites rely on diverse strategies. First, they see to it that European elections remain national in character and that European party federations do not develop fully into transnational parties which would supersede national member parties. Second, in order not to expose intra-party divisions on European integration, mainstream parties' leaderships make an informal agreement not to compete on EU issues. They coalesce (or 'cartelise'[9]) around a common goal: the de-politicisation of EU issues as a potentially relevant dimension of political conflict. As a consequence, EU issues are rarely publicly debated during campaigns for national or European elections: 'Europe becomes a matter for the governing politicians and their bureaucracies' (Mair 2000: 48). Under those conditions, the existence of a new layer of political representation at the EU level results in a highly 'differential empowerment of actors' at the domestic level (Green Cowles *et al.* 2001: 11). While some are provided with new opportunities to exit the constraints of domestic political systems, others remain locked into the national arena. Thus, European integration tends to empower mainstream party elites at the expense of citizens and strengthens governing parties at the expense of opposition parties. Even inside governing parties, it mainly benefits the party leadership (especially heads of governments) at the expense of the rank and file members (Hix and Goetz 2000; Johansson 2002; Raunio 2002b). To a large extent, domestic political elites have been able to prevent the crucial challenge which the development of a European party system could have posed to their authority.[10]

The validity of the above-mentioned assumptions is discussed in more detail below by addressing two sets of correlated questions:

1. How can the persistent non-Europeanisation of domestic political spaces (at mass level) be explained? Is it likely to remain so or are there some trends pointing to a possible change in that respect?
2. Does Europeanisation necessarily empower domestic party elites at the expense of citizens? Doesn't it also create opportunities for citizens, say by providing them with new points of references enabling them to play a more active role in the structuring of political conflict and public debate in the national arenas?

To answer these questions, this chapter proceeds in two steps. In the first section, it is argued that the three theories outlined above aptly depict the attempts of domestic party elites to use Europeanisation in an instrumental way, by trying to benefit from the emergence of a European party system and prevent the emergence of direct channels of communication between the European level of political representation and domestic electorates. In a second section, it is argued that these theories simply tell one part of the story. They are based on the assumption that domestic party elites are still able to maintain themselves as gatekeepers between the domestic and the European levels of political representation. However, the ability to control communication flows between the two levels erodes under the combined impact of developments at the European level (that is, changes in the modes of political representation in the European Parliament) and at the domestic level (political expectations and mobilisations among national electorates, which refer to 'their' understanding of Europe to bring about changes in domestic politics).

8.2 THE 'SELECTIVE' EUROPEANISATION OF DOMESTIC POLITICAL SPACES

8.2.1 The Instrumental Use of the European Level by National Political Elites

The emergence of a European party system has occurred in parallel with another distinct trend, namely an increase in interactions between domestic political parties and European party federations and parliamentary groups (as well as in contacts between like-minded political parties from different member states). Strategies of national political actors are increasingly enmeshed with party politics at the EU level, a trend which has been described as a process of 'party networking' linking national and European political arenas (Ladrech 1999: 100). This process is driven by national political actors who project domestic parties' strategies upwards on to the European level, for example, by coordinating policy initiatives with like-minded parties to legitimise their choices in domestic arenas. In this context, the Europeanisation of domestic political actors refers to an instrumental use of the supranational level for domestic political gains. Some authors contend that this increases the legitimacy of the European polity by better linking the European arena to domestic politics and by associating it to clearly discernible stakes and issues in the eyes of the citizens (Ladrech 1999: 108). However, as argued below, this one-way Europeanisation allows domestic political parties to derive gains from the development of party politics at the EU level, while avoiding the constraints and risks that the Europeanisation of domestic political spaces would imply for them.

What concrete gains can domestic political parties derive from the emergence of a European party system? First, membership in European party federations increases their legitimacy in the domestic arena, especially when this legitimacy is contested. For instance, it has been argued that the decision of the European People's Party (EPP) to accept Forza Italia as a member in 1999 greatly enhanced its fragile legitimacy at home, thus indirectly contributing to its victory in the general elections of 13 May 2001. There was a similar logic when the Spanish People's Party joined the EPP in 1991, which helped the party undermine suspicions regarding its possible links to the Franco period. In a less dramatic way, the attempts by parties to coordinate their policy initiatives at European level, for example, in the Justice and Home Affairs and defence sectors for parties of the EPP or in the fight against unemployment for parties of the Party of European Socialists (PES), and to make reference to like-minded sister parties at the European level are also good examples of this legitimating function of the European party system.

Second, formal membership in European party federations, but also the informal dense relationships resulting from the phenomenon of 'party networking' at the European level place national party leaderships in a privileged position whereby they can 'veto' undesired changes in domestic politics.[11] A good illustration of this is the bilateral measures implemented by fourteen EU governments to protest against the formation of a government coalition between the conservatives of the Austrian People's Party (ÖVP) and the right-wing Austrian Freedom Party (FPÖ) in 2000. Although the democratic credentials of the Freedom Party's leader were highly doubtful, the elections had taken place in a democratic context. Besides, almost half the Austrian electorate wanted an end to the 'grand coalition' between Social Democrats and Conservatives. Indeed, it seems very likely that the leadership of the Austrian Social Democratic party (SPÖ) used its connections among party officials at European level to call for a strong European reaction against a possible ÖVP/FPÖ coalition. Helpfully for the SPÖ, the then president of the Council of the Union, Antonio Guterres, was at the same time head of the Socialist International. This example also corroborates the assumption that 'party networking' at the EU level mainly benefits party leaderships at the expense of the rank and file and the electorate.[12] Indeed, Euro parties and groups mainly interact with national parties' leaderships, not with the members (Raunio 2002a). In the Austrian case, a substantial majority of SPÖ's members and about two-thirds of its electorate strongly disapproved of the party leadership's course at the EU level.

Third, to the extent that the European party system is structured along the same cleavage structures as domestic party systems – with a conspicuous absence of competition on European issues among mainstream parties – it does not risk bringing about the politicisation of politically sensitive issues in domestic arenas. Until recently, the 'cartelised' nature of interactions in the European Parliament, where most decisions were taken either by the grand coalition of the EPP-ED[13] and the PES or by the triangle including EPP-ED, PES and Liberals (Hix 1999), also prevented the projection on to the supranational level of issues raised by citizens at the domestic level.

8.2.2 The Limited Europeanisation of Domestic Political Spaces

At the same time, national political parties do not allow developments at the European level of political representation to reduce in any way their room for manoeuvre in domestic politics and their monopoly over political leadership in domestic arenas.

First, the common rules and disciplines agreed upon at the level of European party federations are often blatantly flouted by domestic political parties in national arenas. The case of Forza Italia illustrates this point. By building a coalition government with a fiercely xenophobic party, the Lega Nord, Forza Italia clearly violated the principles laid down in the EPP Athens programme of 1992, which clearly condemns nationalist and/or extremist positions (European People's Party 1992: 20). It also clearly departed from the official, pro-integration line of the EPP. However, it was never sanctioned by the EPP leadership for violating the party's core values.

Second, domestic political parties tend to make selective use of the principle of 'European democratic interference'. This is highlighted by the behaviour of Austrian and Italian left-wing parties in their relation to 'democratic Europe'. Neither of these parties tried to involve European sister parties in the domestic political debate until it was clear that they would have to go into opposition. For example, during the electoral campaign preceding the Italian general elections on 13 May 2001, none of the leaders of the Italian Left tried to involve European sister parties in a debate on Silvio Berlusconi's control over the Italian media, even though this may have had an impact on the outcome of the subsequent elections. Similarly, the Austrian Social Democrats did not attempt to launch a discussion on the topic of right-wing populism at the level of the European party federation until they found themselves in opposition as a result of the building of the ÖVP/FPÖ coalition. More recently, in March 2004, as the regional section of the SPÖ in Carinthia struck a deal with the FPÖ allowing Jörg Haider to be re-elected as governor of the Land, few voices were raised inside the party to bring the matter before the PES.[14]

Third, domestic political parties try to limit the Europeanisation of domestic political spaces by controlling the channels of communication between the supranational and national levels of political representation. They do so by circumscribing the role, in domestic political debates, of those actors who could act as bridges between the two levels, namely MEPs and European Commissioners. With the significance of the European Parliament (EP) growing, MEPs can challenge national party officials in two main ways. First, they might intervene in domestic political debates or in electoral campaigns in a way which might deviate from the domestic party line (for instance, by defending options which might be seen as 'too pro-integration'). Second, they might gain some recognition and popularity in the domestic political arena. Indeed, with the visibility of the EP increasing, they might become high profile, putting national politicians in the shade. Nonetheless, domestic political parties have a very effective means of control over MEPs as they are the ones who decide on the selection of candidates for European elections and about the later career of MEPs (Lord 2001; Raunio 2002a). Thus, a dissenting MEP can easily be 'sanctioned' by the national party leadership. (For instance, during campaigns for the 2004 European elections, many high-profile and popular MEPs across several member states were allocated low-ranking positions on electoral lists by their parties. Consequently many of them lost their seats in the EP.) To a certain extent, a similar logic applies to European Commissioners. Those who are perceived by national party leaderships as being too supportive of the 'European general interest' can pay a high price for their involvement in the domestic debate. This was the case, for example, of the former French Commissioner Pascal Lamy (who had pleaded in the domestic media for a reform of the Common Agricultural Policy) or the former British Commissioner Lord Cockfield (who had turned too 'pro-European' for the British Conservatives). Despite their recognised expertise in their respective fields, both failed, against expectation, to get (re-)nominated either as Commissioner or as candidate for the Presidency of the Commission (in the case of Pascal Lamy, who had been seen as a possible successor to Romano Prodi). Accordingly, Marquand's (1979: 64) argument still rings true: 'So long as Commissioners depend for their appointment on national governments, and for their future careers on their future acceptability to national governments, they are bound to be reluctant to lead public opinion into battle against national governments'.

However, the control exerted on the Europeanisation of domestic political spaces by national party elites only remained possible because two conditions were met. First, until recently, domestic political elites used to have a monopoly over the signification of 'Europe' in national public spheres. Indeed, there are many occasions when a specific understanding of 'Europe' has been mobilised by national politicians in order to legitimise potentially contested policies or reforms in domestic arenas. This has been analysed by Alberta Sbragia, for instance, in the case of public finance reforms in Italy (Sbragia 2001). The use of the 'misfit' argument (between, on the one hand, the EU embodying sound public finance management and a certain form of 'normality' and, on the other hand, a domestic arena plagued by *malgoverno* and by a political culture described as 'deviant') enabled a coalition of reform-oriented forces in Italy to implement the desired reforms, a policy choice that might have been heavily contested if the reference to 'Europe' had not been made. Indeed, as social constructivist accounts of European integration contend, discourses on integration and the mastering by elites of a certain 'Euro-speak' can be useful power resources in their relationship to civil societies and citizenries (Diez 1999).

Second, until now the emergence of direct links between the European and domestic levels of political representation has been heavily hampered by two elements: the type of political representation prevalent in the EP, which was mainly based on a logic of self-assertion by the institution (at the expense of more politicised modes of representation) and the national character of European elections (a fact which, in some countries like France, was exacerbated by the use, until the 2004 elections, of a single, nationwide list, which prevented the development of direct links between citizens and MEPs).

As argued below, these two conditions are being questioned by evolving political practices at national and European levels, which opens up new perspectives for a more wide-ranging Europeanisation of national political spaces.

8.3 NEW PERSPECTIVES FOR THE EUROPEANISATION OF DOMESTIC POLITICAL SPACES

8.3.1 Bottom-up Europeanisation

Indeed, Europeanisation not only creates new opportunity structures for established actors such as the leaders of governing political parties, but also opens up new opportunities for mobilisation by civil society actors and societal movements (Marks and McAdam 1996). Increasingly, this might also hold true in the non-sectoral sphere of politics as such.

To begin with, Europeanisation has a potentially strong impact on the relationship between parties and national electorates because it influences the overall perception of parties' performance. Even authors who defend the 'selective Europeanisation' thesis recognise that Europeanisation might exacerbate the widely held view that governing parties' ability to 'deliver the goods' in an interdependent world diminishes (Mair 2000: 49). Indeed, Europeanisation influences the dimensions of political spaces because it affects the criteria according to which parties are being assessed by the electorates. For instance, polls conducted recently in Poland show that a large majority of voters see Europeanisation as a way to reform domestic political practices (more transparency, less corruption and better mechanisms of accountability are expected as a result of the country's accession to the EU).[15] The fact that Europeanisation has an impact on the dimensions of political debate and electoral competition in domestic arenas has also been highlighted by recent elections in Bulgaria and Romania. As a result of the accession process, the fight against corruption became a key issue in the elections. In short, Europeanisation influences the criteria according to which parties' competence and legitimacy are being assessed by domestic constituencies.

This shows that national governing parties no longer have a monopoly over the signification of Europe. Citizens' perceptions may differ from the 'official' governmental line. Thus citizens can also mobilise against their governments in the name of a different Europe which they associate with alternative values. In Austria in 2000 and in Italy in 2001 there were mass demonstrations against two coalition governments including the populist right-wing Austrian Freedom Party and the radical right-wing Lega Nord, in the name of 'Europe'. In a more dramatic context, the demonstrations organised by the democratic opposition in the Ukraine during the so-called 'Orange revolution' were at least in part orchestrated in the name of a democratic Europe. In all these cases EU flags were waved by demonstrators to embody this idea. By mobilising in the name of different understandings of European integration, civil society actors and civic movements can also counterbalance elites' tendencies to use the EU as a mere legitimising instrument. The progressive transformation of the 'Justice and Home Affairs' (JHA) sector of intergovernmental cooperation into the wider project of an 'area of freedom, security and justice' also illustrates this. As Klaus Eder and Hans-Jörg Trenz show, cooperation in the JHA sector started as an exclusively intergovernmental forum which performed a clear legitimising function for governments (which could portray themselves as the architects of a protective 'fortress Europe'), while allowing them to insulate security issues from possible scrutiny and contestation at domestic level. However, as civil society organisations working in the field of civic rights mobilised in order to enlarge the JHA agenda, this was expanded to encompass issues such as the harmonisation of defendants' rights in the EU, the fight against racism and xenophobia and so on. What started as intergovernmental cooperation aimed at strengthening national executives eventually fostered the politicisation of domestic public spaces, by producing civic mobilisations centred on the oversight of national executives' action in the JHA sector (Eder and Trenz 2003: 122f).

At a deeper, sociological level, Europeanisation has also indirectly accelerated a process of politicisation in some member states where the traditional ubiquity of political parties had been maintained at the expense of civil society's growth. This was the case in Austria (Pelinka *et al.* 2000) and Italy (Fabbrini and Gilbert 2002: 39). The introduction of EU norms contributed, among other things, to the erosion of the patronage practised by parties in the name of 'consociative values' (Luther and Deschouwer 1999: 261).

8.3.2 Top-down Europeanisation

The Europeanisation of domestic political spaces is also likely to be fostered in the near future by developments at the European level of political representation. The 'EU political space' has experienced some significant developments in recent years. At least three of them are worth stressing. First, the former apolitical and consensual style of interactions between the two major groups in the EP (namely the EPP-ED and the PES) is giving way to more politicised interactions around the Left/Right divide. This may make political conflict in the EP more familiar and meaningful to EU citizens (Van Ecke 2001: 330). Second, the ideological coherence of Euro parties and Euro groups on socio-economic issues has increased, with transnational political orientations increasingly taking precedence over nationality in the voting behaviour of MEPs (at least on the Left/Right dimension) (Thomassen 2002). Third, the 'EU political space' constituted by Euro parties' and Euro groups' positions on the Left/Right dimension looks increasingly similar to the mass-level political space of EU citizens (Gabel and Anderson 2002). According to Gabel and Hix (2002: 953) this should make it easier for citizens to identify with the European level of political representation: 'the coincidence of these political spaces is striking. Among other things, it indicates that were transnational party groups to supplant parties as the primary contestants in European elections, voters and party groups would have a common shorthand language to communicate about policy'. Theoretically, these developments should result in increased links and flows of communication between EU and national political spaces.

Such developments could also be fostered by the emergence of a 'European political public sphere' (Kaelble 2002) in the European Parliament, where the separation between EU politics and domestic politics is being questioned by evolving practices and modes of representation. Indeed, in the name of European norms and values, MEPs now debate issues of domestic politics which were not so long ago considered as purely internal matters. The EP increasingly acts as a tribunal where the once tight border between European and domestic politics erodes, under the impact of new practices and new understandings of national sovereignty. This evolution can be traced back to the beginning of the 1980s and more precisely to 1981, when the EP debated for the first time the Northern Ireland conflict, defining it as a matter concerning the European Community as a whole.[16] Latterly, the EP has taken up a position on the domestic politics of some member states on at least three occasions, thus clearly breaking with previous practices. (Until recently, supranational institutions and their representatives were not supposed to comment on the results of national elections in the member states):

- On 4 May 1994, the EP commented on the Italian general elections which led to the formation of the first government led by Silvio Berlusconi. It passed a resolution calling on President Carlo Azeglio Ciampi to swear in only a government committed to the 'fundamental values of the European Community'.[17]
- On 3 February 2000, the EP passed a similar resolution, backed up by the presidents of the four major parliamentary groups, on 'the project of the Austrian People's Party to form a coalition government with the Austrian Freedom Party'. In this resolution, the EP disapproved of this coalition strategy by stating that it would risk 'legitimizing the extreme right in the EU'.[18]
- On 23 April 2002, the President of the European Parliament, Pat Cox, publicly expressed his concern[19] about the results of the first round of the presidential elections in France.[20] One day later, as the extreme right leader Jean-Marie Le Pen entered the European Parliament, dozens of MEPs protested by standing up and holding 'No' signs.

On all three occasions, debates at the EP level strongly resonated in domestic arenas. In Italy, they prompted President Ciampi to publish a clear warning to Berlusconi, where he stated that the Italian government coalition had to respect principles such as the commitment to Community treaties, the integrity of the Italian state and the rule of law. This was a move unprecedented in Italian political history in the post-war period. In Austria, it triggered a heated debate on the legitimacy of the ÖVP/FPÖ coalition. In France, the media pointed to the parochialism of the domestic political debate before the elections, which created a climate favouring the resonance of the Front National's discourse.

These three examples point to a longer-term evolution of the modes of political representation in the EP and of the self-understanding of their role by MEPs. Increasingly, representatives in the EP perform what French political scientist George Lavau described as the 'fonction tribunitienne' of political parties (Lavau 1981), that is to say, the ability of parties to expose, to 'put on stage' issues and to politicise them by linking them to public debates on fundamental values. This nascent trend is well captured by the green MEP Daniel Cohn-Bendit when he says that 'European politics needs to be more dramatic'.[21] By 'putting on stage' European politics in a way more similar to domestic politics, MEPs can establish a direct link with national electorates and contribute to politicisation processes in domestic arenas. Moreover, increasing media coverage of EP debates fosters this process. For instance, the fact that the EP's specialised commissions now publish the results of the interview sessions of 'applicant' European Commissioners helps politicise the procedure of the Commission's nomination. As a result, the proposing by national governments of individual Commissioners, which used to happen in a private, depoliticised way, is now being increasingly scrutinised at the domestic level. (This was the case with the Italian nominee Rocco Buttiglione in October 2004. His candidacy was eventually withdrawn under pressure from the European Parliament.)

8.4 CONCLUSION: FROM ELITIST 'TWO-LEVEL GAMES' TO MULTI-LEVEL POLITICAL REPRESENTATION

A multi-level policy-making system already exists in the EU in a wide range of policy sectors. In order to address the alleged 'democratic deficit', this policy-making system must be complemented by a multi-level system of political representation. If national political elites do not wish to address the 'democratic deficit' for the EU's sake, they should at least do it for their own sake. Indeed, the disjuncture between 'a Europeanised statehood and non-Europeanised politics' (Hix and Goetz 2000: 23) entails many risks for political elites. For instance, the 'cartelisation' of EU issues in national political spaces has strong backlash effects when 'Europe is forced back in national politics by means of popular referendums' (Mair 2000: 48). Accordingly, anti-elite and Eurosceptic orientations tend to merge at the expense of mainstream political parties, as referenda on the EU Constitutional Treaty in France and the Netherlands in 2005 illustrated.

The crucial question is thus how to articulate better the national and European levels of political representation. Two broad approaches to this question can be identified. One focuses on institutional reforms, the other emphasises the need to increase the quantity and the quality of communication flows between the two levels.

It has been argued elsewhere that a better articulation between the two levels ultimately requires a more coherent division of labour between the national and the European electoral arenas.[22] This would imply changing the division of tasks between the Council and the European Parliament (Mair 2000: 43–7; Bartolini 1999: 42). However, there are two limits to this ambitious scheme. To begin with, EU issues cannot be completely insulated from national issues; therefore, it is misleading to think that EU issues could be debated only in the European electoral arena (Thomassen 2002). Besides, national governments would be reluctant to make such wide-ranging institutional reforms, which would shift the balance of power between the Council of Ministers and the European Parliament. Certainly, some of the reforms entailed in the Constitutional Treaty, such as the 'citizens' initiative', could be useful in order to address the 'communication gap'.

Nonetheless, institutional reforms would not be enough to address the problem. To begin with, horizontal communication flows between national political public spheres should be increased, in order to denationalise debates on EU issues. Political rights entailed in the EU citizenship were certainly a first step in that direction, despite the fact that their use by EU citizens (as measured, for instance, by the proportion of non-national candidates elected for European elections) has been very limited. The setting up of transnational citizens' fora on EU issues could be another step in opening up domestic political public spaces to each other. Moreover, vertical communication links between the European and national levels must be increased. This requires, for instance, a stronger involvement of European political actors (Commissioners, MEPs) in domestic public debates.[23] (As far as MEPs are concerned, a useful way to facilitate this would be to select candidates for European elections at the level of European party organisations, in order to reduce the dependence of MEPs on national political parties). Another useful initiative would be to coordinate regular debates at the domestic level conducted by both the European and national parliaments.[24] In that respect, the fact that politics in the European Parliament loses (albeit in a still limited way) some of its peculiarities and increasingly resembles domestic politics (in terms of both dimensions of political conflict and modes of representation) should not necessarily raise fears of a destabilising 'mass politicisation' of the EU. It definitely opens up new opportunities for a better connection between domestic and European political spaces.

NOTES

1. According to Simon Hix, a political space can be defined by two elements: the dimensions of political conflict, which reflect the dominant socio-political cleavages in a given

polity, and the positions and alignments of political actors within this space (Hix 1999: 71). The 'EU political space' is thus defined by Gabel and Hix as including the dimensions of political conflict within the European Parliament and the positions of the four main European party families 'on a broad range of issues' where the EU is involved (Gabel and Hix 2002: 935). At the level of mass politics, a 'political space' can be defined as the policy space shaped by citizens' preferences on a range of issues (Gabel and Anderson 2002: 894). Ideally, the policy space structured by citizens' preferences should constrain political competition at party level and, ultimately, the behaviour of decision makers.
2. This refers to the definition of 'Europeanisation' given by Simon Hix and Klaus Goetz. For the two authors, understanding Europeanisation is about studying 'how the establishment of a higher level of governance institutions provides new opportunities [for domestic actors] to exit from domestic constraints' (Hix and Goetz 2000: 10).
3. The term 'theory' is used here for practical purposes, although the literature on Europeanisation does not constitute a theory per se but rather an approach to the study of European integration and its implications for domestic changes.
4. To borrow the definition given by Zimmer and Freise, civil society refers here to the 'intermediary sphere' between the state and the market 'populated by voluntary organizations and civic engagement' (Zimmer and Freise 2005: 14). It only partially overlaps with the term citizenry, which refers in the present contribution not only to citizens defined as 'societal and political men and women striving for the betterment of their communities' (Zimmer and Freise 2005: 2) but also includes all members of the polity entitled to civic and political rights.
5. Michael Zürn aptly describes this 'two-level game' based on the informational advantage of elites: 'In two-level games, the agent who is situated at the intersection between the two arenas is better informed than others, which makes strategies of credit-claiming and scapegoating in national politics easier' (Zürn 2000: 103).
6. Consociative theories of European integration apply the model of consociative democracy initially designed by Arend Lijphart (1968) to the EU political system.
7. To take one example, the divisions generated by the debate on the EU constitutional treaty inside the French Socialist Party are illustrative of this cross-cutting impact of EU issues on national parties.
8. The worst case scenario in the eyes of domestic elites would thus be, according to Chryssochoou, the emergence of a 'supranational and politically active demos' (Chryssochoou 1994: 10).
9. Borrowing Richard Katz and Peter Mair's metaphor of the 'cartel party' (Katz and Mair 1995), several authors contend that the leaderships of most mainstream government parties in EU countries tend to 'cartelise' around an officially pro-EU line, thus silencing intra-party divisions on EU-related issues (Bartolini 1999: 13; Hix 1999: 14; Mair 2000: 35).
10. As early as 1979, David Marquand was indicating this challenge: 'If the European Parliament acquires a significant role in Community decision-making, Community political parties will develop; and the national parties will have to transfer power from national party head offices to a Community apparatus' (Marquand 1979: 56).
11. '[D]omestic actors can use the European level to seek a veto on domestic actions. This can occur if an actor is a loser in the domestic arena but can reasonably predict that the direct or indirect impact of European-level outcomes will promote their cause in the domestic arena' (Hix and Goetz 2000: 13).
12. Hix and Goetz rightly point to the limits of EU-level party networking: 'For example, party leaders, who attend party leaders' summits and have access to their party representatives in the Council, the Commission and the Parliament, can pursue exit and informational advantage strategies to strengthen their positions within their party organizations' (Hix and Goetz 2000: 14).
13. European People's Party – European Democrats.
14. *Le Monde* of 15 March 2004: 'En Carinthie, les sociaux-démocrates concluent un pacte de soutien tacite avec Jörg Haider'.

15. Polls quoted in Kolarska-Bobinska (2004).
16. European Parliament, Draft Protocol of the General Assembly of 7 May 1981, point 14: 'Hunger strikes at Long Kesh', 241–56.
17. European Parliament, Resolution on the European Council in Corfu of 4 May 1994.
18. European Parliament, Resolution on the results of general elections in Austria and the project of the Austrian People's Party to form a coalition government with the Austrian Freedom Party of 3 February 2000.
19. Quoted in *Le Monde* of 23 April 2002: 'Inquiétudes des parlementaires européens'.
20. The two extreme right parties' score amounted to 20 per cent of the vote, with roughly 10 per cent going to the extreme left.
21. Quoted in Eder and Trenz (2003: 128).
22. Issues relating to the institutions and scope of the EU would be debated in the European electoral arena, while day-to-day policy making at the EU level would be primarily discussed in the national electoral arena.
23. A measure which is recommended in the Commission's 2005 *Action plan to improve communicating Europe* (European Commission 2005: 5).
24. A list of such measures has been put forward by a network of European policy institutes (EPIN, 2005).

REFERENCES

Bartolini, S. (1999) *The consequences of European integration for national political representation*, Florence: European University Institute, Seminar paper.

Bartolini, S. (2001) 'La structure des clivages nationaux et la question de l'intégration européenne'. *Politique européenne* (4), 15–45.

Chryssochoou, D. (1994) 'Democracy and symbiosis in the EU: Towards a confederal consociation?' *West European Politics* 17 (4), 1–14.

Diez, T. (1999) 'Speaking "Europe": The politics of integration discourse' *Journal of European Public Policy* 6 (4), 598–613.

Eder, K. and Trenz, H.-J. (2003) 'The making of a European public sphere: The case of justice and home affairs' in B. Kohler-Koch (ed.) *Linking EU and national governance*, Oxford: Oxford University Press, pp. 110–34.

European Commission (2005) 'Action plan to improve communicating Europe by the Commission', http://ec.europa.eu/dgs/communication/pdf/communication_com_en.pdf, last access: 4 July 2007.

European People's Party (1992) *General program. Europe 2000: Unity in diversity* Athens, 11–13 November 1992.

European Policy Institutes Network (EPIN) (2005) *A citizens compact: Reaching out to the citizens of Europe* EPIN working paper number 14, September, www.epin.org/pdf/WP14_EPIN.pdf, last access: 19 November 2007.

Fabbrini, S. and Gilbert, S. (2002) 'When cartels fail: The role of the political class in the Italian democratic transition' *Government and Opposition* 35 (1), 27–48.

Gabel, M. (1998) 'The endurance of supranational governance: A consociational interpretation of European integration' *Comparative Politics* 30 (4), 463–75.

Gabel, M. and Anderson, C.J. (2002) 'The structure of citizen attitudes and the European political space' *Comparative Political Studies* 35 (8), 934–64.

Gabel, M. and Hix, S. (2002) 'Defining the EU political space: An empirical study of the European Elections manifestos, 1979–1999' *Comparative Political Studies* 35 (8), 934–64.

Green Cowles, M., Caporaso, J. and Risse, T. (2001) *Transforming Europe: Europeanization and domestic change*, Ithaca and London: Cornell University Press.
Greven, M. and Pauly, L.W. (2000) *Democracy beyond the state? The European dilemma and the merging global order*, New York and Oxford: Rowman and Littlefield.
Hix, S. (1999) 'Dimensions and alignments in European Union politics: Cognitive constraints and partisan responses' *European Journal of Political Research* 35 (1), 69–106.
Hix, S. and Goetz, K. (2000) 'Introduction: European integration and national political systems' *West European Politics. Special issue: Europeanised politics? European integration and National Party Systems* 23 (4), 1–26.
Hooghe, L. and Marks, G. (2001) *Multilevel governance and European integration*, Oxford: Rowman and Littlefield.
Johansson, K.M. (2002) 'Party elites in multilevel Europe: The Christian-Democrats and the single European Act' *Party Politics* 8 (4), 423–39.
Kaelble, H. (2002) 'The historical rise of a European public sphere' *Journal of European Integration History* 8 (2), 9–22.
Katz, R. and Mair, P. (1995) 'Changing models of party organization and party democracy: The emergence of the cartel party' *Party Politics* 1 (1), 5–28.
Kolarska-Bobinska, L. (2004) 'Pologne: L'intégration européenne comme aboutissement de la transformation' in Jacques Rupnik (ed.) *Les Européens face à l'élargissement: Perceptions, enjeux, acteurs*, Paris: Presses de Sciences Po, pp. 165–168.
Ladrech, R. (1999) 'Political parties and legitimacy in the EU' in T. Banchoff and M. Smith (eds) *Legitimacy in the EU: The contested polity*, London: Routledge, pp. 93–112.
Lavau, G. (1981) *A quoi sert le parti communiste français?* Paris: Fayard.
Lijphart, A. (1968) *The politics of accommodation: Pluralism and democracy in the Netherlands*, Berkeley: University of California Press.
Lord, C. (2001) 'Les partis politiques et l'Union européenne: Quel type de concurrence imparfaite?' in P. Delwit, E. Külahci and C. van de Walle (eds) *Les fédérations européennes de partis: Organisation et influence*, Bruxelles: Editions de l'Université Libre de Bruxelles, pp. 39–56.
Luther, R. and Deschouwer, K. (1999) *Party elites in divided societies: Political parties in consociational democracy*, London and New York: Routledge.
Mair, P. (2000) 'The limited impact of Europe on national party systems' *West European Politics. Special issue: Europeanised Politics? European Integration and National Political Systems* 23 (4), 27–51.
Marks, G. and McAdam, D. (1996) 'Social movements and the changing structure of political opportunity in the European Union' *West European Politics* 19 (2), 249–78.
Marquand, D. (1979) *Parliament for Europe*, London: Jonathan Cape.
Moravsick, A. (1993) 'Preferences and power in the European community: A liberal intergovernmentalist approach' *Journal of Common Market Studies* 31 (4), 473–519.
Pelinka, A., Plasser, F. and Meixner, W. (2000) *Die Zukunft der österreichischen Demokratie*, Wien: Zentrum für angewandte Politikforschung.
Putnam, R.D. (1988) 'Diplomacy and domestic politics: The logic of two-level games' *International Organization* 42 (3), 427–60.

Raunio, T. (2002a) 'Beneficial cooperation or mutual ignorance? Contacts between MEPs and national parties' in B. Steunenberg and J. Thomassen (eds) *The European Parliament: Moving toward democracy in the EU*, Lanham: Rowman and Littlefield, pp. 87–105.

Raunio, T. (2002b) 'Why European integration increases leadership autonomy within political parties' *Party Politics* 8 (4), 405–25.

Sbragia, A. (2001) 'Italy pays for Europe: Political leadership, political choice and institutional adaptation' in M. Green Cowles, J. Caporaso and T. Risse (eds) *Transforming Europe: Europeanization and domestic change*, Ithaca and London: Cornell University Press, pp. 79–97.

Scharpf, F. (1999) 'Legitimacy in the multi-actor European polity' in M. Egeberg and P. Laegreid (eds) *Organizing political institutions*, Oslo: Scandinavian University Press, pp. 261–88.

Steunenberg, B. and Thomassen, J. (2002) *The European Parliament: Moving toward democracy in the EU*, Boulder: Rowman and Littlefield.

Taylor, P. (1990) 'Consociationalism and federalism as approaches to international integration', in A. Groom and P. Taylor (eds) *Frameworks for international cooperation*, London: Pinter Publishers, pp. 172–84.

Thomassen, J. (2002) 'The feasibility of a European system of political representation' in B. Thomassen and J. Steunenberg (eds) *The European Parliament: Moving toward democracy in the EU*, Boulder: Rowman and Littlefield, pp. 15–36.

Van Ecke, S. (2001) 'Démocrates-chrétiens et conservateurs au Parlement européen: Marriage d'amour ou de raison?' in P. Delwit, E. Külahci and C. van de Walle (eds) *Les fédérations européennes de partis: Organisation et influence*, Bruxelles: Editions de l'Université Libre de Bruxelles, pp. 323–44.

Zimmer, A. and Freise, M. (2005) 'Bringing society back in: Civil society, social capital and the Third Sector', paper presented at: *CONNEX kick-off meeting*, Bled, 20–22 May 2005.

Zürn, M. (2000) 'Democratic governance beyond the nation-state?' in M. Greven and P. Louis (eds) *Democracy beyond the state? The European dilemma and the merging global order*, Boulder: Rowman and Littlefield, pp. 91–114.

9. The role of interest groups in fostering citizen engagement: the determinants of outside lobbying
Christine Mahoney

9.1 INTRODUCTION[1]

Zimmer and Friese's contribution to this volume (Chapter 2) makes a strong case for recognising the two components of civil society scholarship: social capital and third sector. This chapter focuses on the latter – the role of third sector organisations in mobilising the public and thus fostering citizen engagement and social capital. However, I argue that citizen mobilisation is not restricted to organisations that would traditionally fall into the normatively charged category of third sector or civil society organisations, which either implicitly or explicitly are said to be representing the public interest. If the concern is the way the EU can communicate through the multiple levels of multi-level governance and reach the EU citizens, then any route by which that might happen should be embraced and studied. Other interest groups, including trade, professional, business and regional associations, can also communicate EU issues to the public. Thus this chapter considers how civil society and third sector organisations communicate to the public, but also how other members of the EU advocacy community do this.

The terms 'lobbyist' and 'special interests' are often met with a less than warm reception on both sides of the Atlantic.[2] Today interest groups are seen as a force derailing democracy from its proper course, packing policy with special interest exceptions at the expense of the common good. However, some further thinking of course reminds us of the reality that the interest group community includes the very groups that scholars of social capital championed as vehicles of citizen engagement in politics: environmental groups, women's groups, civil rights groups, groups of older people, anti-globalisation groups, anti-poverty groups, unions, community groups, recreational groups, patient groups, and the list goes on. This tendency to overlook the positive side of lobbying communities may stem from the propensity of the interest group literature to look inside – focusing on direct lobbying tactics; we must also look at outside lobbying tactics.

Interest groups play a critical role in modern democracies by acting as 'mobilisers'. By monitoring policy developments and mobilising the public when policy makers act contrary to their wishes, advocates promote citizen engagement. Arnold (1990) refers to actors acting in this regard as 'instigators'. He argues the availability of an instigator to help reveal citizens' stakes in an outcome affects the probability that citizens will notice if a policy is being proposed that is important to them. He notes that instigators can be political candidates of the opposition that are monitoring the behaviour of policy makers in power with an eye toward unseating them in the next election, or they can be interest groups that monitor the daily policy-making process. If interest groups see policy-making decisions they disagree with, they have an incentive to expand the scope of conflict by involving the offending policy maker's constituents (if that public would be in line with the interest). Thus for citizen groups this is almost always a possibility. However for trade, professional and even individual corporations, it is also a possibility to expand the scope of conflict in instances in which the public shares the goals of the organised interests (see Goldstein 1999).

Through 'outside lobbying' tactics such as mobilising letter writing campaigns, media work, public advertising campaigns in print, radio and TV media outlets, organising grassroots meetings, demonstrations and other outreach programs, organised interests foster citizen engagement.

The degree to which civil society organisations perform their role as 'mobilisers' varies. I argue that three levels of factors must be considered in an explanation of that variation: institutional, issue and interest characteristics. The institutional structure of a political system can facilitate or constrain the use of outside tactics. The nature of the issue – for example whether it is highly salient or arcane – also affects the ability of advocates to engage in outside lobbying tactics. Lastly, advocate characteristics – that is, whether it is a mass membership organisation or a corporation – also play a role in the decision to 'go public'.

Previous literature on EU lobbying has suggested that advocates are generally not employing tactics that lead to mobilisation beyond Brussels (Beyers 2004; Bouwen 2002; Greenwood 1997, 2002; Pedler 2002; Pedler and van Schendelen 1994; Rucht 2001; van Schendelen 1993; Watson and Shackleton 2003). This chapter brings systematic empirical evidence to bear on this general observation, and to assess the determinants of the phenomena. Literature on the lobbying community in the United States has empirically documented the use of outside tactics as well as some of its determinants (Baumgartner and Leech 1998; Gerber 1999; Goldstein 1999; Kollman 1998; Schlozman and Tierney 1986). The comparative framework of this chapter allows us to contribute to that literature, since it will be possible to discern the role of institutional structure in the outside lobbying process.

In order to assess systematically the role of institutional structures, issue-specific factors and interest group characteristics on the decision of lobbyists to mobilise the masses, I present data from a larger project on the lobbying activities of 149 advocates in the United States and the European Union active on a random sample of 47 issues. After reviewing the literature on EU and US lobbying, I highlight the expectations regarding the influence of 1) institutions, 2) issues and 3) interest group factors on the decision to conduct outside lobbying and in doing so to engage the public in the policy-making process. Outside lobbying is not always an optimal strategy or even feasible; issue and interest characteristics are fundamentally important in determining if a given advocate uses outside lobbying tactics on a given policy debate. The second half of the chapter describes the data collection and presents the empirical findings.

9.2 INSTITUTIONS, ISSUES AND INTERESTS: FACTORS INFLUENCING THE DECISION TO MOBILISE THE PEOPLE

I proceed from the argument, as laid out in the introduction, that interest groups foster civic engagement through outside lobbying tactics – aimed at mobilising the public to influence the policy-making process. If we assume that organised interests can promote civic engagement through some of their outside lobbying campaigns, the question then becomes: what influences the lobbyists' decisions to go outside? I argue that three levels of variables are critical in understanding the decision to use outside lobbying tactics: institutional structures, issue-specific characteristics and interest group characteristics. I discuss each of these levels in turn.

9.2.1 Institutions

First, it is important to recognise why a comparative research design is critical for researching the effect of institutional design on outside lobbying. To assess the effect of institutional system characteristics on outside lobbying – which by its definition is *outside* the halls of any one governmental system – it becomes critical to do so by comparing across systems.

A number of recent scholars have come to a similar conclusion after assessing the state of the literature. In Woll's review of the literature she concludes 'In all of these studies, there is a consensus that EU lobbying cannot be understood without looking at the institutions and policy context in which groups are trying to act . . . Increasingly, scholars have thus turned their attention to cases beyond Europe to understand more about EU lobbying' (2005: 6). It is not difficult to make the case that to study the effect of institutions, you need variation in institutions, which is lacking in a single-system study. But the question then becomes: which systems to compare, and the answer for many is the EU with the US.

Michalowitz makes a strong case for an EU–US comparison in researching influence, arguing that:

> Firstly, the question as to why EU lobbying may be less influential than it appears from literature is difficult to answer from looking at the EU alone . . . Since US literature provides data already, it appears most useful to begin with a comparison of EU and US lobbying before going into more detailed studies of EU interest group influence (2005: 2).

In addition: 'The availability of US literature on the topic is the second reason to decide for a comparative analysis of the EU and the US' (ibid.). And of course she notes that there is the simple fact that observers – academic and practitioner alike – are increasingly making the comparison and noting similarities.

In addition to the strong similarities in the group systems, Kreppel analyses the legislative systems in detail, concluding that the US and EU legislatures share a number of similarities (2005: 7). Menon notes that the US and the EU 'share several traits, including: potentially comparable institutional landscapes; apparently parallel developmental trajectories and strikingly similar institutional dynamics stemming from comparable federal structures' (2005: 3). In sum, the US and the EU share numerous similarities in their institutions, norms and lobbying communities. Moreover, the wealth of scholarly treatment of lobbying in the two systems provides a strong foundation for pursuing comparative research. This is not to say, however, that there are not differences – there are; their existence is the very advantage of the comparative design.

In recent literature on EU lobbying and the fairly young literature considering lobbying in a transatlantic perspective specifically, two key institutional factors emerge as important: the method of selecting officials and the presence of a broad-reaching media system. I discuss each of these in turn, how scholars have suggested they should influence the use of outside lobbying, and finally, my hypotheses related to each.

First, there is the democratic accountability of policy makers – or the selection process. While there is variation on this variable within the EU, with the European Parliament (EP) being more democratically accountable than the Commission and Council, the EU institutions are largely not democratically accountable to the people – as is often lamented in the large literature on the democratic deficit. In the US, on the other hand, members of both the House and the Senate are highly aware of their electoral vulnerability and are thus highly accountable to the people in direct elections. The democratic accountability of an institution will influence which type of tactics a lobbyist pursues on an issue. Some lobbying tactics are designed to evoke the will of the people and tap the fear of policy makers accountable to those citizens. Other strategies are designed to convey technical information about policy proposals. Lobbyists are more likely to employ the former strategy if they are active in an arena where the officials are driven by the re-election motive. That is, I hypothesise that outside lobbying tactics such as grassroots letter writing campaigns, advertising, press releases, press conferences or protest activity should be more prevalent when lobbying in a venue that is highly democratically accountable.

Second, many observers of EU politics have noted the lack of a pan-EU media system, or what some have termed a 'European Public Space'. Due to the 23 official languages of the EU, and the lack of any widespread EU newspaper or television channel, there is no simple way to relay information directly about the EU to the people. It has to be funnelled through the national outlets, which vary in their interest and their spin on EU affairs. Rucht in his study of the lobbying and protest strategies of environmental groups notes 'Virtually all communication via mass media remains within the boundaries of national languages and discourse. Journalists located in Brussels report only for the national papers of their respective home countries' (2001: 139). Princen and Kerremans suggest that:

> the EU lacks an integrated 'European Public Space.' As a result, there are no or very little European news media and European-wide debates, especially when compared with the media and public debates in the EU's member states . . . this puts those groups at a disadvantage that rely on direct political actions to mobilise public opinion and the media (2005: 8).

Similarly Saurugger notes that 'What seems to be missing is a European demos with a shared identity, a common deliberative forum and an open system of communication' (2005: 6).

Michalowitz sees this lack of a pan-European media space as a result of a lack of a European public: 'Outside lobbying is also the reason for a strong significance of the media in US lobbying. Media are needed to create a public for the interest represented . . . EU lobbyists rarely concentrate on media lobbying, most likely because no European public exists' (2005: 10).

Considering previous literature and the logistics of lobbying, I hypothesise that certain outside lobbying tactics such as issue advertisements (in print, radio or TV), press releases or press conferences should be more prevalent when lobbying in an institutional setting with a broad-reaching media system. However, not all outside lobbying tactics should be suppressed by the lack of a media machine – specifically, mobilising letter writing campaigns of organisational members and the mass public should still be possible. Both of these tactics can be coordinated at the EU level and the mobilisation of the people carried out by the national associations. Neither requires complex media campaigns and either would foster citizen engagement.

Knowing the institutional system within which an advocate is lobbying, however, is not enough; in addition we must consider the characteristics of the issue at hand as well as the type of advocate and its resource set. I discuss these factors below.

9.2.2 Issues

The second source of variation that influences the use of outside lobbying is at the issue level. Issue-specific characteristics shape the way advocates carry out their advocacy strategy. In any society, the number and range of social problems which the government might attempt to solve – thus forming a 'political issue' – is enormous. To study the effect of issue characteristics on advocacy in a way that is generalisable to the system at large requires a research design with variation in issue characteristics and that the issues be a random sample. As mentioned in the introduction, the research presented here is based on a random sample of 47 issues identified by a random sample of advocates.

Following the initial issue identifier interview, in order to collect accurate contextual data on an issue, I carried out additional interviews, triangulation and collection of additional, publicly available information – that is, I conducted small-scale case studies on a large number of issues. In this way I was able to code my 47 issues for a number of critical variables that are likely to influence advocacy, and the decision to conduct outside lobbying specifically.

First is the scope or size of the proposed policy – the magnitude of the impact on individuals (Baumgartner and Leech 2001; Browne 1990). The larger the issue and the bigger its impact on citizens, the more likely an organisation might be to attempt to mobilise the masses. Second is the salience of the issue to the mass public (Kollman 1998). Clearly, the more salient an issue is to the people – the more they are engaged in the topic and following its developments – the more likely an advocate will go 'outside'. Third, the presence of a focusing event is an important factor influencing advocacy (Kingdon 1984). If a crisis has occurred related to the policy, this event can crystallise the need for policy action and create a concrete example with which to mobilise people. The presence of a focusing event should increase the likelihood that an organisation will engage in outside lobbying. Fourth, the level of conflict is also a determinant of the character of lobbying (Salisbury *et al.* 1987). The hypothesised impact of this variable is that the more conflict, the more outside lobbying. A high conflict issue may compel one side of the debate to engage in outside lobbying – those that want to expand the scope of conflict (Schattschneider 1960). And the media always like controversy; it gets ratings. While the opposition may not like the coverage, once the scope of conflict is expanded, they will probably also have to go public to combat the other side's outside communications. Finally, the history of the issue is important. New issues have more room for manipulation of the dimensions of debate and alliance and opposition patterns, compared to older reoccurring issues (McKissick 1995). A new issue that is a 'hot' topic may be used by advocates to spark the interest of the people, thus making outside lobbying a good tactical option. In sum, it is critical to consider the set of issue-specific variables of scope, salience, focusing events, conflict and reoccurrence when investigating the determinants of the decision by advocates to lobby outside.

9.2.3 Interests

The third level of analysis provides the final set of independent variables that influence the use of outside lobbying tactics. Organisational characteristics also have an impact of the decision of advocacy organisations to 'go public' (Dür 2005; Schlozman and Tierney 1986). The range of interests active in the EU has mushroomed along with the expansion of the polity's competencies. The wide range of group types has been well documented (Balme, Chabanet and Wright 2002; Greenwood 1997; Mahoney 2003). Groups vary not only by group type but by a number of other factors, and each of these has implications for advocacy activity. First, the type of organisation, and thus its goals or purposes, determines whether the entity can engage in outside lobbying (Beyers 2002; Clark and Wilson 1961). For example, a sectoral association of chemical manufacturers might be much less happy with their Washington or Brussels representative organising a blitz media campaign then an association of green activists. Kriesi, Jochuma and Tresch note that the number and type of interests engaging in political debates has grown: 'The struggle for the attention of the public includes elected political decision-makers, but also an increasing number of collective political actors' (2005: 6). They distinguish between state actors, political parties, interest groups and social movement organisations. Another common distinction is between civil society and industry interests; while others divide the community by diffuse versus concentrated interests (Pollack 1997; Schneider and Baltz 2003). My coding of actor type is a bit more detailed, in an effort to identify differences between different types of interest groups. The general expectation is that citizen groups will be more likely to go public while organisations representing industry will be less likely to do so.

Second, the level of financial resources is a major determinant of outside lobbying. It plays a critical role in the type and number of outside lobbying tactics an organisation can engage in (McCarthy and Zald 1977; Schlozman and Tierney 1986). Staff size is a good indicator of the level of financial resources an advocate controls – establishing a capital office (Washington DC or Brussels), and staffing it is an expensive undertaking. Staffing has also been shown to correlate highly with other, more difficult to gather indicators of financial resources like annual budget or money spent on lobbying. The more financial resources an organisation controls, the more likely it should be to engage in outside lobbying tactics.

The size, type and spread of an organisation's membership is also an important determinant of its tactic options (Bacheller 1977; Kollman 1998). If an actor has a broad membership, it is much easier and more likely to be effective at public mobilisation than an organisation that is comprised of only a few hundred individuals; and thus it is expected to engage in outside lobbying at a higher rate. Finally, it is also important to consider how the group is organised, as this also affects lobbying strategies (Marks and McAdam 1996). If an advocate has a network of membership organisations in place in the states or member states, it should be much more likely to attempt to mobilise the masses than an interest that has no member organisations, such as a corporation or lobbying firm. In the EU this is coded as whether the organisation's structure is federated, direct membership, mixed membership or no membership. In the US it is coded as a dichotomous variable if the organisation maintains local, state or regional sub-units.

In sum, a range of interest-group-specific variables including monetary and membership resources as well as group type and organisational structure can be expected to affect the decision to go 'outside'. Institutional, issue-specific and interest-group factors are all critical pieces of the advocacy puzzle and thus each will be measured and analysed so that a complete image of influences on outside lobbying can be constructed.

9.3 DATA COLLECTION

As mentioned, the data presented in this chapter stem from a larger project aimed at analysing the determinants of each of the stages of the entire advocacy process. I carried out the American interviews during 2002 under the Baumgartner, Berry, Hojnacki, Leech and Kimball project.[3] The European field work was carried out during 2004–5. The American actors were randomly drawn from a database created from the *Lobbying Reports* for 1996 that were filed with the Secretary of the Senate, compiled by Baumgartner and Leech (see Baumgartner and Leech 1998, 2001). In the European arena, I developed a sampling frame from the 2004 *Registry of the European Parliament*, the 2004 *Commission Registry of Civil Society Organisations* (CONECCS) and the 2004 *European Public Affairs Directory*. Randomly selected advocates identified a random sample of issues, and snowball sampling completed the process.

Interviewees were asked about the background of the issue they were working on, the other major players on the issue, the tactics they were engaging in, coalition participation, the arguments they were employing, the opposition they were facing and the allies they found to support their cause, among others. The coding of their tactical strategy forms the basis of the data for this chapter. Each interview transcript is coded (0 – not mentioned, or 1 – mentioned) as to whether the advocate reported using a range of outside lobbying tactics including:

1. Grassroots mobilisation of the organisation's membership (contacting members, encouraging them to write, email, call, attend town meetings or otherwise communicate with policymakers);
2. Grassroots mobilisation of the mass public;
3. Media usage (issuing press releases, organising press conferences, talking with the press, doing interviews);
4. Issue advertisements;
5. Public education campaigns/PR (coordinating large-scale public relations strategy including multiple routes to communicate to the public);
6. Protest, demonstration or rally; and
7. Writing or opinion editorial (op-ed) (writing op-eds, encouraging elite organisation members or other experts to write op-eds).

These are the very types of strategies that organisations can use to influence policy making but that simultaneously promote civic engagement.

9.3.1 Additional Data Collection from Publicly Available Sources

In addition to data collected through the in-person interviews, I also collected information on the individual organisations and issues. In the US I gathered information on group type, founding date, membership size, membership type, staff size and annual budget from *Associations Unlimited* – an online directory of Washington organisations. For groups in the EU, I gathered information including group type, founding date, type of membership and membership size from their websites.

On issues in the US, I monitored *Roll Call* and the *Washington Post* and conducted research on the websites of the House of Representatives, Senate, administration, any relevant agencies and the Library of Congress' legislative tracking system. In the EU, I monitored the *European Voice* and *EurActiv* weekly as well as researching the issues on the Commission archives and EP Legislative Observatory OEIL as well as Pre-LEX. This issue research was the basis for the coding of the issue variables of: scope (coded as 0: impacts small sector, 1: impacts large economic sector, 2: impacts multiple sectors and 3: has pan-EU or pan-US impact); conflict (coded as 0: only one perspective or viewpoint on issue, 1: multiple viewpoints but not directly opposed and 2: directly opposing viewpoints); presence of a focusing event (0: absence, 1: presence); and the history or the issue (0: for reoccurring or ongoing issue, and 1: new issue). The hypothesised directions are: the larger the scope, the higher the probability of outside lobbying; the higher the conflict, the higher the probability of outside lobbying; the presence of a focusing event, the higher the probability of outside lobbying and the newer the issue, the higher the probability of outside lobbying.

A measure of salience was collected for each issue by assessing the amount of news coverage from a major paper in each sphere. In the US, salience is indicated by the number of *New York Times* articles on the issue in the two-year period of research. This variable was collected through Lexis-Nexis searches. Searches were limited to the two-year time span of the 107th Congress (1 January 2001–31 December 2002), during which the US interviews were conducted. For a salience measure of the EU issues, I conducted Lexis-Nexis searches of the *Financial Times*. Searches were similarly limited to a two-year time span surrounding the time period during which I conducted my EU fieldwork (1 June 2003–1 June 2005); this insures comparability between the US and EU media coverage measures. The expectation is that the more salient the issue to the public, as indicated by news coverage, the more likely it is that advocates will engage in outside lobbying on the topic.

9.4 EMPIRICAL FINDINGS

9.4.1 Institutions

As expected, there is a marked difference in the use of outside lobbying in the US and the EU. Every outside lobbying tactic is used more by lobbyists

Table 9.1 Outside tactics by institutional system

	US		EU	
	Freq.	Per cent	Freq.	Per cent
Grassroots – Organisational	16	25	1	1
Grassroots – Mass Public	3	5	1	1
Media	26	40	19	23
Issue Ads	4	6	2	2
Public Education/PR	5	8	3	4
Protest/Rally	1	2	1	1
Op-ed/Editorial	9	14	2	2

in the US than the EU. Table 9.1 shows the number and percentage of US and EU advocates reporting using each of the outside lobbying tactics. So, for example, 26 US advocates out of all 65 interviewed (or 40%) reported using media strategies, while only 19 out of the 82 EU advocates interviewed (or 23%) reported doing so. Also, quite notable is the difference between grassroots mobilisation of organisational members which 25% of US advocates reported using while only 1% of EU advocates did so.

To look at the results a slightly different way, I calculated a summary variable – and additive index of the total number of outside lobbying tactics used by each advocate. Only 51 per cent of advocates in the US reported not engaging in any outside lobbying activity, whereas in the EU outside lobbying was not employed at all by 76 per cent of lobbyists. In addition, in only 6 cases out of 82 did EU advocates pursue more than one outside lobbying tactic, while combined strategies were much more prevalent in the US at 23 per cent.

While the quantitative evidence is striking, the numbers alone cannot convey the difference in intensity of outside lobbying between the US and the EU. An advocate in both the US and the EU may be coded as using a media strategy, but for the American advocate this may be a concerted media effort, whereas in the EU it is a simple press release. In many instances, media usage in the US is a fully fledged campaign, as one lobbyist active in the debate over anti-terrorism regulations explained:

> We were constantly commenting on these issues in the media, speaking personally I probably gave a dozen newspaper interviews on this particular subject and half a dozen to a dozen radio interviews . . . Also we've had editorial published on the topic. We relied pretty heavily to advance our agenda through the media.

A similarly aggressive media campaign was launched on the cloning prohibition case, as a professional association lobbyist described:

Interest groups and citizen engagement 181

> We've had a very aggressive media strategy both as part of the coalition and as individual organisations . . . I've done talk radio all over the country, I've done CNN a couple of times and we have a very strong relationship with a half dozen or so sort of leading national reporters that are covering the issue . . . And you know we did an op ed campaign, and we did paid advertising, we did a lot of talk show appearances, everybody from me to Christopher Reeve, and anybody in between, anybody that could get anybody on.

Media is often an important part of an advocacy strategy in the US and this is facilitated by the presence of a vigorous media community in the capital. In the EU, the media-intensive tactics are more difficult to employ. A humanitarian organisation active on the issue of trafficking in children explained that the Brussels press corps is often only covering the narrow topic of what dossiers are up for a vote:

> We haven't done any press, Brussels media is interested in what's on the legislative agenda so there is not much interest in this, but that is just a fact of what Brussels news covers; not about if the issue is interesting; but they just follow the legislative agenda and there hasn't been much legislative action on this.

While the presence or absence of an extensive media system is important, electoral accountability also plays a role. The electoral connection was quite apparent in a number of discussions with American lobbyists. One citizen group advocate active on the TANF (Temporary Assistance for Needy Families) reauthorisation explained the importance of the constituency link:

> What I do is to go to my constituency and say here's what you need to be telling them. They need to hear from you. It's important that I go and talk to them . . . until they hear from you, people who are actually out there, living there, breathing this, eating and sleeping it every day of your life, they need to hear from you to better understand and to really bring home that impact of what's happening at the state level.

A professional association active on the maths and science education debate echoed the point that mobilising the constituents matters:

> One of the most valuable lobbying tools we have is our legislative action network . . . Five or six times a year we will send out an action alert to 7000 of our members saying Congress is about to vote on this math and science education bill, here's the background, here's our position, here's the key players, please go to our website, type in your zip code, read more about the issue, and if you support our position then send an email to your Member of Congress . . . What we do know is that all those Members of Congress do listen to constituents . . . So that's grassroots, getting your wide membership involved in the process, getting them to weigh in.

The level of constituent mobilisation found among US advocates is markedly absent in the EU arena. Thus, we see support of both parallel hypotheses – media presence and electoral accountability – predicting less outside lobbying in the EU. However, the two tactics of grassroots mobilisation of organisational members and the mass public allow us to parse out the effects to a degree. That is, the two grassroots mobilisation tactics do not require a broad-based media system. Both tactics could be accomplished by EU organisations encouraging citizens, either directly or through their national associations, to write, email, fax or call policy makers. The fact that both of these tactics are used to a much smaller degree in the EU suggests that the first institutional characteristic – the democratic accountability of the institutions – is also at play, and that the lack of media tools are not the only explanation for the limited use of outside lobbying.

9.4.2 Issues

In order to see how the use of outside tactics varies by issue characteristics, I tabulated each of the seven dichotomous variables of outside lobbying tactics by: scope, conflict, the presence of a focusing event, the recurring or new nature of the issue, and salience. Table 9.2 A–C reports a subset of the results for the US system. The table shows, in part A for example, that 25 per cent of all groups used grassroots techniques associated with their own members (reported in the 'Total per cent' row) across all issues, but only 13 per cent of advocates used the tactic if they were lobbying on a small-sector issue. The last column shows the Ns on which each of the individual sets of percentages are calculated.

There is a clear upward trend in relation to the scope of the issue with regard to grassroots mobilisation of the membership, grassroots mobilisation of the mass public and media usage. As the issue increases in size each of these outside lobbying tactics is used by a larger percentage of advocates. There are no discernable patterns in advertising, public relations, protests, or op-ed writing.

For the issue characteristics of conflict, as issues exhibit higher conflict, the outside lobbying tactics of media use, protest, PR and op-ed writing all increase as we move from no conflict to issues with conflict. Advertising and grassroots mobilisation do not exhibit any clear patterns. It is understandable that we see more outside lobbying as conflict increases. As one side of the debate gets coverage, the other side responds in kind, as one citizen group explained:

> I don't want to say most importantly, but very important was also getting this information out to the media. Because this issue had not been debated in a really

Table 9.2 Percentage of advocates using outside tactics by issue characteristics in the US

A. Scope	Grassroots							
	Members	Public	Media	Ads	PR	Protest	Op-ed	N
Small sector	13	4	30	4	4	0	13	23
Large sector	27	5	46	14	14	0	18	22
Multiple sectors	40	10	20	0	10	10	10	10
System-wide	30	0	70	0	0	0	10	10
Total per cent	25	5	40	6	8	2	14	65

B. Conflict	Grassroots							
	Members	Public	Media	Ads	PR	Protest	Op-ed	N
None	19	5	33	0	0	0	5	21
Multiple views	33	0	33	33	0	0	0	3
Opposing	27	5	44	7	12	2	20	41
Total per cent	25	5	40	6	8	2	14	65

C. Salience	Grassroots							
	Members	Public	Media	Ads	PR	Protest	Op-ed	N
0 stories	27	7	23	7	7	0	7	30
1–5 stories	14	0	36	0	0	0	7	14
6–50 stories	36	9	55	9	18	9	27	11
51 or more	20	0	80	10	10	0	30	10
Total per cent	25	5	40	6	8	2	14	65

comprehensive way, in over ten years . . . and there was a need to really rebut the industry's arguments and help people in the media and policymakers and the public kind of see an alternative point of view.

There is less evidence of a clear pattern for the presence of a focusing event; only two tactics trend in the hypothesised direction: media and op-ed writing (shifting from 33 per cent to 55 per cent and 11 per cent to 20 per cent respectively as we move from an issue with no event to an issue with a related focusing event). All the others tactics exhibit no pattern, or, as in the case of mobilisation of the grassroots, suggest the opposite direction: this type of outside lobbying happens on issues that have no focusing event. Similarly for the variable of issue history – whether the issue is a new topic or an older reoccurring issue – the evidence does not support the hypothesised direction. Save for the slightly higher usage of media on new issues, the data would suggest that the opposite is in fact the case: that the older the issue, the more likely there is to be outside lobbying – with every other outside lobbying tactic registering higher usage percentages when the issue is older.

Regarding salience, the hypothesised direction is exhibited for every outside lobbying tactic: the more salient the issue is to the mass public, the more advocates are engaging in outside lobbying techniques. It is extremely difficult to parse out the causation here but the fact that letter writing campaigns among the public, grassroots mobilisation of the membership and protest activities are all also trending upward, in addition to the specifically media-oriented tactics, suggests that highly salient issues correlate with outside lobbying by advocates.

Now we turn to the same analysis but for issues in the EU system. As in the US arena, the use of outside lobbying tactics by advocates is related to the five issue characteristics of interest. In some cases, due to the much lower prevalence of outside lobbying in the EU, patterns are difficult to discern.

In the EU case we see essentially no pattern between issue scope and the use of any of the seven outside tactics. For conflict there is generally an upward trend from zero for six of the seven tactics, with the exception of media, which trends upward but with no cases registering in the middle category of 'multiple but not conflicting viewpoints'. For the variable of the occurrence of a focusing event, the majority of the cells indicate very low usage; however, the two tactics that have a more significant level of use confirm the hypothesised direction: as in the US, media and op-ed tactics are employed more on issues that have had some type of attention grabbing event related to them (shifting from 21 per cent to 75 per cent for media and 1 per cent to 25 per cent for op-ed). Regarding the variable of issue history, it similarly trends in the expected direction for media and op-ed but in the opposite direction for all other five tactics.

Finally, to look at the role of salience on outside lobbying usage in the EU, all seven tactics increase in usage as we move from no news coverage to any news coverage. When the public isn't concerned with an issue it is difficult for advocates to engage the media, as one trade association lobbying against the packaging environment indicator on the Packaging and Packaging Waste case study noted: 'We don't use the media much, our targets are the institutions, so maybe sometimes the *European Voice*, but the media isn't interested in packaging waste, and if you went to your average Joe on the street, and tried to talk with him about packaging and packaging waste! – good luck!'

In conclusion, we see support for the first two hypotheses that lobbyists active on larger issues and highly conflictual issues are more likely to employ outside lobbying tactics – working to engage the citizens in the policy-making process. The support for the hypotheses regarding the second two

Table 9.3 *Percentage of advocates using outside tactics by issue characteristics in the EU*

A. Scope	Grassroots		Media	Ads	PR	Protest	Op-ed	N
	Members	Public						
Small sector	0	0	13	4	0	0	0	24
Large sector	4	4	39	4	9	0	9	23
Multiple sectors	0	0	21	0	5	0	0	19
System-wide	0	0	19	0	0	6	0	16
Total per cent	1	1	23	2	4	1	2	82

B. Conflict	Grassroots		Media	Ads	PR	Protest	Op-ed	N
	Members	Public						
None	0	0	19	0	0	0	0	16
Multiple views	0	0	0	0	0	0	0	7
Opposing	2	2	27	3	5	2	3	59
Total per cent	1	1	23	2	3	1	2	82

C. Salience	Grassroots		Media	Ads	PR	Protest	Op-ed	N
	Members	Public						
0 stories	0	0	9	3	0	0	0	32
1–2 stories	5	5	35	5	5	0	5	20
3 or more	0	0	30	0	7	3	3	30
Total per cent	1	1	23	2	4	1	2	82

issue characteristics is more mixed, suggesting that knowing the issue's history and whether a focusing event occurred may not be quite enough to predict lobbying strategies. Finally, there is evidence supporting the hypothesis that there will be more outside lobbying on more salient issues.

9.4.3 Interests

The final level of independent variables that should have an effect on the use of outside lobbying is organisational characteristics. As readers of the literature would expect, in the US citizen groups are much more inclined to employ outside lobbying tactics: they use them to a greater extent than the average on every tactic except advertisements (and protests, but only one advocate reported employing a protest strategy out of all 65 respondents). They are the only type of actor mobilising the mass public (at 22 per cent) other than trade associations, of which only 8 per cent reported doing so. Professional associations are also large users of outside strategies, exhibiting higher-than-average use of five of the seven outside lobbying strategies. This category of actors is especially inclined to use grassroots mobilisation of the membership, with 57 per cent of professional associations reporting that they used this tactic on the issue on which they were interviewed. Also interesting to note is the types of actors that are dominating certain tactics: issue advertisements are used by only 6.15 per cent of actors on average, but it is the professional associations and the corporations that are the only types of actors engaging in this activity; 43 per cent of professional organisations are advertising related to their policy fights, and 14 per cent of corporations. Advertising requires a significant amount of resources to design, produce and air. One advocate described the blitz advertising campaign being financed by industry in the Corporate Average Fuel Economy debate:

> A big part of their ad campaign, before the vote in Congress this past year was, they had ads running in rural America saying: Congress is going to take away your pickup truck and you're going to be hauling hay in the back of a little Pinto.

All the think tanks reported pursuing media strategies and a third also reported engaging in public relations campaigns and writing editorials. Multinational corporations were not engaging in any form of outside lobbying. One company lobbyist described how they try to stay out of the media:

> We generally stay behind the scenes, we are not one to go grab a microphone or a spot light very often, we will call people, rather than go see them, we are a company that draws a lot of criticism because we are so big . . . So we basically keep to ourselves, sort of lurk in the shadows and try not to put our fingerprints on anything.

Regarding the interest group characteristic of staff, the data does not clearly support the hypothesised relationship – larger staff sizes seem to be related to a higher use of outside lobbying tactics only in the case of media, where we see 43 per cent of small offices reporting media tactics, 50 per cent of medium-sized offices and 57 per cent of large offices. For both types of grassroots mobilisation and protest, it appears that you need to cross some threshold of staff resources to engage in these outside tactics, but the largest offices are not 'going public' as much as the mid-range offices. This finding might not be as surprising as it seems at first blush, for it is the well-heeled lobbying firms, corporations and business associations that have the well-staffed offices – the very types of advocates that are unlikely to engage in large public mobilisation campaigns. Thus it appears, when you do not have the money and inside-the-beltway staff (that is staff located in the District of Columbia surrounded by the Capital Beltway highway) to engage in incessant direct lobbying, you rely on the masses and mass membership to communicate your message to lawmakers. However, you need enough staff to put into motion the outside strategy.

Organisational structure seems to have a clear influence on the decision to go outside or not: advocates that have sub-units at the regional, state or local level use outside lobbying strategies at a higher level than groups with no local groups, and this goes for every outside lobbying tactic except for op-ed writing, which is often done by expert members or Washington staff. This finding follows logic: it is easier to mobilise the members, citizens in the communities, coverage in local papers, public education campaigns and protests if you have established offices already active in the field. This was exemplified by one of the environmental organisations I interviewed; as their lobbyist explained:

> We are the largest grassroots environmental organisation in the country. We have about 750 000 members and the real strength of our organisation is the ability to mobilise people across the country, so we often help in the release of other organisation's reports because they don't have that field staff, they don't have the regional offices, and the chapter office in every state and volunteers that can put on a press conference in just about any city you would want.

To assess the relationship between membership size and outside lobbying, I distinguished between individual members and organisational members – be they organisations, corporations or institutions. The larger the individual membership, the higher the percentage of outside lobbying usage – and that goes for every single lobbying tactic. A similar pattern also holds for corporate membership – the more members, the more outside lobbying – but only for the tactics of grassroots mobilisation of organisational members, grassroots mobilisation of the public and media use. The other four tactics are not used by organisations with corporate or institutional members, regardless of how large that membership is.

Turning to the EU and investigating the relationship between group type and outside lobbying, a pattern similar to the US emerges: domination by the citizen groups. It is they who use the majority of outside lobbying tactics more than the average of all groups. In addition, they are the only category of actors mobilising the mass public. Second to citizen groups though are trade associations, using four of the seven outside tactics at a higher-than-average rate. As in the US, it is the industry associations that are the only category of actors using advertising. A number of actor categories reported using no outside tactics: professional associations, business groups, lobbying firms and the governmental actors. While the governmental actors are, of course, unlikely to mobilise letter writing campaigns or protest events, media, advertising, public relations and op-ed tactics are all open to them.

When it comes to the relationship between staff and outside lobbying, the opposite of the hypothesised relationship is exhibited, with more outside lobbying being done by the smaller and mid-range offices. Again, as in the US, this makes sense, since it is the well-heeled offices that can engage in aggressive inside lobbying strategies; they do not need to resort to outside mobilisation.

Again, as expected, organisational structure has a clear relationship to outside lobbying. Organisations without sub-units in the member states use only one type of outside lobbying – media – and they do so at a level lower than the average. It is the organisations that have a federated structure – composed of member associations – that exhibit higher-than-average outside lobbying on every type of tactic. These types of umbrella organisations can spread the message and call for action through their member associations down to the individual members. The one organisation that reported mobilising the masses and membership described its strategy on the live animal transport debate:

> So we try to coordinate with our member associations, and get the media done at the same time, so we did that on this issue. Citizens write to their MPs and to their MEPs. MEPs say that animal welfare is the largest number of letters they get, that is, the most letters they get about one topic is on animal welfare. People care about this, people care about animals and they write.

The EU differs from the US in that there are few mass membership organisations. Only one organisation that fell into my sample had direct individual members, of which there were only 91. This organisation was not pursuing any outside lobbying tactics. Thus, for the EU arena the membership analysis is limited to organisations with institutional members, which could be associations, corporations or institutions. In the EU arena, differing from the US findings, it is the mid-range category of advocates – those that have members but not a large number – that are employing outside lobbying tactics at a higher rate.

In sum, the findings fit with previous suggestions by political observers: it is the citizen groups and those with a weak insider presence that resort to outside lobbying. In addition, organisational composition also plays a role. Those groups that have local offices in the field are better able to engage in outside lobbying and thus draw the public into the policy debates in the capitals. In the US, organisations with more members, whether individual or institutional, are using outside lobbying at a higher rate, while in the EU, it is the groups with medium-sized institutional membership.

9.5 CONCLUSION

Thus we see evidence that the political context as well as individual interest group characteristics play a role in determining if a lobbyist pursues an outside lobbying campaign. Knowing any single factor is not enough to predict if outside lobbying tactics are the way to go. It is the melding of factors from all three levels that influences the ultimate tactical strategy.

The findings showed that civil society groups are most likely to use outside lobbying, and members of the business community are less so inclined. Small and medium staff sizes also suggest an outside approach. In the US, a large membership base further suggests more outside lobbying, while in the EU it is the mid-range groups that are pursuing outside tactics rather than the largest membership organisations. And in both polities we saw that an established on-the-ground network of local and regional offices facilitates going public.

At the issue level, evidence from both polities supported the hypotheses that more outside lobbying is exhibited on issues that are high in conflict and salience. In addition, in the US, issues large in scope also lead to more outside lobbying. A clear pattern was lacking when it came to the history of the issue and if a focusing event was linked to the issue by a policy entrepreneur.

It is clear from comparing the EU and the US findings that EU advocates are not mobilising European citizens as much as they might be. The institutional structure plays a large role in explaining the lack of outside lobbying. And the requirements of the various outside lobbying tactics – some requiring a media system, and some not – have allowed us to confirm that both institutional factors are likely to be at play: the presence of a media system and the selection of officials. Even if the constellation of organisational and issue characteristics is that which would suggest high use of outside lobbying, in the EU such an advocate is still unlikely to mobilise the masses, and foster citizen engagement, due to contextual constraints.

Two institutional reforms could bring about a change in that tendency, which would open the door for more citizen involvement via outside lobbying. First, the lack of a pan-EU media machine could change in time; with the rise of the blogosphere and other on-line papers, it may be more and more possible to bypass the slow-moving traditional forms of media and spread a pan-EU message through the internet and mass emails. The Commissioner for Communication, Margot Wallström, called for just this following the constitutional crisis and budgetary crisis of 2005: 'innovative steps must be taken to create cross-border "public space" for debate at the European level. This might include translation facilities, venues for exchanging articles and exchange programs for journalists' (21 June 2005,

International Herald Tribune). If this is the case we may begin to see more outside lobbying in the EU, but orchestrated through virtual news outlets rather than traditional print editorials.

However, even the two outside lobbying tactics that do not require a pan-EU media system – mobilisation of members and the mass public to produce grassroots communications – are also less prevalent in the EU, suggesting that the democratic responsiveness of policy makers is also very much at play. Thus, changes in the democratic accountability of the primary political institutions seem to be required – to impose a re-election concern on policy makers, making them more responsive to communications from the citizenry.

While organised interests may be using citizen-mobilisation techniques to a lesser degree in the EU, that does not mean citizen interests are going unnoticed in the EU while dominating the political scene in DC. Conversely, when we look at lobbying success rates in the two systems we see more balanced outcomes in the EU, favouring both citizen and industry groups, while industry tends to win absolute victories over civil society in the US (for more on this see Mahoney 2008). Outside lobbying then is, of course, only one piece of the puzzle we study when investigating the role of civil society in political processes.

NOTES

1. Thank you to Frank Baumgartner, Donna Bahry, Jeffrey Berry and the participants in the CONNEX meeting at Bled, Slovenia, May 2005 for comments on an earlier draft of this paper. Thank you also to the Fulbright Commission for the Fulbright Fellowship that supported the data collection and to the Pennsylvania State University for the Fellowship that supports the analysis.
2. Much debate surrounds the proper term to use when studying lobbying. Interest groups, organised interests, civil society organisations and lobbying groups, all connote some type of 'group', leaving out the other important players in all lobbying communities, such as individual firms, institutions, other governmental units and lobbying, law and PR firms. The term 'advocate' – any entity attempting to influence the policy-making process – successfully captures all these actor types.
3. The Baumgartner, *et al.* project, entitled 'The Advocacy and Public Policymaking Project', studied the lobbying activity on 98 issues in the United States and was funded by NSF grants #SES0111224 and SBR-9905195.

REFERENCES

Arnold, R.D. (1990) *The logic of congressional action*, New Haven: Yale University Press.
Bacheller, J. (1977) 'Lobbyists and the legislative process: The impact of environmental constraints' *American Political Science Review* 71 (1), 242–63.

Balme, R., Chabanet, D. and Wright, V. (2002) *L'action collective en Europe*, Paris: Presses de Sciences Po.
Baumgartner, F.R. and Leech, B.L. (1998) *Basic interests: The importance of groups in politics and in political science*, Princeton, NJ: Princeton University Press.
Baumgartner, F. and Leech, B. (2001) 'Interest niches and policy bandwagons: Patterns of interest group involvement in national politics' *Journal of Politics* 63 (4), 1191–213.
Beyers, J. (2002) 'Gaining and seeking access: The European adaptation of domestic interest associations' *European Journal of Political Research* 41 (5), 586–612.
Beyers, J. (2004). 'Voice and access: Political practices of European interest associations' *European Union Politics* 5 (2), 211–40.
Bouwen, P. (2002) 'Corporate lobbying in the European Union: The logic of access' *Journal of European Public Policy* 9 (3), 365–90.
Browne, W.P. (1990) 'Organized interests and their issue niches: A search for pluralism in a policy domain' *Journal of Politics* 52 (2), 477–509.
Clark, P.B. and Wilson, J.Q. (1961) 'Incentive systems: A theory of organisations' *Administrative Science Quarterly* 6 (2), 129–66.
Gerber, E.R. (1999) *The populist paradox: Interest group influence and the promise of direct legislation*, Princeton, NJ: Princeton University Press.
Goldstein, K.M. (1999) *Interest groups, lobbying, and participation in America*, New York: Cambridge University Press.
Greenwood, J. (1997) *Representing interests in the European Union*, New York: St. Martins Press.
Greenwood, J. (2002) *Inside the EU business associations*, New York: Palgrave.
Kingdon, J.W. (1984) *Agendas, alternatives, and public policies*, Boston: Little, Brown.
Kollman, K. (1998) *Outside lobbying: Public opinion and interest group strategies*, Princeton, NJ: Princeton University Press.
Kreppel, A. (2005) 'Understanding the European Parliament from a federalist perspective: The legislatures of the USA and the EU compared', paper presented at: *EUSA 9th Biannual International Conference*, Austin, Texas, 31 March 2–April 2005.
Kriesi, H., Jochuma, M. and Tresch, A. (2005) '*Going public in the EU: Changing strategies of Western European collective political actors*', Unpublished working paper, University of Zürich.
Mahoney, C. (2003) 'Influential institutions: The demand side of lobbying in the European Union', paper presented at: *The American Political Science Association Annual Meeting*, Philadelphia, Pennsylvania, August 2003.
Mahoney, C. (2008) *Brussels versus the Beltway: Advocacy in the United States and the European Union*, Washington DC: Georgetown University Press.
Marks, G. and McAdam, D. (1996) 'Social movements and the changing structure of political opportunity in the European Union' *West European Politics* 19 (2), 249–78.
McCarthy, J.D. and Zald, M.D. (1977) 'Resource mobilization and social movements: A partial theory' *American Journal of Sociology* 82 (6), 1212–41.
McKissick, G.J. (1995) 'Interests, issues, and emphases: Lobbying Congress and the strategic manipulation of issue dimensions', paper presented at: *The Annual Meeting of the Midwest Political Science Association*, 1 September, Chicago, Illinois.
Menon, A. (2005) 'The limits of comparative politics: International relations in the European Union', paper presented at: *EUSA 9th Biannual International Conference*, Austin, Texas, 31 March–2 April 2005.

Michalowitz, I. (2005) 'Service bureaux of decision makers or successful spin-doctors: Assessing interest group influence in the EU and the US', paper presented at: *EUSA 9th Biannual International Conference*, Austin, Texas, 31 March–2 April 2005.

Pedler, R.H. (2002) *European Union lobbying: Changes in the arena*, Basingstoke: Palgrave Macmillan.

Pedler, R.H. and van Schendelen, M.P.C.M. (eds) (1994) *Lobbying the European Union: Companies, trade associations and issue groups*, Aldershot: Dartmouth.

Pollack, M. (1997) 'Representing diffuse interests in EC policy-making' *Journal of European Public Policy* 4 (4), 572–90.

Princen, S. and Kerremans, B. (2005) 'Opportunity structures in the EU multilevel system: Reviewing the state of the art', paper presented at: *CONNEX WP1 – The State of the Art in EU Interest Representation*, Leiden, Netherlands, 14–16 April 2005.

Rucht, D. (2001) 'Lobbying or protest? Strategies to influence EU environmental policies' in D. Imig and S. Tarrow (eds) *Contentious Europeans: Protest and politics in an emerging polity*, Lanham, MD: Rowman and Littlefield Publishers.

Salisbury, R.H., Heinz, J.P., Laumann, E.O. and Nelson, R.L. (1987) 'Who works with whom? Interest group alliances and opposition' *American Political Science Review* 81 (4), 1211–34.

Saurugger, S. (2005) 'Associative democracy and the democratic legitimacy of the European Union', paper presented at: *CONNEX WP1 – The State of the Art in EU Interest Representation*, Leiden, Netherlands, 14–16 April 2005.

Schattschneider, E.E. (1960) *The semi-sovereign people*, New York: Holt, Rinehart and Winston.

Schlozman, K.L. and Tierney, J.T. (1986) *Organized interests and American democracy*, New York: Harper and Row Publishers.

Schneider, G. and Baltz, K. (2003) 'The power of specialization: How interest groups influence EU legislation' *Rivista di Politica Economica* 93 (1–2), 1–31.

van Schendelen, M.P.C.M. (ed.) (1993) *National public and private EC lobbying*, Aldershot: Dartmouth.

Watson, R. and Shackleton, M. (2003) 'Organized interests and lobbying in the EU', in E. Bomberg and A. Stubb (eds) *The European Union: How does it work?* Oxford: Oxford University Press.

Woll, C. (2005) *Research agenda: Lobbying in the European Union: From sui generis to a comparative perspective*. Unpublished paper, CERI, Sciences Po.

10. Coalition structures in national policy networks: the domestic context of European politics

Silke Adam, Margit Jochum and Hanspeter Kriesi

10.1 INTRODUCTION

Today the European Union is regarded as the most ambitious project of multi-national governance (Hirst and Thompson 1996). Some authors even call it a state-like structure (Lepsius 1999; Lord and Beetham 2001). As a result, no other region in the world has a comparatively high level of state surpassing regulations as the European Union (Kohler-Koch 2000). This might lead us to the expectation that, at least in those policy domains that are jointly regulated, European nation states might converge, leaving behind their national characteristics. However, research points to the puzzling fact that, despite these common European structures and regulations, member states still respond differently to these challenges and changes at the European level (for example, Cowles *et al.* 2001; Héritier and Knill 2001). The reason for these specific domestic adaptations (Risse *et al.* 2001: 1) refers to the fact that European regulations and policies meet with different domestic contexts. These are the key to understanding responses to European policies. Wallace (2001: 593) for example argues that 'the adaptations of behaviour and the outcomes of policy need to be read against significant and persistent diversity between Member States'.

Although research has pointed out the importance of the national level in European integration (for example, Imig and Tarrow 2000; Wallace 2001; Maurer *et al.* 2003), there is so far little understanding of how the national level affects adaptation processes in relation to EU policies (Knill and Lehmkuhl 2002: 255). These domestic adaptation processes, we argue, take place in policy-domain-specific subsystems, which operate more or less independently of one another in a parallel fashion. As a consequence thereof, it is not sufficient to look for general country differences to explain national filter processes; we also need to take into account characteristics of policy domains within each country (see Kriesi *et al.* 2006). Domestic adaptation processes are furthermore not determined by national state actors alone. Rather, they involve a large number of actors – from state actors to civil society and NGOs – that interact with each other. This domain-specific perspective and the concern with a large variety of actors and their interactions have given prominence to the concept of policy networks. This term – as we use it here – is to be understood as a generic label that embraces different forms of relations between state and private actors (Jordan and Schubert 1992; Rhodes and Marsh 1992). Policy networks can be used as a descriptive tool that helps characterise domestic constellations as filter mechanisms for the common European input.

These domain-specific policy networks are not constituted by single actors but by coalitions (Sabatier 1993). Accordingly, we seek to describe domestic coalition structures within policy networks. To this end, we draw on a typology that identifies the crucial dimensions of policy networks and apply these dimensions to coalition structures within policy networks. Subsequently we analyse empirically the coalition structures in six European countries – Germany, Spain, France, Italy, the Netherlands and the UK – and one closely associated country (Switzerland) regarding three policy domains (EU integration, immigration and agricultural policies). While our data do not allow an analysis of the actual influence of coalition structures on concrete policy adaptation processes, we can provide a clear description of the coalition structures in our 21 cases and show that the domestic policy-specific coalition structures, with which EU policies are confronted at the domestic level, vary strongly. Linking these results to arguments about policy change, we are able to formulate hypotheses about the varying potentials for and the different ways of policy change at the national level induced by EU policies and regulations.

10.2 A TYPOLOGY OF DOMESTIC POLICY NETWORKS APPLIED TO COALITION STRUCTURES

In order to capture the essential features of policy networks, various typologies have been developed. As these typologies are hardly comparable (van Waarden 1992), we make a fresh start (see Kriesi *et al.* 2006). Social networks consist of two basic elements: a set of actors and the relations between them. Accordingly, networks are characterised by two types of variables (Wasserman and Faust 1999: 29): variables describing actors' attributes and variables specifying the type of ties. The first dimension of our typology refers to the actors' attributes. Actors have specific capabilities, perceptions and preferences. As the aspect of capabilities seems most crucial to us for the way policy networks operate, we characterise a policy network in regard to the distribution of capabilities, which means the 'distribution of power' (see also Atkinson and Coleman 1989; Rhodes and Marsh 1992; van Waarden 1992). This dimension is above all concerned with whether power is concentrated in the hands of one dominant actor or distributed between actors. The existing literature also commonly refers to the relative share of power attributed to different types of actors. We consider this aspect as a subsidiary element qualifying the overall distribution of power. This perspective shows whether and to what extent state actors have to share power with political parties, interest groups and non-governmental organisations.

The dominant type of interaction between actors constitutes our second basic dimension to describe policy networks (see for example van Waarden 1992; Scharpf 1997). Depending on the degree of cooperation among actors, we distinguish between three forms: (predominance of) conflict/competition, (predominance of) bargaining and (predominance of) cooperation. Bargaining constitutes an intermediary or ambivalent type of interaction that is characterised by both conflict/competition and cooperation.

By combining the above specified dimensions, six types of policy networks can be derived (see Figure 10.1). The distribution of power qualifies the interaction modes in each case: the concentration of power introduces a hierarchical element into the pattern of interactions. In the case of conflict, we distinguish between a situation of 'dominance', where a few powerful actors are challenged by peripheral actors. This situation is different from the one we call 'competition', where power is shared between challengers and those in power. With respect to bargaining, we distinguish between symmetric or asymmetric bargaining, depending on the power distribution. Similarly, we distinguish between horizontal and hierarchical cooperation. In both instances, we follow Scharpf's (1997: 197ff) suggestion that bargaining or cooperation 'in the shadow of hierarchy' is conducted under conditions significantly different from those obtaining among actors who are all more or less equally powerful. In Scharpf's analysis, the

Type of interaction **Distribution of power**	Conflict	Bargaining	Cooperation
Concentration	Dominance	Asymmetric bargaining	Hierarchical cooperation
Fragmentation	Competition	Symmetric bargaining	Horizontal cooperation

Figure 10.1 Typology of policy networks

hierarchically superior actor is the state, but we do not want to preclude that a non-state actor could also have a predominant position in the network.

So far we have treated a policy domain as if it were constituted of individual actors who interact with each other. The literature however indicates that these individual actors cluster together forming coalitions (Sabatier 1993; Sabatier and Jenkins-Smith 1999). Each coalition can be characterised by a specific belief system – that is, a set of common values, causal attributions and perceptions. At a given moment, in a given policy domain, we are likely to find a limited number of coalitions. It is an empirical question whether or not domain-specific policy making is dominated by one of these coalitions exerting what Baumgartner and Jones (1993) have termed a 'policy monopoly'.

Consequently, the proposed typology should be applied to coalitions instead of individual actors. As a result, one needs to delimit the coalitions within a specific policy domain and then ask for the type of interaction and the distribution of power between these coalitions. Measuring these indicators on single actors only reveals the average degree of fragmentation of power and the average type of interaction. It does not show, however, whether fragmented power between single actors also means fragmented power between coalitions. If all powerful actors clustered together in the same coalition, power might be concentrated at the coalition level, but fragmented at the actor level. Additionally, such a coalition perspective allows us to determine whether state actors and the actors from the system of interest intermediation group together (heterogeneous coalitions), or whether the different types of actors form separate coalitions (homogenous coalitions). Finally, such a coalition perspective reveals the course of the major conflict lines running between coalitions within policy domains and thus shows which coalitions might cause change and which direction change might take.

10.3 MEASURING POWER AND INTERACTIONS IN COALITION STRUCTURES – OPERATIONALISATION AND DATA

The analysis is based on 306 semi-structured interviews with four categories of actors; state actors, political parties, interest associations and SMO-NGOs (social movement organisations/non-governmental organisations) present in three policy fields (immigration, agriculture and European integration) in seven countries (Switzerland, France, Germany, Italy, the Netherlands, Spain, the UK). The most important person in charge of designing an organisation's mobilisation and communication strategy was interviewed. The interviews were conducted face to face or by phone by members of the different country teams of the Europub.com project in 2003.[1] The interviews are distributed as follows over the countries in question: Switzerland: 48; Germany: 47; Spain: 43; France: 32; Italy 49; the Netherlands: 45; the UK: 42.

For each policy field, we intended to select the four most important organisations in each one of our four categories of actors. Note that this selection procedure does not necessarily include all the most important actors in a policy domain. It could be that all the SMO-NGOs were marginal in one of the policy domains, while several additional state actors played a key role. While neglecting some key actors, this procedure has the advantage of providing us with information about all four types of actors.

In order to study coalition structures and the type of interactions we asked each organisation questions regarding their relations within the policy domain. These questions on networks are very much inspired by earlier work about political elites and their involvement in specific policy areas (Laumann and Pappi 1976; Kriesi 1980; Laumann and Knoke 1987; Knoke et al. 1996; Kriesi and Jegen 2001). The 16 interviewed organisations per country and policy domain were presented with a list of 40 organisations, which included all the actors the country teams considered to be the most important in the respective domains based on media content analysis performed earlier in the project. The interviewed organisations constituted a subset of the 40 organisations on the list. For each actor on the list, the respondents were asked questions about three types of interactions – alliances, oppositional relationships and targeting relations. In particular they were asked whether they had 'closely collaborated' (cooperation), had 'some major disagreements' (conflict) and/or 'tried to influence' (target) a specific actor in the last five years. Note that we only have complete information on systematic network analyses for the organisations interviewed. This means that, at best, we can only identify a complete network of 16 organisations per issue domain and country.

To determine the dominant type of interaction, that is, the average degree of conflict and cooperation within a network, we calculate the density of each type of tie within the network and compare these densities to each other. This procedure allows us to identify whether conflict, bargaining or cooperation prevails within a network. This view however does not reveal how conflict divides specific actors and specific actor coalitions and how cooperation unites them. To identify the pattern of conflict between and within coalitions we draw on block model analysis. A block model consists of two elements (Wasserman and Faust 1999: 395). First, it divides actors in the network into discrete subsets called 'positions' or 'blocks'. Actors are placed within the same block if they have similar relations to all the other actors and are therefore regarded as 'structurally equivalent'. Actors thus form a coalition if they have the same allies and enemies. Thus it is not necessarily the consent within a block, but the overall pattern of similar ties that defines a coalition.[2] For each policy domain in each country, four blocks have been identified. Second, for each network a block model represents the pattern of ties between and within the blocks. The presence or absence of a tie between two blocks or within a block depends on the density of the ties among the actors comprising them. We regard a relation as present if the density of ties is above 0.1. The advantage of block model analysis is that we can analyse all types of interaction at the same time.

So far we know whether a network is conflict- or cooperation-driven, which actors cluster together as they have the same allies and opponents and where conflict or cooperation lines run through these resulting coalitions. However, as policy networks are not only defined by the type of interaction, but also by the power distribution, we need to operationalise this second dimension as well. The power of an actor is operationalised by reputational measures. The interviewees were asked to name all organisations on the list of 40, which, from their point of view, had been particularly influential in the relevant policy domain over the past five years. Next, they were asked to name the three most influential organisations, and finally, the most influential one. For each actor on the list of 40, an overall indicator is calculated out of these three questions that shows the power that is attributed to the respective actor. For each policy domain in each country, the maximum value of this indicator has been set to 1 and the remaining values have been adjusted accordingly. To indicate whether power is fragmented or concentrated we use the standard deviation. Power is equally distributed (fragmented) if the standard deviation is low. In contrast, power is concentrated if the standard deviation is high. For a general overview of the distribution of power within a network, this measure can be calculated at the individual actor level. If we seek to describe coalition structures in terms of power distributions, we need to calculate the standard deviation for the power distribution between 'blocks' (or coalitions). This measure indicates whether a policy field is dominated by a leading coalition or whether different, equally powerful coalitions struggle with each other. For such an analysis we start out by calculating the mean of the actors' power in each block. The standard deviation of these mean power values indicates whether power is concentrated or distributed between blocks.

It must be kept in mind that, for each country-specific policy domain, only a limited number of actors has been interviewed. In order to check whether these actors include the most powerful ones at the domestic level, we compared their power with that of the remaining actors on the list of 40. The results of the respective comparisons were quite satisfactory. With some exceptions – mainly, but not exclusively, from France and Italy – the actors we interviewed include the most important ones overall, and the most important ones in each category. Knowing about the possible shortcomings of our selection procedure and the limited number of interviews, these results give us confidence in the quality of our data. Nevertheless, we should mention that, in two cases, the respondents were less than willing to provide us with information on their network ties (agriculture in France, and EU integration in Italy). Therefore, the corresponding networks are not analysed in detail.

10.4 COALITION STRUCTURES – EMPIRICAL FINDINGS

To characterise coalition structures as domestic contexts of European politics, we present results concerning the distribution of power between national coalitions, the composition of these coalitions and the way the type of interaction shapes specific conflict constellations. For these analyses we draw on the results of block modelling.

Power Distribution among Coalitions

Our typology distinguishes between policy domains where power is fragmented and those where power is concentrated in the hand of one coalition only. In reality, however, this binary structure must be replaced by a continuum indicating varying degrees of power concentration (see Table 10.1). The higher the standard deviation in this table, the more concentrated the power within the specific policy domain. This analysis clearly shows that power between coalitions is not equally distributed in any of the analysed policy domains as the standard deviation is always above zero. However, the unevenness of the power distribution over coalitions varies between countries and policy domains. This variation is smaller in the domain of EU integration than in immigration or agriculture. In EU integration, it is Germany that shows the highest concentration of power, followed by the UK and France. In Switzerland, by contrast, the only non-member country of our sample, power is most strongly fragmented between the competing coalitions. Spain and the Netherlands are intermediate cases.

Turning to the domain of agricultural policy, we find concentrated power structures in Spain and Italy. In each of these cases there is one leading coalition which dominates the field (see Appendix 10.1, Table 10.A1). Germany, by contrast, shows the most balanced power constellation, followed by the UK, the Netherlands and Switzerland. While one could characterise the Southern European countries as concentrated in the domain of agricultural policy, power within the other countries is more equally shared.

Table 10.1 Power distribution among coalitions

Standard deviation between blocks	CH SD	CH n	D SD	D n	E SD	E n	F SD	F n	I SD	I n	NL SD	NL n	UK SD	UK n
EU integration	0.11	16	0.25	16	0.16	9	0.21	9	–	–	0.16	12	0.22	16
Agriculture	0.21	16	0.14	15	0.39	8	–	–	0.37	15	0.20	15	0.17	15
Immigration	0.18	16	0.17	16	0.11	11	0.29	12	0.14	16	0.21	11	0.40	11

Notes:
SD (between blocks B; B = square root of the variance of B; B = mean power value of each block
Empty cells: information is not sufficient

Table 10.2 Composition of coalitions and average power

Block type	Power	State (%)	Party (%)	Int.Gr. (%)	NGO (%)	Total (%)	N
1 State block	**0.65**	**67.1**	16.5	15.2	1.3	100.0	79
2 Party block	0.33	15.2	**56.1**	21.2	7.6	100.0	66
3 Interest-group block	0.37	13.5	14.9	**44.6**	27.0	100.0	74
4 SMO block	0.29	4.9	8.6	23.5	**63.0**	100.0	81
All blocks	0.42	25.7	22.7	26.0	25.7	100.0	300

Note: Basis: averages taken across all issues and countries. Case numbers for the block membership (N = 300) is higher than case numbers for power as here data are missing (N = 281).

Finally, in the domain of immigration policy, the UK and France stand out as the countries with the most concentrated power structures. In both countries there is one dominant coalition (see Appendix 10.1, Table 10.A1) within the policy domain. On the other side of the continuum, we find Spain and Italy with coalition structures that reveal strong fragmentation of power. Here one can hardly determine which coalition leads the game. Germany, Switzerland and the Netherlands can be characterised as intermediate cases. Although in each of these countries there is a dominant coalition, it is surrounded by other coalitions that hold at least some power.

To qualify our dimension 'distribution of power', we are interested in its distribution over the different actor types. Table 10.2 shows that the block model procedure results in coalitions which are relatively homogenous with regard to the type of actors. This means that state actors have similar relations to other state actors and interest groups define the allies and opponents in a similar way to other interest groups. Independent of the policy domain or the country, the first block is typically dominated by state actors and it is also typically the most powerful block. Roughly two-thirds of the actors in the first block are state actors, and their average power is almost twice as high as that of the next two blocks. The second block is dominated by parties, but it also includes an important share of state actors. The remaining two blocks are typically composed of interest groups and SMO-NGOs – with the former dominating the third block and the latter dominating the fourth block. This result vividly shows that non-state actors hardly make it into the ruling coalitions. Not only do they predominantly form coalitions with similar organisations, but these non-state coalitions are also characterised by a lack of power.

Type of Interaction and Course of Conflict Lines among Coalitions

To determine whether conflict, bargaining or cooperation prevails within a policy domain, we compare the density of conflictual and bargaining relations to the cooperative ones. Countries with high ratios of conflict or bargaining compared to cooperative ties are classified accordingly (see also Kriesi et al. 2006).[3] Regarding the domain of EU integration, conflict dominates in Switzerland, the UK and Germany whereas in Spain, France and the Netherlands cooperation prevails. The domain of agricultural policy can be characterised by bargaining relations in most of our countries (Switzerland, Germany, the Netherlands and Spain). In Italy however conflict prevails. In the UK cooperation is dominant. Turning to the domain of immigration, it seems that only the UK and the Netherlands have settled the conflicts inherent in this field. Here cooperation or bargaining prevails whereas in all other countries under study conflict is dominant.

However, with this type of analysis, we still do not know anything about the pattern of conflict lines among coalitions. To locate conflict or cooperation and to show, at the same time, power distributions visually, we present graphs based on block model analysis for each of our three policy domains and all the countries with sufficient information in the corresponding domain (Figures 10.2–10.4). Tables 10.A1 and 10.A3 contain the relevant information for drawing these graphs. The blocks are represented by circles, the ties by arrows. The circles are shaded accordingly to the power of the block. Very powerful blocks (mean power > 0.60) are dark, moderately powerful blocks are grey (mean power 0.30–0.60) and weak blocks are white (mean power < 0.30). The arrows refer to the type of tie: bold arrows indicate cooperation, normal arrows bargaining, interrupted ones conflict. The absence of an arrow indicates that there is no relationship whatsoever between two blocks. Note that the first two blocks and the last two were split in the second step of the block model procedure. This means that the first couple of blocks and the second couple of blocks are generally more similar than blocks from different couples. These graphs allow us to go beyond a pure analysis of the degree of conflictuality of policy domains, by pointing to the actual course of conflict lines and thus revealing a more qualitative view of the interaction patterns within a country's policy domain.

EU integration
There are two possible types of conflict that shape the policy field of EU integration. The first is a fundamental one and refers to the question of whether a nation should join or remain within the European Union. The second type of conflict deals with the way European integration should proceed. Here the debates centre around a supranational versus intergovernmental or a liberal versus social Europe. In Switzerland and the UK, the conflicts are of the fundamental type. Its relationship with the European and global context has become the key political cleavage in the non-EU Switzerland over the past decade (Kriesi 2007). For the UK, the EU integration process is still a heavily disputed project, as illustrated by the widespread rejection of and mobilisation against the common currency, the Euro. The struggle might have been domesticated in the last years, as Blair was said to have had a more positive stance towards Europe than the former governments (Armstrong and Bulmer 2003: 389). By contrast, in the countries where cooperative structures prevail – Spain, France and the Netherlands – the conflicting relations refer to the way integration should proceed. Germany is a special case to which we come back in a moment.

The block models of the domestic coalition structures in Figure 10.2 reveal these conflict constellations. In those countries with fundamental conflicts (Switzerland and the UK) there is a pro-EU coalition – in

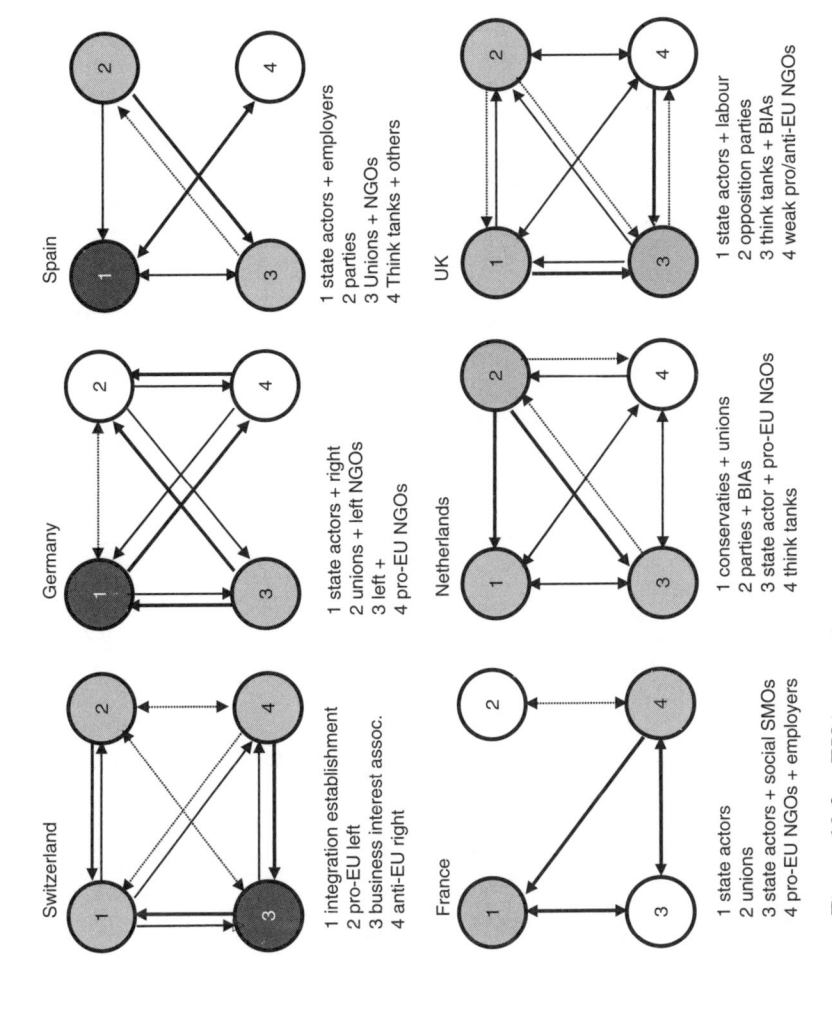

Figure 10.2 EU integration

Switzerland

1 agricultural establishment
2 right, business, cantons
3 environmentalists
4 consumer groups

Germany

1 state actors, regional units
2 alternative agriculture
3 right + farmers' associations
4 left + environ/consumer groups

Spain

1 primarily state actors
2 right, farmers' associations
3 left + environmentalists
4 alternative agriculture

Italy

1 state actors + farmers' associations
2 state actors + left
3 unions + environmentalists
4 alternative agriculture

Netherlands

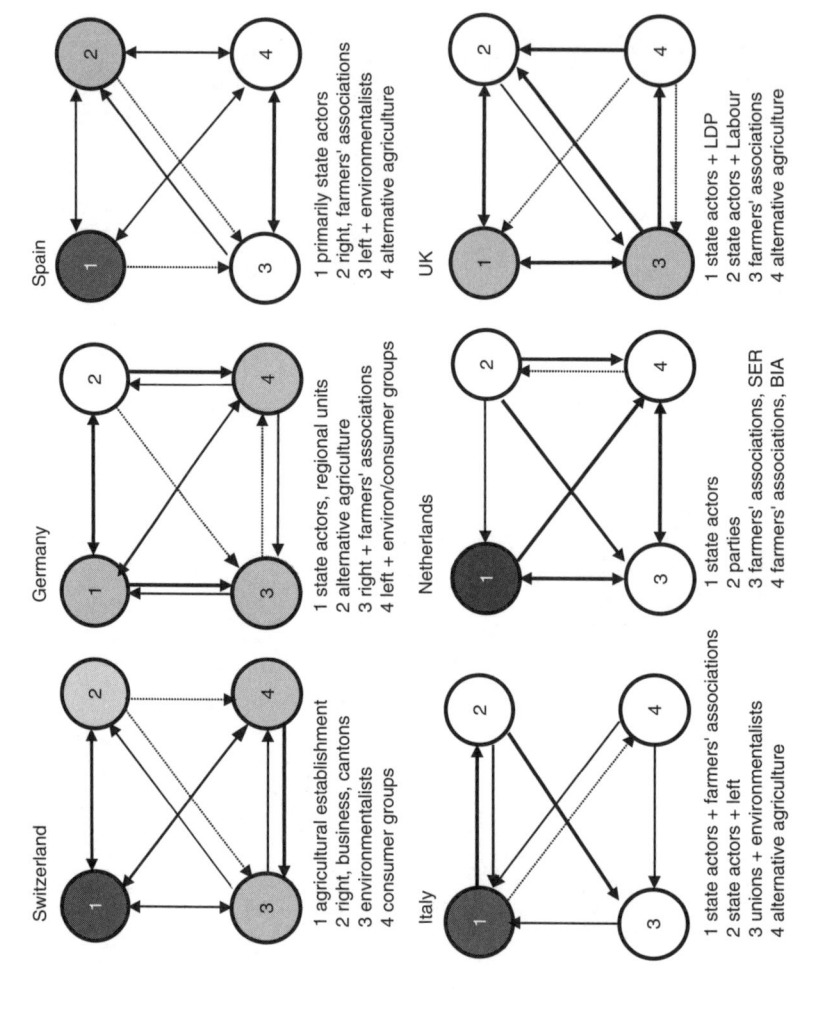

1 state actors
2 parties
3 farmers' associations, SER
4 farmers' associations, BIA

UK

1 state actors + LDP
2 state actors + Labour
3 farmers' associations
4 alternative agriculture

Figure 10.3 Agriculture

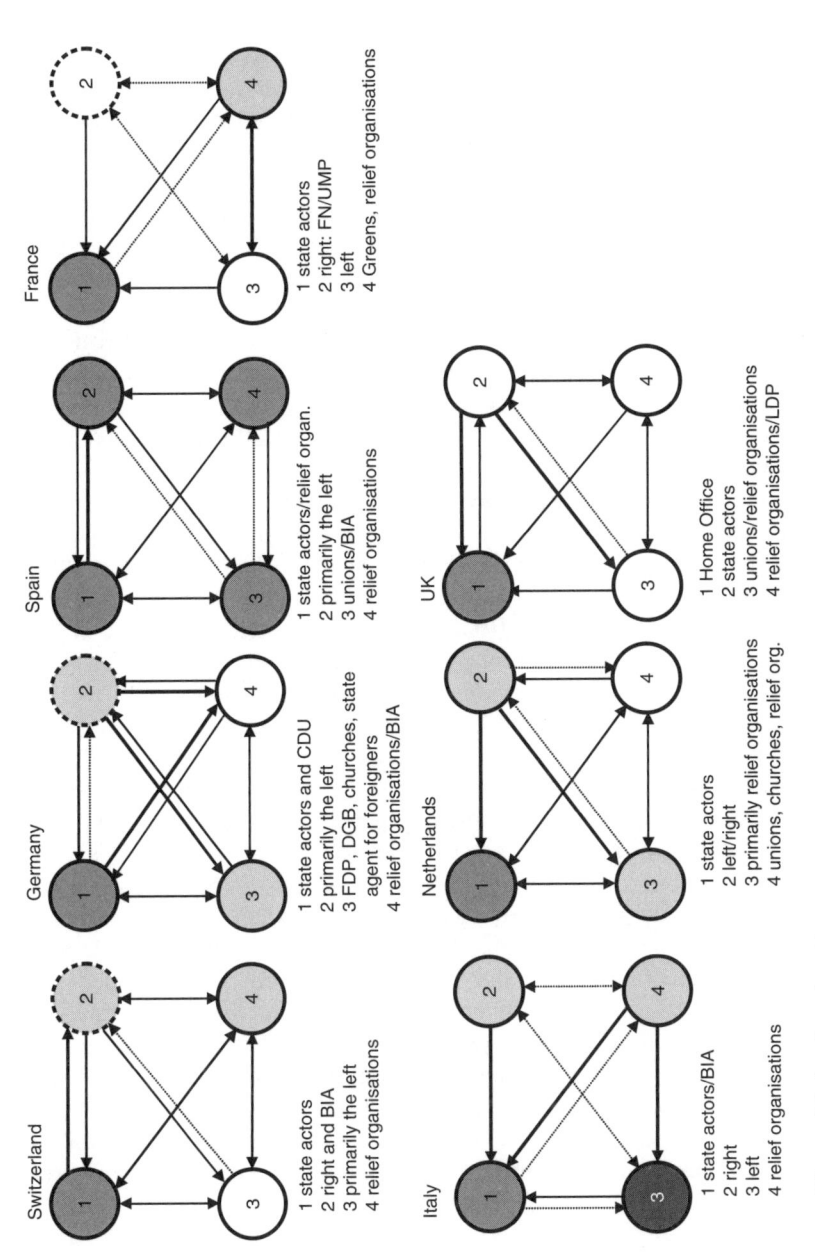

Figure 10.4 Immigration

Switzerland it is composed of the integration establishment and the pro-EU left, in the UK of the state actors and the Labour party.[4] The anti-EU coalition in Switzerland is dominated by the SVP, the Swiss People's Party – the single most powerful actor in the field of EU integration in Switzerland (in block 4). In the UK, the opposition parties – internally divided – are the main sources of critique and also of opposition towards the integration process. Business interest associations emerge as a third important block in both countries. In Switzerland they serve as brokers despite being divided by major internal disagreements: they cooperate with the integration establishment, reject the pro EU-left (including the unions) and bargain with those not willing to join the EU at all. In the UK, business interest associations (including the unions and the Confederation of British Industry) cooperate with the state actors and the Labour party, while having disagreements with all other blocks. In both countries, power is shared between the pro- and anti-EU coalitions. There is however a difference between the UK and Switzerland (see Table 10.1). Whereas power is completely fragmented in Switzerland, which means that the major EU opponents have as much power as the traditional integration establishment, we find a more concentrated structure in the UK. Here the pro EU-left has a higher share of power compared to the anti-EU coalition. Thus the only non-EU member Switzerland shows a structure of competition in the domain of EU policies, whereas the UK, as a long-term member of the integration project, reveals stronger tendencies towards a situation of dominance.

Surprisingly, the interactions between German actors prove to be dominated by conflicts regarding the EU integration project too. Germany is normally characterised by a strong elite consensus on the integration project in support of the development of a European Constitution. For the main part of the German elite, the EU is an extension of their national constitutional system that does not lead to fundamental problems of legitimacy (Jachtenfuchs 2002: 283). A more detailed analysis of the German conflict constellation reveals that 75 per cent of all conflictual relations originate from four out of the sixteen interviewed actors, namely the *Euromärsche*,[5] the unions, both part of block two, and the conservative and liberal opposition parties, both part of block one. Thus critiques originate primarily from the left movements and from the opposition parties.

In fact, with its conflict centered on left movements, Germany resembles Spain and France. In all three countries, there is domestic conflict about the form of EU integration, which lacks the fundamental character symbolised in the existence of pro- and anti-EU coalitions. The degree of this domestic conflict is higher in Germany, followed by Spain then France.[6] The latter two have been rated as cooperative. The main conflict line regarding the process of EU integration in these three countries refers to the question of a liberal versus a social Europe. In all three countries – as the block model reveals – the unions and left NGOs constitute the focal point of conflict. As the distribution of power reveals, these left challengers are powerful actors in Spain, whereas in France they lack any substantial influence (see Table 10.A1). In Germany, block two is not powerful as a whole, but it includes one powerful actor: the German union federation (DGB). In all of these countries however – even if the power distribution is not identical – the integration establishment of block one (state actors) constitutes the leading coalition that holds most power. The German situation thus resembles the configuration of strong dominance, the French and Spanish ones that of a hierarchical cooperation. Finally, in the case of the Netherlands, a relatively far-reaching power sharing is combined with a cooperative climate. In this situation of horizontal cooperation it is hard to deduce a clear-cut conflict line from the block model.

Agriculture
The main cleavage in agricultural policy is one between the 'agricultural establishment' and the 'agricultural opposition'. The members of the establishment largely defend the model of agricultural production and support that has been developed in Europe over the last 60 years. It corresponds to a highly subsidised mass production paradigm, excluding simultaneously agriculture from liberalised markets. The advocates of the opposition are not only concerned with environmental, health, food safety and animal protection issues related to agricultural production, but also more generally with the role of agriculture in our societies. Far from being a homogeneous group, the agricultural opposition constitutes a conglomerate of interests, united only by its opposition to the established regime and the most likely foreseeable future development: the inclusion of agriculture in a free market regime. This is rejected on the basis that agriculture provides not only food, but a greater common good, most notably the preservation of landscapes and rural development.

Our block models (Figure 10.3) are clearly marked by this cleavage. Regardless of the country, the first two blocks include the actors commonly associated with the 'agricultural establishment', most notably state actors and political parties of the right as well as farmers' associations. Blocks 3 and 4 are composed of (non-governmental) environmental agencies, consumer groups and 'alternative' agricultural associations, such as *Uniterre* in Switzerland. Only Germany is an exception to this general picture. Here, farmers' associations (block 3) are part of the second grand coalition of blocks, while (the powerless) part of the agricultural opposition (block 2, composed of *Euronatur* and *Arbeitsgemeinschaft bäuerliche Landwirtschaft*) falls together with block 1 and has strong collaborative ties with it.

Switzerland resembles Germany insofar as in both countries – contrary to all other cases – the agricultural opposition (or at least parts of it) shares a significant amount of power, which allows it to engage in bargaining relations with the establishment. This 'privileged' situation is – in the case of Germany – to a large extent the consequence of the considerable political clout of the Green party as well as a Red–Green coalition government (Grant 1997; Koestner 2000) at the time of our study. In Switzerland, it was a series of popular initiatives in the mid-1990s that forced the agricultural establishment to acknowledge claims put forward by the agricultural opposition, granting the latter access to decision making and power. Nonetheless, the coalition of state actors and major agricultural associations (block 1) has managed to hold on to its traditionally dominant position, which results in the fact that, in Switzerland, power is more strongly concentrated than in Germany. Along with Germany and Switzerland, Spain is equally characterised by bargaining. However, its agricultural opposition, which is composed of NGOs such as WWF-Spain, Intermon Oxfam and Global Nature as well as the socialist party, not only entirely lacks power, but constitutes so-called 'zero blocks', that is, its components are only loosely, if at all, linked to each other. It seems thus that in the domain of agricultural policy, it is only Germany that comes close to what we have called symmetric bargaining, whereas the other countries show a stronger element of hierarchy in this policy domain.

The Netherlands is a borderline case (on the individual actor level), falling into the bargaining category, but showing strong cooperative ties between coalitions. To that extent, it resembles Britain, the only genuine example of the cooperative type. In both cases, the first block, composed primarily of state actors, is a zero block. The absence or low level of cooperation within these establishment coalitions is all the more astonishing as they both have a considerable amount of power in their respective networks. In Britain, the block composed of the UK government, Parliament and the Liberal Democrats is one of only two blocks that have moderate power. The Dutch agricultural ministry, the ministry of economic affairs and the Second Chamber of the Dutch Parliament constitute the most powerful block in the Dutch agricultural network. Both countries thus show hierarchical elements in their network structure. It seems that the leading coalitions are well installed in power.

Italy has to be classified overall as a conflictual network – a result less visible in the block models, which seem to indicate a considerable amount of cooperation and bargaining. Interestingly, though, in Italy, power is strongly concentrated in the hands of state actors and agricultural associations, a coalition which maintains cooperative ties only with other state actors and with the left, while being entirely opposed to the coalition of alternative agriculture. No ties exist between the second block, a somewhat strange mixture of the ministry for European affairs, the social democrats, the green party and the WWF, on the one hand, and the fourth block, that is, the advocates of alternative agriculture, on the other. The agricultural domain in Italy thus can be described as a situation of dominance in which the agricultural establishment, despite the high level of conflict, is not challenged by other coalitions.

Immigration

As Lavenex (2001: 10f) argues, refugee policy is characterised by an intrinsic tension between the principles of human rights and national sovereignty: 'As a consequence, the notions of refugees and refugee protection are contested concepts, whose perception and definition follow either more statist or more humanitarian concerns'. According to these conflicting principles, there are two basic points of view in refugee policy – the realist view, which gives priority to the defense of national sovereignty, and the idealist view, which gives priority to the individual who seeks protection. In each country, we find this confrontation between a 'realist' coalition led by the government and its administrative offices, and a 'humanitarian' coalition composed of unions, churches, relief organisations and often (when they are not part of the government) social democratic, green and sometimes also liberal parties. This overall configuration is complicated by the presence of a nationalist-conservative opposition that takes a particularly restrictive view with regard to the defense of the national sovereignty and the national cultural traditions. With the increased influx of refugees in the 1990s and the more pervasive opening up and unbundling of national borders, this opposition from the nationalist-conservative right has become ever more important. It has decisively contributed to the relatively high level of conflict in the immigration subsystems.

Switzerland illustrates this point. The dominant block in the Swiss case is composed of the administrative offices in charge of the policy. This block is closely linked to a second block composed of the three major governing parties on the right and the peak employers' association. Together they form the dominant 'realist' coalition. However, the second component of this coalition is not a homogenous entity, but is internally divided between the two moderate parties and the employers' association, and the nationalist-conservative party (the Swiss People's Party). This division is all the more important as the Swiss People's Party constitutes the most important actor in this subsystem.[7] For years, this party has led an intensive populist campaign in favor of tightening asylum policy. Moreover, the members of this second block also have major disagreements with the dominant block of state actors and, of course, with the two blocks (blocks 3 and 4) of the 'humanitarian' coalition. The third block is composed of the social-democratic party, the major Swiss unions and a state actor close to the left – the Federal Commission against Racism. This block does not have much power, however, and is clearly second to the fourth block composed of the major relief organisations. The latter are quite powerful and cooperate closely with the state actors in the implementation of policy measures in favour of refugees. The peculiarity of this configuration consists in the combination of, on the one hand, the internal division within the dominant 'realist' coalition and, on the other hand, the close cooperation between the core blocks of the two coalitions.

Such conflictual configurations can also be found in Italy, France, Spain and to a lesser degree in Germany. A closer look at the patterns of interactions reveals that France and Italy resemble the configuration already described for Switzerland. In both countries, the core state block is associated with a block composed of the right parties, which are internally heavily divided (in France: FN and UMP), or have major disagreements between themselves (in Italy: AN, CCD-CDU, Lega). The state block is also allied to the major relief associations. In both France and Italy, this alliance is more subject to conflict than in Switzerland. In all three countries, the left constitutes the third block, with the only difference that it is much stronger in Italy than in the other two countries. In one respect, France is different from the other countries characterised by intense conflicts in the domain of immigration. In France we find a high concentration of power, which means that it comes close to what might be called a situation of dominance. By contrast, Spain and Italy – countries where one cannot even identify a leading coalition – as well as Switzerland and Germany are characterised by competitive situations.

Only the British and the Dutch seem to have settled the conflict on the immigration issue. Both countries show relatively low levels of conflict. In the Netherlands, this reflects the elite consensus which has presided over the important reforms in immigration policy since around 1980 (Thränhardt 2000: 170). After lengthy discussions, the large parties found a compromise about the key points of the reform – a compromise which favoured a multicultural coexistence between immigrants and the residential population. While the left clearly was more open and pleaded for inclusive reforms, there were also powerful voices among the Christian democrats and liberals for such a reform. This consensus was put into question by the mobilisation of the radical-populist right party *Lijst Pim Fortuyn* (LPF), which made its entry into national politics in the national elections of 2002. In the Dutch configuration, the LPF is part of block 2, which also includes the Christian democrats and the social democrats. What seems to have happened in the Netherlands is that the established parties have repositioned themselves in reaction to this new challenge and a new, much harsher consensus on immigration has been established. In contrast to the situation in the previously mentioned countries, the Dutch 'realist' coalition is not divided by conflicts, but there are noticeable conflicts between the two coalitions. The overall situation in the Netherlands is thus one of (symmetric) bargaining though with a moderate level of power fragmentation.

Whereas in the Netherlands power is partly shared in the immigration field, in the UK the low level of conflict goes along with an extremely strong concentration of power. Here the Home Office constitutes the leading coalition without any other coalitions having any substantial share of power. Other state actors, the unions and relief organisations cooperate or bargain with this uniquely strong central coalition. This co-occurrence of cooperation and concentration of power leads us to classify British immigration policy as a network of hierarchical cooperation.

10.5 CONCLUSION

This analysis of policy-domain-specific coalition configurations in six different European countries and one closely associated country shows that despite common EU regulations and policies in the course of EU integration, there is still considerable variation between nation states in terms of the national context that these EU policies are confronted with at the domestic level. This variation is assumed to be responsible for different responses to EU integration. So far, however, we have remained on a descriptive level, claiming that power distributions and the type of interaction between and within coalitions are relevant variables to account for these different responses to EU policies and regulations. In order to use network analysis as more than a descriptive tool it is necessary to link such typologies of policy networks – applied here to coalition structures – to the types and potentials of change and thus to policy outcomes. Such changes, as we understand them, are not independent of policy networks (Stones 1992). Rather, as is observed by Marsh and Smith (2000: 8), 'the extent and speed of change is clearly influenced by the network's capacity to mediate, and often minimise, the effect of such change'. Domestic policy networks in this perspective are regarded as independent variables accounting for differential responses to EU integration.

Accordingly, we would like to suggest that the type of interaction within a policy network determines the form of policy change. In conflictual situations we expect rapid (serial) policy shifts, whereas incremental changes are most likely to result from bargaining situations. Cooperative structures stabilise the status quo. It is possible to develop more detailed hypotheses if we also take into consideration the pattern of conflict lines among coalitions. The location of conflict, bargaining and cooperation helps to identify the possible future directions of change. In the domain of EU integration, for example, the UK, Switzerland and Germany were rated as conflictual policy fields. The location of conflict, however, shows that in the UK and Switzerland there are pro- and anti-EU coalitions fighting with each other and making radical shifts possible. In Germany, on the other hand, the focal point of conflict is constituted by left organisations that do not reject the project of EU integration in general, but call for a stronger emphasis on social aspects. In this case, even if we were to find serial shifts, these shifts should cause less fundamental alterations.

Linking the second crucial characteristic of policy networks to change, we expect that the power distribution influences the potential for change. We assume the potential for each type of change to be greater, if power is fragmented. If power is fragmented between coalitions, the scales are more easily tipped in favour of the challenging coalition. By contrast, if power is concentrated between coalitions, challengers lack resources to break the 'policy monopoly'. In the cases of Swiss and British EU politics, one might not only expect fundamental serial shifts given the type of interaction, but, given the kind of power distribution, also a high likelihood of such changes. In Switzerland the relatively fragmented power structures make radical shifts more likely than in the UK, where the pro-EU coalition is leading the game. Figure 10.5 summarises how characteristics of policy networks can be systematically linked to policy changes.

Whether these hypotheses prove useful is unfortunately not part of this chapter. Evidence provided by Héritier and Knill (2001) is promising, however. Their analysis of how nation states in Europe mediate the impact of European input in road haulage and railway policies shows that reform is more likely to be triggered by European regulations if domestic constellations are contested and characterised by uneven power distributions.

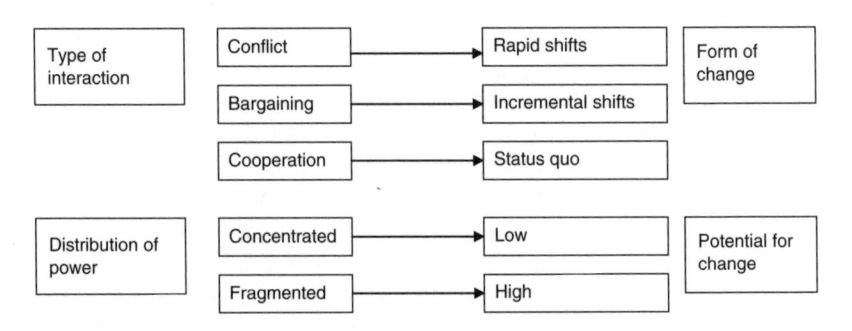

Type of interaction	Conflict → Rapid shifts	Form of change
	Bargaining → Incremental shifts	
	Cooperation → Status quo	

Distribution of power	Concentrated → Low	Potential for change
	Fragmented → High	

Figure 10.5 Policy networks as determinants of policy change

APPENDIX 10.1

Table 10.A1   Power distribution among coalitions

EU integration Block-POWER	CH	D	E	F	I	NL	UK
Block 1 (Mean)	0.40	0.73	0.71	0.59	0.57	0.43	0.57
Block 2 (Mean)	0.40	0.25	0.44	0.22	0.50	0.39	0.36
Block 3 (Mean)	0.63	0.53	0.42	0.11	0.46	0.48	0.38
Block 4 (Mean)	0.53	0.21	–	0.33	0.47	0.13	0.05
n	16	16	9	9	15	12	16
Agriculture Block-POWER	CH	D	E	F	I	NL	UK
Block 1 (Mean)	0.75	0.51	1.00	0.67	0.87	0.66	0.46
Block 2 (Mean)	0.30	0.25	0.46	0.02	0.16	0.25	0.16
Block 3 (Mean)	0.31	0.58	0.25	0.00	0.11	0.23	0.36
Block 4 (Mean)	0.37	0.42	–	0.00	0.09	0.27	0.09
n	16	15	8	11	15	15	15
Immigration Block-POWER	CH	D	E	F	I	NL	UK
Block 1 (Mean)	0.60	0.66	0.65	0.75	0.69	0.73	1.00
Block 2 (Mean)	0.43	0.35	0.70	0.19	0.47	0.40	0.22
Block 3 (Mean)	0.17	0.35	0.90	0.08	0.60	0.37	0.19
Block 4 (Mean)	0.33	0.26	0.75	0.30	0.38	0.24	0.18
n	16	16	11	12	16	11	11

Note: Empty cells: power indicators are missing.

Table 10.A2   Density ratios of conflict/cooperation and bargaining/cooperation by country and policy domain

Density Ratios	CH	D	E	F	I	NL	UK
European Integration							
Conflict/cooperation	0.83	0.54	0.38	0.10	–	0.12	0.52
Bargaining/cooperation	0.09	0.11	0.10	0.05	–	0.15	0.22
Agriculture							
Conflict/cooperation	0.47	0.29	0.39	–	0.50	0.32	0.24
Bargaining/cooperation	0.41	0.24	0.43	–	0.14	0.16	0.14
Immigration							
Conflict/cooperation	0.82	0.49	0.62	0.67	0.70	0.27	0.16
Bargaining/cooperation	0.30	0.32	0.36	0.23	0.00	0.24	0.28

Table 10.A3 Complex image matrices for three policy domains in each country

country	block	EU integration				immigration				agriculture			
		1	2	3	4	1	2	3	4	1	2	3	4
1 CH	1	**3**	2	2	2	**2**	3	2	2	**2**	2	2	2
	2	3	**3**	−1	−1	2	**−1**	2	2	2	**0**	−1	−1
	3	3	−1	**2**	2	2	−1	**3**	3	2	2	**2**	2
	4	−1	−1	3	**3**	2	2	2	**3**	2	0	3	**2**
2 D	1	**2**	−1	2	3	**2**	−1	2	3	**2**	3	3	2
	2	−1	**2**	2	2	2	**−1**	3	3	3	**3**	−1	3
	3	3	3	**3**	3	2	2	**2**	2	2	1	**2**	−1
	4	2	3	3	**3**	2	2	2	**3**	2	2	2	**2**
3 E	1	**2**	0	2	3	**2**	3	2	2	**3**	2	−1	2
	2	2	**2**	3	1	2	**0**	2	2	2	**3**	−1	2
	3	2	−1	**3**	0	2	−1	**2**	−1	1	2	**0**	3
	4	3	1	0	**0**	2	2	2	**2**	2	2	3	**0**
4 F	1	**3**	1	3	1	**3**	0	0	−1	**0**	−1	3	3
	2	0	**3**	0	−1	2	**−1**	−1	−1	2	**−1**	0	0
	3	3	0	**0**	3	2	−1	**3**	3	3	0	**1**	0
	4	3	−1	3	**3**	2	−1	3	**3**	3	0	0	**0**
5 I	1	**0**	3	0	0	**3**	0	−1	−1	**2**	3	0	−1
	2	3	**3**	−1	0	3	**2**	−1	−1	2	**3**	3	0
	3	2	3	**3**	1	2	−1	**3**	0	2	0	**3**	0
	4	−1	0	0	**0**	3	−1	3	**3**	2	0	2	**3**
6 NL	1	**2**	2	2	0	**3**	0	2	2	**1**	0	3	3
	2	2	**0**	1	0	3	**2**	3	−1	2	**2**	3	3
	3	3	3	**3**	3	2	−1	**2**	2	3	0	**3**	3
	4	2	1	2	**3**	2	2	2	**3**	1	−1	3	**2**
7 UK	1	**3**	2	3	2	**0**	2	0	0	**0**	3	3	0
	2	−1	**−1**	−1	2	3	**3**	3	2	3	**3**	2	1
	3	2	2	**2**	−1	2	−1	**2**	2	3	3	**3**	3
	4	2	2	3	**0**	2	2	2	**2**	−1	3	−1	**3**
8 EU	1	**1**	0	0	0	**0**	3	−1	−1	**2**	2	2	2
	2	0	**0**	0	0	−1	**2**	2	3	2	**2**	−1	3
	3	1	0	**2**	0	−1	2	**2**	3	2	2	**2**	2
	4	2	0	3	**2**	−1	3	2	**1**	2	1	3	**3**

Notes:
3 = cooperation (possibly also target)
2 = ambivalence (possibly also target)
1 = only target
0 = no relation
−1 = conflict
Bold: Type of relationships within a given block

NOTES

1. More information about this seven-country project sponsored within the 5th framework of the EU (HPSE-CT2000-00046) can be found at http://europub.wzb.de.
2. We are aware of the fact that this definition of coalition emphasises another aspect of coalition formation than most approaches do in political science (e.g. Sabatier 1993). Nevertheless, we think that coalitions can not only be determined by internal cohesion, but also by the same relations to other actors in a field. This latter perspective could be called an indirect approach for coalition building.
3. Appendix 10.1, Table 10.A2 shows the density ratios on which this classification is based. The breaking points are defined as follows: where ratios for conflict/cooperation take on intermediary values (between 0.3 and 0.5) and those for bargaining/cooperation are roughly equally prominent, we attribute the network to the bargaining category. Where conflict/cooperation ratios are equal to or greater than 0.5, we class the network in the conflict category.
4. Wallace (2000: 2) claims that the UK has turned from a 'regime-taker' to a 'regime-maker' in some areas in the field of EU integration under the Blair government.
5. *Euromärsche* claims to have conflicts with all other 15 interviewed actors. This biases the results and leads to an overestimation regarding the degree of conflict in Germany.
6. The lack of conflict in France regarding EU integration is a result of the fact that the actors who have taken up the debate on EU integration, namely the party actors, were not interviewed. France is one of those few countries where EU integration has substantially altered the party landscape. There are communist, socialist, conservative and right-wing extreme EU adversaries. Part of these (new) parties are founded as split-offs of the traditional parties. But even within the main parties in France EU integration is one of the strongly debated issues (Goulard 2002) that has polarised the nation and shadowed French EU politics (Ziebura 2003: 305).
7. This does not become visible in the image matrix, since we only provide the average power of the members of a block.

REFERENCES

Armstrong, K.A. and Bulmer, S. (2003) 'The United Kingdom: Between political controversy and administrative efficiency', in W. Wessels, A. Maurer and J. Mittag (eds) *Fifteen into one? The European Union and its member states*, Manchester and New York: Manchester University Press, pp. 388–410.

Atkinson, M.M. and Coleman, W.D. (1989) 'Strong states and weak states: Sectoral policy networks in advanced capitalist economies' *British Journal of Political Science* 19 (1), 47–67.

Baumgartner, F.R. and Jones, B.D. (1993) *Agendas and instability in American politics*, Chicago: University of Chicago Press.

Cowles, M.G., Caporaso, J. and Risse, T. (eds) (2001) *Transforming Europe. Europeanization and domestic change*, Ithaca, NY: Cornell University Press.

Goulard, S. (2002) 'Frankreich und Europa: Die Kluft zwischen Politik und Gesellschaft', in M. Meimeth and J. Schild (eds) *Die Zukunft von Nationalstaaten in der europäischen Integration: Deutsche und französische Perspektiven*, Opladen: Leske und Budrich, pp. 173–95.

Grant, W. (1997) *The common agricultural policy*, Basingstoke: Macmillan Press.

Héritier, A. and Knill, C. (2001) 'Differential responses to European policies: A comparison', in A. Héritier (ed.) *Differential Europe: New opportunities and*

restrictions for member-state policies, Lanham: Rowman and Littlefield, pp. 257–94.
Hirst, P.O. and Thompson, G. (1996) *Globalization in question: The international economy and the possibilities of governance*, Cambridge: Polity Press.
Imig, D. and Tarrow, S. (2000) 'Political contention in a Europeanising polity' *West European Politics. Special Issue Europeanised Politics* 23 (4), 73–93.
Jachtenfuchs, M. (2002) 'Deutschland, Frankreich und die Zukunft der Europäischen Union', in M. Meimeth and J. Schild (eds) *Die Zukunft von Nationalstaaten in der europäischen Integration: Deutsche und französische Perspektiven*, Opladen: Leske und Budrich, pp. 279–94.
Jordan, G. and Schubert, K. (1992) 'A preliminary ordering of policy network labels' *European Journal of Political Research* (21), 7–27.
Knill, C. and Lehmkuhl, D. (2002) 'The national impact of European Union regulatory policy: Three Europeanization mechanisms' *European Journal of Political Research* (41), 255–80.
Knoke, D., Pappi, F.U., Broadbent, J. and Tsujinaka, Y. (1996) *Comparing policy networks: Labor politics in the U.S., Germany, and Japan*, Cambridge: Cambridge University Press.
Koestner, U. (2000) 'The role of Germany in the common agricultural policy', in S. Tangermann (ed.) *Agriculture in Germany*, Frankfurt am Main: DLG Verlag, pp. 209–29.
Kohler-Koch, B. (2000) ‚Europäisierung: Plädoyer für eine Horizonterweiterung', in M. Knodt and B. Kohler-Koch (eds) *Deutschland zwischen Europäisierung und Selbstbehauptung*, Frankfurt am Main: Campus, pp. 11–31.
Kriesi, H. (1980) *Entscheidungsstrukturen und Entscheidungsprozesse in der Schweizer Politik*, Frankfurt am Main: Campus.
Kriesi, H. (2007) 'The role of European integration in national election campaigns' *European Union Politics* 8 (1), 83–108.
Kriesi, H., Adam, S. and Jochum, M. (2006) 'Comparative analysis of policy networks in Western Europe' *Journal of European Public Policy* 13 (3), 341–61.
Kriesi, H. and Jegen, M. (2001) 'The Swiss energy policy elite: The actor constellation of a policy domain in transition' *European Journal of Political Research* (39), 251–87.
Laumann, E.O. and Knoke, D. (1987) *The organizational state: Social choice in national policy domains*, Madison: The University of Wisconsin Press.
Laumann, E.O. and Pappi, F.U. (1976) *Networks of collective action: A perspective on community influence systems*, New York: Academic Press.
Lavenex, S. (2001) *The Europeanization of refugee policies: Between human rights and internal security*, Aldershot: Ashgate.
Lepsius, R.M. (1999) 'Die Europäische Union: Ökonomische Integration und kulturelle Pluralität', in R. Viehoff and R.T. Segers (eds) *Kultur. Identität. Europa*, Frankfurt am Main: Suhrkamp, pp. 201–22.
Lord, C. and Beetham, D. (2001) 'Legitimizing the EU: Is there a "Postparliamentary Basis" for its legitimation?' *Journal of Common Market Studies* 39 (3), 443–62.
Marsh, D. and Smith, M. (2000) 'Understanding policy networks: Towards a dialectical approach' *Political Studies* 48 (1), 4–21.
Maurer, A., Mittag, J. and Wessels, W. (2003) 'Preface and major findings: The anatomy, the analysis and the assessment of the "beast"', in W. Wessels, A. Maurer and J. Mittag (eds) *Fifteen into one? The European Union and*

its member states, Manchester, New York: Manchester University Press, pp. XIII–XVII.
Rhodes, R.A.W. and Marsh, D. (1992) 'New directions in the study of policy networks' *European Journal of Political Research* 21 (1–2), 181–205.
Risse, T., Green Cowles, M. and Caporaso, J. (2001) 'Europeanization and domestic change: Introduction', in M. Green Cowles, J. Caporaso and T. Risse (eds) *Transforming Europe: Europeanization and Domestic Change*, Ithaca and London: Cornell University Press, pp. 1–20.
Sabatier, P.A. (1993) 'Advocacy-Koalitionen, Policy-Wandel und Policy-Lernen: Eine Alternative zur Phasenheuristik', in A. Héritier (ed.) *Policy-Analyse, Kritik und Neuorientierung, Politische Vierteljahresschrift 34, Sonderheft 24*, Opladen: Westdeutscher Verlag, pp. 116–48.
Sabatier, P.A. and Jenkins-Smith, H.C. (1999) 'The advocacy framework: An assessment', in P.A. Sabatier (ed.) *Theories of the policy process*, Oxford: Westview Press, pp. 117–66.
Scharpf, F.W. (1997) *Games real actors play: Actor-centered institutionalism in policy research*, Boulder, CO: Westview Press.
Stones, R. (1992) 'International monetary relations, policy networks and the Labour government's policy of non-devaluation 1964–67', in D. Marsh and R.A.W. Rhodes (eds) *Policy networks in British Government*, Oxford: Clarendon Press.
Thränhardt, D. (2000) 'Conflict, consensus, and policy outcomes: Immigration and integration in Germany and the Netherlands', in R. Koopmans and P. Statham (eds) *Challenging immigration and ethnic relations politics: Comparative European perspectives*, Oxford: Oxford University Press, pp. 145–61.
van Waarden, F. (1992) 'Dimensions and types of policy networks' *European Journal of Political Research* 21 (1–2), 29–52.
Wallace, H. (2000) *Possible futures for the European Union: A British reaction*, Jean Monnet Working Paper 7/00 Symposium: Responses to Joschka Fischer www.jeanmonnetprogram.org/papers/00/00f0701.html, last access: 19 November 2007.
Wallace, H. (2001) 'The changing politics of the European Union: An overview' *Journal of Common Market Studies* 39 (4), 581–94.
Wasserman, S. and Faust, K. (1999) *Social network analysis: Methods and applications*, Cambridge: Cambridge University Press.
Ziebura, G. (2003) 'Frankreich am Beginn des 21. Jahrhunderts: Zwischen Europäisierung, Globalisierung und nationaler Selbstbehauptung: Eine Problemskizze', in G. Ziebura (ed.) *Frankreich: Geschichte, Gesellschaft, Politik: Ausgewählte Aufsätze*, Opladen: Leske und Budrich, 297–324.

11. European Union support for civil society in the Baltic states

Susan Stewart

11.1 INTRODUCTION

This chapter provides an assessment of EU activities that have affected the development of civil society in the Baltic states of Estonia, Latvia and Lithuania from the early 1990s to the present, focusing particularly on the period 1998–2004. In order to assess these activities we will examine three issues: 1) the contextual conditions specific to the Baltic states, 2) the structural changes in civil society brought about *inter alia* by EU involvement and 3) the transfer of values and norms promoted by the EU and their incorporation into the Baltic context. These latter two issues will be addressed primarily within the period during which the Baltic states were candidate members to the EU. However, in the conclusion we will also provide some tentative remarks on changes in funding programmes and instruments, and the consequences thereof, which can be observed or anticipated in the post-accession phase.

In the case of the Baltic states, it is important to keep in mind that the developments analysed here occur in a context of ongoing democratization. While the academic literature offers no consensus on when democratic consolidation can be considered complete (see for example Linz and Stepan 1996), and the current debate on the 'democratic deficit' in the EU highlights the need for continuing concern with democratic developments even in consolidated environments, it is nonetheless significant that the Baltic countries were part of the Soviet Union (and thereby an authoritarian regime) as little as fifteen years ago. This implies that they are dealing with recent historical legacies which set them apart from the old member states of the European Union (Ekiert and Hanson 2003). These legacies have consequences for the level and type of civic engagement, the functioning of public institutions, elite and mass attitudes, and the degree of international and transnational involvement in the Baltic states. Furthermore, the rapidity of the transition to democracy and the strict conditionality imposed by the EU have created a situation in which 1) many democratization issues are still to be addressed and 2) civil society development has taken a back seat to other, more pressing concerns. Therefore, many of the legal, institutional and socio-economic conditions which can be taken for granted in the old member states simply do not hold for the Baltic countries.

Throughout the chapter we explore the implications of the investigated developments for the evolution of both vertical and horizontal multilevel governance in the EU. These concern channels of communication and support both between EU institutions and local/national civil society organizations (CSOs), and among these CSOs in their respective national contexts, as well as between the CSOs and the relevant national and local governments. We understand civil society to be 'an intermediary sphere between the privacy of the individual, the family, the enterprise etc., and the realm of the political, in which primarily collective actors organise and articulate public interests' (Croissant, Lauth and Merkel 2000: 16). Civil society organizations are those which can be attributed to this sphere. A subset of these, non-governmental organizations (NGOs), will constitute our primary focus here. These must be: 1) organized (have an institutional reality), 2) private (institutionally separate from government), 3) non-profit-distributing, 4) self-governing and 5) voluntary (utilizing volunteer labour and without automatic membership) (Salamon, Anheier *et al.* 1999: 467f). As these definitions indicate, our analysis is located at the interface of the civil society and third sector approaches as outlined by Zimmer and Freise (Chapter 2).

11.2 THE HISTORICAL CONTEXT OF CIVIL SOCIETY DEVELOPMENT IN THE BALTICS

In research on transitional societies, the concept of path dependency is frequently used to explore the impact of historical legacies on more recent developments. When applying this concept to the development of civil society in the three Baltic states of Estonia, Latvia and Lithuania, three phases can be seen as crucial: the period of 'national awakening' in the nineteenth century, the period between the First and Second World Wars, and the Soviet era. Although the interwar phase is temporally closer to current developments, the nineteenth-century occurrences are considered by the few scholars who have explored the role of such legacies to be more important in their influence on the emergence of the national movements in the Baltics in the late 1980s (Hackmann 2003: 59; Lux 2000: 147). While Hackmann emphasizes the explicit references made by recent civil society discourses to nineteenth-century developments, Lux (2000: 147) points to the overlapping thematic foci of the nineteenth-century movements and their 1980s counterparts, which dealt with 'folklore, language, national myths and an almost idealised relationship to nature'. The interwar republics are seen as having more symbolic importance as a period of independence to which the later national movements could refer than as having a thematic link with those movements. This is especially the case because of the increasingly authoritarian nature of the interwar governments, which could not serve as models for a potential democratic evolution in the 1990s.

With respect to the Soviet era, the reflections on civil society development range from the denial of the existence of civil society in any form, to the identification of it solely with dissident activities, to assertions of the presence of a type of civil society different from those types which developed in Western countries (Hackmann 2003: 49; Lux 2000: 147). Here most scholars are careful to distinguish between different parts of the former Soviet bloc. The first distinction lies between the republics of the former USSR and the 'satellite states' of East Central Europe. However, even within the USSR, developments varied from place to place. According to Hackmann: 'The small nations along the Baltic rim showed structures of voluntary associations that were older and obviously further developed than those in Russia herself' (2003: 57). While Richard Rose (1999) has posited the presence of an 'anti-modern' form of social capital in Russia, based on personal relationships and clientelist structures, the Baltics appear to have been preserved from (or able to shed) this phenomenon to a large extent due to their different historical trajectories. Toward the end of the Soviet period, environmental and heritage protection movements became especially strong in the Baltics, and both were closely connected to the development of national discourses (Hackmann 2003: 53). Environmental groups were especially important because they could attract a significant number of followers since they were in only indirect opposition to the regime. This distinguished them from, for example, human rights groups, which went further in their demands but therefore tended to remain small and persecuted (Lux 2000: 148).

The late 1980s saw the development in all three Baltic countries of 'people's fronts', which combined reform-oriented Communists and moderate opposition forces. These movements became 'flagships' of the new civil society (Lauth and Merkel 1997 cited in Lux 2000: 151), and it was in large part thanks to them (and comparable developments in the Visegrad countries) that scholarly interest in the role of civil society in political and societal transition was stimulated. However, the emergence of such movements was accompanied by a phenomenon that turned out to be indicative of social problems which would persist long into the post-Soviet period. The primarily Russian-speaking minorities in the Baltics, who experienced little or no 'cultural discomfort' during the Soviet era, were now disadvantaged because they often did not know the relevant Baltic language well, nor could they necessarily identify with the national goals of the people's fronts. This meant that civil society development proceeded apace, but mainly with respect to the titular nation, leaving the Slavic minority groups behind. According to Lux: 'The creation of organizations relevant to civil society among the Russian minority or its participation in the people's fronts did not occur during the phase of liberalization in the Baltics' (2000: 153). This cleavage in terms of civil society development has persisted in the post-Soviet period (Lagerspetz et al. 2004: 33). It was exacerbated by the formation of 'civic committees' which demanded a return to the interwar status quo, under which only citizens of the interwar republics or their descendants could vote and possess other attributes of citizenship. Immigrants, who were mostly Russian or at least Russian-speaking, were seen as intruders by adherents to this position, which was in large part a reaction to the Soviet policy of resettling Slavs in large numbers in Estonia and Latvia (less so in Lithuania) in the 1960s and 1970s to serve as political functionaries on the one hand and industrial workers on the other.

Thus the decision taken by all three Baltic countries following their independence to restore the interwar states rather than to found new ones was demoralizing for the ethnic minorities, especially the recent immigrants. This cleavage was at least temporarily overcome due to Moscow's military intervention in Vilnius in January 1991, which induced all ethnic and linguistic groups to rally around a common banner against violence perpetrated by the 'imperial centre'. Civil society actors were also able to be influential between the spring of 1990 and August 1991 in the process of creating environmental and minority policy for the new (or restored) states (Lux 2000: 159). However, while Lithuania opted for the so-called 'zero option' in the citizenship question (thus granting citizenship to all legal residents of Soviet Lithuania without major hurdles), Estonia and Latvia chose in large part to return to interwar citizenship regulations, thereby including a number of Slavs but excluding many others. This has had major consequences both for integration of non-Balts into the respective societies and for EU (and other international) involvement in the region, both inside and outside the civil society sphere. Such developments have led Lux (2000: 157f) to claim that democratization increasingly took a back seat to national concerns, including in the civil society realm. This allowed civil society actors to become unified across the Baltics in their striving for independence, but reinforced the cleavages between the titular nations and the ethnic minorities. Data from the Latvian context show that non-citizens (mainly Russophone Slavic minorities) participate in civil society activities significantly less than does the primarily Latvian group of citizens (Baltic Data House 1998: 14–16).

In the post-Soviet period, civil society has gone through its own type of transition, which has involved increasing exposure to Western concepts and institutions, resulting in a blend of legacies from the Soviet and earlier periods with more immediate influences. The most important shift has been away from the mass national movements of the late 1980s and early 1990s and toward the creation of smaller, more fragmented organizations, primarily in the form of NGOs (Lux 2000: 164). The leadership of the national movements in large part migrated to the sphere of 'political society' (Linz and Stepan 1996), in line with the trajectory outlined by Lauth and Merkel (1997), who point to different roles for civil society at different stages in the transition. Thus, as Hackmann (2003: 61) states: 'The point . . . is not that civil society totally disappeared with the downfall of socialism, but that it changed its role in the political process'. Much of this evolution involves the need for the emerging civil society institutions to come to terms with their relationship to the state. As Hackmann (2003: 60) points out, during the Soviet era 'civil society in its opposition to the state was foremost a negative notion, pointing at the lack of freedom and basic rights, but its positive conceptualisations remained, to a high degree, utopian'. This corresponds to the normative component of the civil society approach highlighted by Zimmer and Freise (Chapter 2). The ongoing discourse on the relationship between civil society and the public sector in the Baltics has been one in which the EU has had an influential role.

11.3 EU EFFORTS TO SUPPORT CIVIL SOCIETY IN THE BALTIC STATES AND THEIR IMPACTS

11.3.1 Phare and Other EU Involvement

Phare is a pre-accession instrument originally designed in 1989 to assist Poland and Hungary in restructuring their economies. It has since been significantly expanded to cover ten countries: the eight new member states in Central and Eastern Europe plus Bulgaria and Romania, which had candidate status at the time of writing but are now member states.[1] Phare's complete 'pre-accession' focus was established in 1998 after the Luxembourg Council launched the current enlargement process.[2] While 2003 was the final year for Phare programming in the new member states, contracting of Phare projects continued until 2005 and payments related to these contracts could be issued until 2006. However, since May 2004 the new member states have been required to assume complete responsibility for the management of the Phare programme.³

Phare priorities are divided into two components: 1) institution building and 2) investment support in regulatory infrastructure (to ensure compliance with the *acquis*) and in economic and social cohesion (ESC) (Marsh 2003: 4f). Projects related to civil society development can be found under both components. While in the component on institution building the projects targeting civil society generally focus on strengthening its capacity, in the ESC-related component more of a monitoring role for civil society is envisaged. This differentiation points to a general difficulty associated with assessing EU support for civil society development in the candidate and new member states, namely that it occurs not only via specific projects directed toward civil society strengthening, but also through the dissemination of EU attitudes toward the role of civil society actors in those programmes affecting candidate countries and new members.

Phare financing in the civil society realm can be found in the Phare Democracy Programme, the LIEN Programme (primarily for NGOs in the social sector dealing with disadvantaged groups), and the Partnership Programme (focused on local economic development) (see Raik 2003: 206). There have also been national Civil Society Programmes funded by Phare, but these were only established in six countries. Of these the only Baltic country was Lithuania, and it was represented with only one programme worth 0.8 million Euro, five times less than Romania and twelve times less than the Czech Republic (OMAS Consortium 2001: I).

The LIEN Programme stands for Link Inter-European NGOs and was established to fund projects which develop connections between Central and Eastern Europe (CEE) NGOs and those in EU member states. In 1999 the LIEN and Partnership programmes were combined into a new programme entitled ACCESS, which reflected the increasing emphasis on preparing the candidate countries for EU membership. Thus ACCESS was geared toward supporting those types of civic activity believed to promote the implementation of EU legislation (such as consumer and environmental protection) and to assist disadvantaged social groups. According to Raik, the Phare programmes thus focused both on developing civil society institutions and on improving the quality of the democratic environment in which these function (2003: 206). However, other analysts believe that Phare involvement in the civil society sphere has been too narrowly focused on transposal of the *acquis* and its implementation, rather than on the broader goals of civil society development and related governance issues (OMAS Consortium 2001).

Phare involvement in civil society strengthening in the candidate countries has been surprisingly low, considering the emphasis placed on civil society participation in the EU itself. This lack of involvement is partially explained by the perception which underlies comments such as that of John O'Rourke, Counsellor and Phare and ISPA Coordinator for the European Commission Delegation in Warsaw: 'It is not the job of the European Union to build civil society' (Krzeczunowicz 2004, title page). Initial stages of Phare did not pay much attention to impacts on civil society, and this relative neglect led to recommendations for a greater emphasis on civil society development (Multi-Country Thematic Report 2001). The ACCESS programme has in part remedied this lack of emphasis. However, the Phare civil society focus remains dispersed across various areas, without being mainstreamed into EU support for applicant or new member states as a whole. The focus includes not only attention to advocacy organizations, but also (and perhaps especially) an emphasis on service organizations providing assistance to politically and socio-economically disadvantaged groups. Despite the fact that consequences for civil society flow from a variety of Phare components, Phare involvement in the Baltics has remained quite low in the civil society arena, at least in terms of projects explicitly addressing civil society development, although this has begun to change since 2002, as we will see in more detail below.

11.3.2 EU Impacts on Civil Society Development

This section focuses primarily on developments in the NGO sphere, as this is the component of civil society which has undergone the most rapid evolution since the collapse of the USSR. The concept of civil society has historically developed differently in Western and Eastern Europe, while within each of these regions further differentiation can be made. The EU conception of civil society is clearly described by Zimmer and Freise (Chapter 2). The introduction here of the Estonian definition can prove useful in locating similarities and differences between the EU and Baltic treatments of the term. The Estonian Civil Society Development Concept (EKAK, Public Policy Centre 2002) states: ' "Civil society" means self-initiated cooperation of people for pursuing their interests, discussing public issues and participating in decision-making processes, as well as the associations, networks and institutions which enable such cooperation' (EKAK Article I, final paragraph). Here individuals are at the core of the definition, although the associations they form are also included. The larger document supplies a normative connection between civil society and democracy. On the whole the EU and Estonian definitions appear to be compatible, and in both cases civil society is positively connoted.

While in both the EU and Baltic cases civil society is seen as necessary for an adequately functioning democracy, different conceptions of what democracy entails do emerge. For example, whereas the EKAK explicitly claims that co-operation with CSOs will increase the legitimacy of politicians, this is much more controversial in the older member states, where the non-elected nature of CSO representatives is commonly pointed to as a defect with regard to their involvement in policy processes. This difference stems in part from the dissimilar regime experiences of Western and Eastern Europe in the past decades. In the Baltics, the involvement of civil society in policy processes represents a great improvement over a system in which there was little or no genuine popular input. In the West, however, well-established patterns of electoral democracy have created a benchmark against which other types of input are measured. Thus the question of legitimacy (usually associated with some form of election) is viewed more critically in the older than in the newer member states. In the Baltics, democratic institutions were created rapidly and this was less a process of mutual consent than an imposed version of democracy more or less dictated by the EU Copenhagen criteria and the stipulations of the *acquis communautaire*. For this reason the institutions do not always function as the EU officials associated with the process anticipated. This affects civil society development because national and local officials often have interpretations different from those propagated by the EU of the utility and necessity of involving civil society in the policy process. CSOs may also not be prepared to enter into dialogue with the authorities or may need time to develop the required expertise and confidence. Thus the different phases of democratic development in which the EU, the older member states and the newer members find themselves can lead to unanticipated and contradictory developments in the civil society sphere.

One realm in which the EU has contributed to changes in the civil society sphere has been the creation of a particular balance between service provision and advocacy organizations. As programmes such as LIEN indicate, the EU is inclined to emphasize service provision. This is perhaps unsurprising as many older EU states have civil society models in which services are provided by a variety of CSOs, often in co-operation with state institutions. However, while such arrangements are present in the Baltics, the structure of civil society is nonetheless different due to Soviet traditions of an omnipresent state. Furthermore, many of those civil society leaders willing to co-operate with state institutions were absorbed into political society shortly after independence, leaving in particular those with antagonistic attitudes toward the public sector to remain in the civil society realm. Thus it is not surprising that numerous 'watchdog NGOs', which see their primary task as the independent monitoring of government, have sprung up since the early 1990s. A discussion initiated by the Polish professor Wiktor Osiatynski within the Open Society Institute network (financed by George Soros) led to lobbying in Brussels which resulted in the inclusion in the EU 2004 budget of a pilot programme for an annual facility of 3 million Euro to support the work of watchdog NGOs (Krzeczunowicz 2004: 7). Previously the EU had not been in the forefront of supporting this type of NGO – funding had come from other western donors. Krzeczunowicz (2004: 8) argues that the work of watchdog organizations will increase in importance with enlargement because new laws and funding sources open up new opportunities for corruption and lack of implementation.

Nonetheless, watchdog organizations are seen by some observers inside and outside the new member states as problematic because they embody the antagonistic civil society–state relationship prevalent in the late Soviet era. Such observers believe a more complex model is required whereby civil society actors to some extent co-operate with government, for example, in the sphere of service provision or as partners in agenda setting and policy implementation. Actually, this is the case in practice; many service provider NGOs have been established to assume functions that the state has (at least temporarily) been unable or unwilling to fulfil. For example, in a 1995 survey undertaken by the Latvian Ministry of Welfare, the major NGO activity was found to be social assistance, especially to the disabled, children and the sick (Baltic Data House 1998: 12, 14). Evidence of this perspective on civil society organizations can also be found in the Estonian Civil Society Development Concept (Public Policy Centre 2002), or EKAK, which emphasizes co-operation between civil society and the Estonian parliament.

In addition to influencing the balance between advocacy and service provision, the EU has also affected the civil society realm through its emphasis on particular thematic foci. Thus the sphere of human and minority rights has been one exception to the relative lack of EU support for watchdog organizations. In the Baltic states (especially Estonia and Latvia), this has often taken the form of concern with the integration of Russian speakers into the respective societies (Pabriks 2003; Semjonov 2003). While funding for human and minority rights projects has been welcomed by many, it can also be seen as a symptom of a larger problem with EU support: its tendency to focus on specific issues which may or may not reflect the needs of the particular societies involved. More recently, within this general focus on rights, an even more precise emphasis on Roma communities has been reflected in EU rhetoric and funding practices (Phare 2001: 10). Thus certain types of NGO have been promoted more than others, and priorities for funding have been based primarily on EU documents such as the Copenhagen criteria or selected sections of the *acquis* rather than on the situations prevailing in the candidate countries. This has sometimes meant that organizations have jumped on the relevant bandwagon and/or shifted their focus regularly in order to obtain international funding. This in turn has made their work excessively project-oriented, and resources have had to be expended on grant applications and on achieving the necessary levels of expertise rather than on establishing a sustainable institutional base.[4] Unlike some other international donors, the EU does not usually offer core funding on the national or sub-national level to keep organizations afloat between projects and allow them to focus on aspects such as developing an institutional identity and projecting it to the broader society as well as to potential partners in the public and private sectors. These practices tend to keep the NGOs subordinate to the EU, strengthening the EU–civil society link, but in a hierarchical manner. A more partnership-oriented relationship can conceivably emerge over time, as the NGOs acquire more expertise and gain more influence in their national political and societal spheres, but the EU will continue to hold the purse strings for the foreseeable future.

Related to the thematic foci has been an increasing emphasis on issues concerning the *acquis communautaire*, which understandably gained in prominence as the accession process proceeded. However, the desirability of this emphasis in the civil society sphere was called into question by an evaluation of the Phare programme. The assessment recommended giving 'issues of governance, public administrations, judiciaries and civil society bodies as much prominence as the *acquis*' (European Commission 2004: 22). While issues of participation and their link to democratization are given lip service, it is clear from overarching Phare projects such as 'Development and Strengthening of Civil Society' in Latvia that the main priority is to achieve complete transposal of the *acquis*, here in the realms of environmental protection and socio-economic development (Standard Summary Project Fiche 2002). Furthermore, the emphasis is on service provision, especially relating to 'social reintegration' or 'support for marginalized groups'. There is one section focused on 'building the functional and administrative capacity of NGOs', but this appears to be subordinated to *acquis*-related concerns. Nonetheless, projects funded under this rubric do to some extent aim at greater involvement of NGOs in certain aspects of social and economic development and thereby in the policy process (see for example Baltic Environmental Forum).

The EU has also had an impact on civil society development through its advocacy of particular types of funding and means of channelling grant monies. In fact, EU (and to some extent other foreign) funding has arguably hindered the development of longer-term domestic financing opportunities by orienting certain NGOs toward EU priorities. This has now been recognized by some international funders, especially those who are pulling out of the new member states, and attempts are currently being made to raise awareness among NGO activists in the respective countries of the need to diversify funding sources and to create an environment more receptive to public and private financing of civil society activity.[5] Since the EU is not in the group of donors advocating diversity of funding sources, but rather assumes that NGOs with EU links will continue to receive EU funding (for example, through the structural funds) or will be financed by local or national governments, it would appear to have contributed little to the financial sustainability of the civil society sphere in terms of avoiding dependency on one particular funding source.

In its civil society programmes, the EU has often granted funds directly to NGOs rather than channelling them through national and regional authorities. This differs from its practice in other areas. Youngs (2001) argues that 'the EU has developed a distinctive "grass-roots" approach to democracy promotion, which clearly differs from American aid that has been predominantly top-down and focused on the formal elements of democracy' (cited in Raik 2003: 207). This approach has had a variety of effects on the development of civil society in the candidate countries. It has increased the capacity and resources of a number of NGOs directly, allowing them to take responsibility for administering EU programmes and to participate in decisions about grant allocation. This has contributed to an intensive learning process among the NGO representatives involved and has helped to prepare them for interaction with the EU in terms of utilizing resources from the EU structural funds. This type of preparation has constituted a major EU goal in the candidate countries and is also advocated by NGO activists in the region (Krzeczunowicz 2004). However, this practice has also tended to privilege a few large and well-connected NGOs in each of the countries involved, increasing their capacity and resources while failing to involve a large variety of smaller, more geographically dispersed NGOs to the same extent. This creates or reinforces existing hierarchies and makes it more difficult for smaller, more remote NGOs to tap into potential funding sources and acquire expertise in working with foreign donors. This tendency is exacerbated by the extremely bureaucratic nature of EU application procedures, although attempts have been made to simplify these for smaller organizations (Raik 2003: 213f).

Another aspect of the EU's support of civil society has involved its use of local and national NGOs in the applicant countries to disseminate information on the EU and the implications of accession. Although this type of support affects only a minority of NGOs, it has multiplier effects and strengthens the identification of NGOs with the EU level, both for NGO members themselves and for the general public. This identification of NGOs with EU topics may even extend to involve EU officials and national governments. For instance, partially in response to EU overtures, former

Estonian Foreign Minister T.H. Ilves established a consultative council to deal with EU-related matters (unique in the candidate countries), consisting of representatives from labour market organizations, other NGOs and academia. While this council has issued some recommendations to the Estonian government, its primary function has been to serve as a clearinghouse for developments concerning EU integration (Raik 2003: 215). Also, prior to Estonia's accession to the EU in May 2004, the Estonian government funded numerous NGOs to carry out projects involving information dissemination about the process and consequences of enlargement (Raik 2003: 215).

What are the implications of these structural developments for civil society in the Baltics and for multilevel governance in the EU? First of all, while the EU has contributed to the already existing emphasis on service provision in the civil society realm, it has also taken account of more recent local trends by supporting advocacy organizations in a limited way. Second, the thematic and *acquis*-based approach, combined with the bureaucratic nature of EU grant procedures, has tended to create a hierarchy both between the EU level and the relevant national NGOs and within the NGO realm. As an increasingly significant source of NGO funding, the EU has been able to dictate its conditions and has proceeded to 'groom' a number of strong NGOs in each country for more intensive future cooperation with EU institutions. Rather paradoxically, the creation of such a hierarchy has emerged from an EU attempt at 'bottom-up' support for civil society in which it assists the NGOs directly rather than through national or local governments. This EU–NGO relationship has led to a hierarchy in the NGO sphere on the ground as well, since those NGOs which have developed the competence necessary to collaborate with the EU possess significant advantages in both funding and capacity over smaller organizations. Third, the EU's failure to stress diversity of funding sources has, while strengthening its own role, tended to hamper the overall financial sustainability of the NGO sphere. While this specific and pragmatic approach has certainly gained the EU some reliable partners in the Baltic states, it has arguably hindered the EU in its ability to influence broader issues of governance as they relate to civil society in the region. In the following section we explore whether the EU has been able to address such broader questions through the mechanisms of value and norm transfer.

11.3.3 EU Attempts at Value and Norm Transfer in the Civil Society Sphere

As indicated above, EU efforts in the context of the Phare programme have largely referred to the relatively narrow field of *acquis* transposal rather than to the broader arena of improving governance. Enlargement, however, is arguably first and foremost a question of value transfer, as illustrated by a statement on goals from the enlargement commissioner Olli Rehn: 'Enlargement is a matter of extending the zone of European values, the most fundamental of which are liberty and solidarity, tolerance and human rights, democracy and the rule of law' (Rehn 2005). Due to this overarching character of enlargement, it is particularly important to examine the informal and unintended aspects of EU involvement, as it is often through these less formal mechanisms that value and norm transfer occurs.

By promoting or even requiring increased civil society participation in political decision-making processes, the EU has granted increased legitimacy to NGOs both in their own eyes and in those of government officials. According to Raik, the Phare programme has contributed to the density of informal contacts between candidate countries (now new member states, for the most part) and EU members. She introduces the concept of 'indirect empowerment' to capture this type of value transfer, claiming that the EU 'supports civil society in the applicant countries indirectly by legitimising the demands of civic organisations and offering new opportunities for them to make themselves heard in public' (Raik 2003: 209). This process is a slow one, as NGOs must have time to gain the necessary expertise and capacity to participate in political agenda setting and implementation, and officials' attitudes toward civil society involvement in political processes change only gradually and are conditioned by Soviet-era practices. Nonetheless the inclusive model provided by the EU (even if primarily rhetorical) raises the stature of civil society in the candidate and new member states and allows the relevant actors to seek ways of adapting this EU practice to domestic conditions.

The evolution and eventual passage of the EKAK can be viewed as one example of such an adaptation. While similar documents exist in several other countries, the Estonian one is unique in the sense that the initiative for drafting it came from NGO representatives (Lagerspetz 2004: 90). However, there was and is no consensus among these representatives on the model of the relationship between civil society and the state to be advocated. The process of EKAK's elaboration allowed three discourses identified by Lagerspetz and associates to crystallize and compete openly. Lagerspetz believes that while the discourse of a 'participant society', in which NGOs represent the pluralism of opinions prevalent in society vis-à-vis the public sector, emerged the strongest among NGO representatives by the end of the EKAK debates, the final document does not fully reflect this development because the parliamentarians involved subscribe to this discourse to a very limited degree. Raik (2003: 216), while welcoming the passage of EKAK, urges caution at an approach which potentially 'spells danger for the independence and critical function of civil society'. In her eyes, the passage of EKAK indicates the strength of a model of civil society which emphasizes its partnership role with the public sector and focuses on civil society organizations that cooperate with and relieve the state of certain service provision tasks, rather than monitoring government behaviour. In addition, it tends to subordinate NGOs to the state, relegating them to an implementing role rather than creating an equal partnership in which they can contribute conceptually to societal design. To the extent that it emphasizes service provision and co-operation, the EKAK would appear to coincide with the prevailing EU inclination as discussed in the previous section.

According to Raik (2003: 219) the EU has implicitly contributed to the promotion of this concept of civil society because 'some of the aid programmes (LIEN and to some extent ACCESS) have positioned NGOs in the role of a substitute of the state by supporting voluntary work aimed at alleviating social problems'. Even though the EU has not consistently promoted one particular model of civil society in the CEE countries, it has 'influenced domestic developments largely indirectly, by shaping visions and ideas about civil society, and by conditioning civic activity and especially its relations to the state' (Raik 2003: 225). Thus EU influence has gone far beyond the relatively meager financial support aimed directly at civil society strengthening. In this broader, less formal perspective, the EU has on the one hand supported an upgrading of the status of CSOs overall and on the other encouraged a strong emphasis on service provision within the civil society sphere.

Within this overall paradigm encouraging a larger role for civil society in policy processes, competing models of civil society have been present, not only in the old EU, but also within each of the new member states. While 'it is important to look at how EU policy interacts with domestic conditions and choices, and how EU norms become appropriated into the domestic context' (Raik 2003: 200), this becomes a complex undertaking, since each individual country presents a different platform for the interaction of domestic and international discourses. In the Estonian example, the three different discourses about the role of the NGO sector mentioned above focus on: 1) the potential economic contribution of NGOs as service providers; 2) the mobilizing role of NGOs in support of state and nation building; and 3) NGOs as elements of a pluralist democracy (Lagerspetz 2004). If we accept Raik's conclusion that the EU has indirectly supported two discourses by its actions in the accession process, then we can see that the path toward the establishment of a stable civil society with a relatively clear relationship to the public and private sectors is by no means linear.

Rather it is characterized by the presence of a variety of competing models which interact in a struggle for prominence.

Raik further argues that the introduction of democratic norms and values into the NGO sector in Estonia is unnecessary because the NGO activists there already subscribe to democratic values. Instead, it is more an issue of providing ideas on how to better implement democratic norms in practice in the Estonian situation. However, elite conceptions of democracy in the new member states do not always include the involvement of civil society in the political process, even if tolerance of such involvement has grown in the Baltics in recent years (see USAID 2004). This in turn means that the necessary 'channels of participation' to facilitate interactions between NGO representatives and government institutions may need to be created (Lagerspetz *et al*. 2004: 44). Considering the complexity inherent in both the national societal level and in the EU level regarding the role and functions of civil society, it appears logical that the EU has not been able to introduce clarity into national discourses on these questions. Instead, it has presented a conception of civil society which, while possessing certain recurring hallmarks, is both in flux itself and capable of interacting differently with the various national discourses.

Issues involving values include not only the question of the relationship between civil society and other spheres, but also the internal evolution of the civil society realm. For example, the EU focus on a few large NGOs has consequences for norm transfer in the area of democracy. It sends the message that smaller organizations closer to their social base are less worthy of being funded than increasingly bureaucratic larger organizations which become more attuned to EU demands and less to local constituencies (compare Krzeczunowicz 2004: 6f). These larger organizations are usually located in capital cities, which increases the concentration of resources and expertise there vis-à-vis other areas of the country. While there have been efforts by the EU (and other foreign donors) to counteract some of these tendencies (see Raik 2003: 213f), there is a difference between allocating grant money and allotting the organizations an administrative role. Although providing grants is important, it does not usually address issues of capacity building and institutional strengthening which allow the NGO sphere to become more stable and sustainable (see for example McMahon 2002; Richter 2002).

Corroboration for the 'larger is better' tendency in the Phare realm is provided by Anders Engström of the Union of the Baltic Cities, who cites officials from the Estonian Ministry of the Interior. According to Engström, the Estonian civil servants were told by a Phare delegation to prioritize larger Phare projects of 2 million Euros or more (Engström 2000). This certainly would make it more difficult to involve smaller NGOs in many of the project stages. While evaluations of EU activities in other contexts have acknowledged that small projects are often successful in terms of impact and sustainability, they are nonetheless characterized as 'burdensome to manage' (Towards a new Tacis concept, Part II[6]). The focus on larger projects limits the number of civil society actors with which the EU can productively interact and points to an approach which privileges depth of interaction over breadth of organizational involvement.

The developments in the realm of value and norm transfer have multiple implications for Baltic civil society and for multilevel governance. First of all, it appears quite clear that, through a variety of both formal and informal activities, the EU has supported an increasing role for civil society in decision-making processes. However, the EU has not consistently promoted one unified model for the civil society sphere, but instead has presented a discourse which, while possessing certain recurring features, has been flexible enough to interact with the prevailing models developing in the relevant national contexts. As we saw in the previous section, the EU advocated privileging a few large NGOs and therefore sent a clear message about the type of organization most highly valued as a partner for the EU and, by implication, perhaps for national governments as well.

11.4 CONCLUSIONS

At the time of writing, over two years have passed since the Baltic states joined the EU and changes in the civil society realm in response to accession are occurring only gradually. Phare programmes are concluding and other international donors are pulling out of the Baltics slowly. However, an internal shift is taking place among NGOs, many of which realize they will need to work increasingly with the EU bureaucracy and/or seek new domestic sources of funding. Thus there are some indications of how the NGO landscape might look in the years to come.

One activist predicts that '[o]nly some parts of the civil society sector will get a shot at using EU funds to carry out their work' (Krzeczunowicz 2004: 2). This appears to dovetail with developments outlined above, for example, the tendency of the EU to rely on large NGOs with specific resources and expertise as administrative partners, and the EU emphasis on particular thematic foci, which privileges certain segments of the NGO sphere. The increasing complexity of the policy and funding landscape introduced by EU involvement has resulted in 'the need for legislative advocacy work of NGOs to become much more sophisticated and international' (Krzeczunowicz 2004: 3). This makes it all the more likely that only large and well-established

NGOs will be able to connect with EU funding opportunities. Thus a more stratified and hierarchical civil society realm appears likely to emerge, especially since this development is convenient for many national government officials as well (see Lagerspetz 2004: 98).

It therefore seems highly probable that the EU–civil society direct link will remain limited primarily to a few powerful NGOs which correspond to the priorities set by the EU structural funds. Most local and the majority of national NGOs will stay more closely connected to domestic networks, be they governmental, corporate or community in nature. The hierarchy created by the EU will have consequences for the internal functioning of the civil society sphere as well, since a few privileged NGOs have benefited disproportionately from accession. Overall, however, the status of NGOs as potential partners in policy processes has been raised due to EU involvement, although the particular developments in each country have depended on the type and quality of interaction between EU and national discourses. The continuation of this improved NGO status, however, is likely to depend more on national developments than on EU involvement, since the Baltic states are now full-fledged EU members and no longer under particular scrutiny. Nonetheless, due to a number of parallel developments both within and outside the immediate EU context, NGOs and the civil society realm in general continue to grow stronger and more active, and local and to some extent national governments have begun to realize the benefits of co-operating with NGOs and to better conceptualize their role in the democratic process. While these developments are most advanced in Estonia, they have certainly taken root in Latvia and Lithuania as well. So even if the EU emphasis shifts more completely to formalized support for a small number of NGOs through the structural funds, it appears likely that the incorporation of a variety of civil society actors into the political process, to which the EU has been contributing substantially in the past decade, will prove itself irreversible.

The consequences of EU support for civil society in the Baltics for multilevel governance have been multiple. While direct links have been established between EU institutions and certain civil society organizations in the Baltic states, thus strengthening the EU–civil society link, this has occurred at the expense of other relationships. CSOs with EU funding have been more focused on the EU level than on networking with other local CSOs, and the latter have often turned to local, regional and national governments as potential alternative funding sources. Thus two parallel tracks of CSO development have emerged, and this has also reduced the potential linkages between the EU level and the national, regional or local government level in the relevant states, since government structures have been circumvented in order to lend direct assistance to civil society. While contributing to the greater involvement of civil society actors in political, social and economic processes in the Baltics, the EU has been constrained by local conditions as well as by its own enlargement priorities, which at times have run counter to a concept of multilevel governance espousing the engagement of a wide variety of non-state actors.

NOTES

1. Until 2000 several western Balkan countries (Albania, Bosnia-Herzegovina and Macedonia) also benefited from Phare, but as of 2001 this assistance was replaced by the CARDS (Community Assistance for Reconstruction, Development and Stability in the Balkans) Programme.
2. See www.eu.int/comm/enlargement/pas/phare/index.htm.
3. See www.eu.int/comm/enlargement/pas/phare/index.htm.
4. This phenomenon is not limited to the EU or to the Baltic states. For examples from the US funding context in Central and Eastern Europe see Mendelson and Glenn (2002).
5. For examples of such attempts see Baltic-American Partnership (n.d. a and b)
6. See http://ec.europa.eu/external_relations/consultations/cswp_tacis.htm.

REFERENCES

Baltic–American Partnership Fund (n.d.a) 'Summary of BAPP-Latvia 2005–2007 Strategy' www. bapf.org/BAPP-LV_2005-7_Strategy.pdf, last access: 26 September 2005.

Baltic–American Partnership Fund (n.d.b) 'Summary of BAPP-Lithuania 2005–2007' www.bapf.org/BAPP-LT_2005-7_Strategy.pdf, last access: 26 September 2005.

Baltic Data House (1998) *Conditions of enhancement of civic participation* www.policy.lv/index.php?id=102360&lang=en, last access: 26 September 2005.

Baltic Environmental Forum (n.d.) *Project: Involvement of non-governmental organisations (NGOs) in water management policy* http://river.bef.lv/data/file/about_the_project.pdf, last access: 26 September 2005.

Croissant, A., Lauth, H.-J. and Merkel, W. (2000) 'Zivilgesellschaft und Transformation: Ein internationaler Vergleich', in W. Merkel (ed.) *Systemwechsel 5: Zivilgesellschaft und Transformation*, Opladen: Leske und Budrich, pp. 9–49.

Ekiert, G. and Hanson, S.E. (eds) (2003) *Capitalism and democracy in central and Eastern Europe: Assessing the legacy of communist rule*, Cambridge: Cambridge University Press.

Engström, A. (2000) 'Statement by Mr Anders Engström at the CBSS meeting, Brussels, 8 February' www.ubc.net/today/08th0200.html, last access: 26 September 2005.

European Commission (2004) *From pre-accession to accession: Interim evaluation of Phare support allocated in 1999–2002 and implemented until November 2003*: Consolidated Summary Report, March 2004.

Hackmann, J. (2003) 'Civil society against the State? Historical experiences of Eastern Europe', in N. Götz and J. Hackmann *Civil society in the Baltic Sea Region*, Aldershot: Ashgate, pp. 49–62.

Krzeczunowicz, P. (2004) *European Union funding after enlargement – Blessing or curse for civil society*, paper commissioned by: Trust for civil society in central and Eastern Europe.

Lagerspetz, M. (2004) 'From NGOs to civil society: A learning process', in M. Lagerspetz, A. Trummal, R. Ruutsoo and E. Rikmann (eds) *Non-profit sector and the consolidation of democracy: Studies on the development of civil society in Estonia*, Tallinn: Avatud Eesti Fond, pp. 86–103.

Lagerspetz, M., Rikmann, E. and Ruutsoo, R. (2004) 'The structure and resources of NGOs in Estonia', in M. Lagerspetz, A. Trummal, R. Ruutsoo and E. Rikmann (eds) *Non-profit sector and the consolidation of democracy: Studies on the development of civil society in Estonia*, Tallin: Avatud Eesti Fond, pp. 28–47.

Lauth, H.-J. and Merkel, W. (1997) 'Zivilgesellschaft und Transformation: Ein Diskussionsbeitrag in revisionistischer Absicht' *Forschungsjournal neue soziale Bewegungen* 10 (1), 12–34.

Linz, J. and Stepan, A. (1996) *Problems of democratic transition and consolidation: Southern Europe, South America, and Post-Communist Europe*, Baltimore and London: Johns Hopkins University Press.

Lux, M. (2000) 'Drei Staaten – ein "Baltischer Weg"? Die Zivilgesellschaft in der Transformation im Baltikum', in W. Merkel (ed.) *Systemwechsel V: Zivilgesellschaft und Transformation*, Opladen: Leske und Budrich, pp. 145–72.

Marsh, H.B. (2003) *The Phare Programme: What is Phare and how to work with Phare?* Brussels: The European Commission's Information Centre on Enlargement, May.

McMahon, P. (2002) 'International actors and women's NGOs in Poland and Hungary', in S.E. Mendelson and J.K. Glenn (eds) *The Power and limits of NGOs: A critical look at building democracy in Eastern Europe and Eurasia*, New York: Columbia University Press, pp. 29–53.

Mendelson, S.E. and Glenn, J.K. (eds) (2002) *The power and limits of NGOs*, New York: Columbia University Press.

OMAS Consortium (2001) *Assessment of the European Union Phare Programmes by OMAS Consortium*: multi-country thematic report, Report No. S/ZZ/CIV/01004, 10 September.

Pabriks, A. (2003) 'Ethnic limits of civil society: The case of Latvia', in N. Götz and J. Hackmann (eds) *Civil society in the Baltic Sea Region*, Aldershot: Ashgate, pp. 133–44.

Phare (2001) *Phare programming guide 2001: guidance for Phare country coordinators*, http:/www.mfcr.cz/cps/rdex/bcr/mfcr/PHAREprogrammingguide2001_pdf.pdf, last access: 19 November 2007.

Public Policy Centre (2002) 'Estonian civil society development concept' www.policy.lv/index.php?id=102546&lang=en, last access: 26 September 2005.

Raik, K. (2003) *Democratic politics or the implementation of inevitabilities? Estonia's democracy and integration into the European Union*, Tartu: Tartu University Press.

Rehn, O. (2005) 'Values define Europe, not borders' *Financial Times*, 3 January.

Richter, J. (2002) 'Evaluating Western assistance to Russian women's organizations', in S.E. Mendelson and J.K. Glenn (eds) *The power and limits of NGOs: A critical look at building democracy in Eastern Europe and Eurasia*, New York: Columbia University Press, pp. 54–90.

Rose, R. (1999) 'How Russians cope: Living in an antimodern society' *East*

European Constitutional Review 8 (1–2).
Salamon, L.M., Anheier, H.K., List, R., Toepler, S. and Sokolowski, S.W. (eds) (1999). *Global civil society: Dimensions of the Nonprofit Sector*, Baltimore: The Johns Hopkins Center for Civil Society Studies.
Semjonov, A. (2003) 'Ethnic limits of civil society: The case of Estonia', in N. Götz and J. Hackmann (eds) *Civil society in the Baltic Sea Region*, Aldershot: Ashgate, pp. 145–57.
Standard Summary Project Fiche 2002, Désirée Number 2002/000-590-01-02. Title: *Development and strengthening of civil society (Latvia)*.
USAID (2004) *NGO sustainability index for Central and Eastern Europe and Eurasia* www.usaid.gov/locations/europe_eurasia/dem_gov/ngoindex/, last access: 26 September 2005.
Youngs, R. (2001) 'European Union democracy promotion policies: Ten years on' *European Foreign Affairs Review* 6 (3), 355–73.

PART IV

In conclusion

12. Conclusion: Europeanization, multi-level governance and civil society

William A. Maloney and Jan W. van Deth

12.1 INTRODUCTION

Europeanization, multi-level governance and civil society appear to be related in manifold and complex ways. Analyses dealing with these phenomena and their interdependencies usually start with the claim that many policy areas within EU member states have been Europeanized. Yet even a cursory glance at the various approaches clearly demonstrates that the conceptual, theoretical and empirical complexities in this area are immense. While Olsen (2002: 921) notes that ' "Europeanization" is a contested but fashionable concept' that can be 'applied in a number of ways to describe a variety of phenomena and processes of change', other authors try to pin down the most important features in a single sentence. Green Cowles and Risse (2001: 217) define Europeanization 'as the emergence and development at the European level of distinct structures of governance, that is, of political, legal, and social institutions associated with political problem solving that formalize interactions among the actors, and of policy networks specializing in the creation of authoritative rules'. The rise of these 'institutions' and 'networks' clearly presents a challenge to the conventional approaches to democratic decision making and the role of civil associations. This volume has examined various aspects of Europeanization and its consequences for democratic decision-making processes by addressing greater citizen involvement in EU governance, increasing identification with and confidence and trust in EU political institutions, and the issues of transparency, legitimacy and accountability of decision-making procedures within the EU.

While the links between civil society and democracy have been relatively well established at the local and national level, much less is known about the opportunities that exist for associations to contribute to European integration or the functioning of democracy at the European level. The contributors to this volume all aimed to assess the extent to which local and/or national associations empower civic actors in the European and/or international arena. Do civil society organizations at various levels contribute to good governance in terms of democracy and efficiency?

It is clear that, at the European level, establishing and improving democratic decision-making processes is certainly not a straightforward task. For analytical purposes we distinguished between 'top-down' approaches for the study of relationships within the developing EU multi-level system (that is, the consequences of Europeanization for civil society at the local level), and 'bottom-up' approaches (that is, the consequences of civil society for the process of European integration and democracy in the EU). The exploration of these recursive linkages requires a rethinking of the relationships between (local, national and trans-national) civil society and multi-level governance. In various ways, several of the contributions also employ – or at least touch upon – the 'social capital' concept, which was seen as especially relevant given the EU's and the EC Commission's enthusiasm for addressing the democratic deficit and engendering the more 'meaningful' (grassroots) involvement of EU civil society. In theory and practice these institutions see social capital as a means to promote democratic and efficient governance.

Civil society associations are expected to play a key role in the various links between the local and national levels and the trans-national level. In this way, they are at the core of our analyses of decision-making processes in Europe. New forms of active citizenship and NGO engagement are required to deal with internationalization and Europeanization, and a new 'civil society elite' has emerged in various regions and areas in recent years. In this concluding chapter we summarize and assess the extent to which civil society associations and political organizations have the capacity to, or have actually contributed to plugging the democratic deficit, offering more meaningful opportunities for citizen involvement in EU matters and accentuating the Europeanization process.

12.2 MAIN FINDINGS

We started our explorations of the consequences and interdependencies of ongoing Europeanization with a broad distinction between top-down and bottom-up approaches based on the question whether civil society associations are mainly considered as a starting point or as objects of these processes. Essentially, the volume is divided into two main parts dealing with these distinct perspectives.

Before the first empirical studies were presented, Zimmer and Freise (Chapter 2) provided a theoretical tenet for all contributions to the volume.

They analysed three concepts that are predominately society-centred and that have gained momentum during the last decades: civil society, social capital and third sector. None of these concepts constitutes a 'grand theory', but each claims to have some utility in the sense of a so-called middle-range theory that highlights the innovative capacity of civic engagement and societal activity. In their analyses, the specific background and origin, methodology and scientific (and common) understanding of each concept is discussed. Against this background a closer nexus between the civil society and the third sector approaches is proposed by drawing on the terminology used by the European Union that defines third sector organizations as 'organised civil society'. Finally there is the question of what the civil society approach might add to the further development and democratic underpinning of multi-level governance in Europe. Civil society as an analytical concept has much in common with the third sector and the social capital approaches. In sum, there is much need for further research with regard to theory development. This may involve a fundamental reappraisal of the meaning of democracy and the role of representative institutions within nation states. The three concepts scrutinized and redefined – civil society, social capital and third sector – offer very useful analytical tools for the empirical studies presented in this volume.

The first part of the book contains five contributions focusing on the opportunities for civil society associations to contribute to democratic decision-making processes in the European multi-level system. Maloney and van Deth (Chapter 3) argue that while much of the contemporary focus is on the (alleged) impact of associations on members, there is a paucity of research that actually links the citizen to the association, and of course the local associations or local activists to the EU. In their analyses the (local) organizational context in Germany and the UK is connected to various attitudes towards Europe. Maloney and van Deth show the types of organizations European citizens join and assess what impact, if any, associational type has on the levels of attachment to, confidence in, or engagement with the EU (compared to other local, regional and nation political or state institutions). They also assess the impact of organizational size and levels of membership involvement on attachment to, and interest in the EU. Drawing on a typology of attachment to various political objects, it is demonstrated that German respondents are more pro-European than their British counterparts – something that accords with the commonplace notions of the Euro-sceptic British. However, there is not much comfort for EU architects because the levels of attachment and confidence in European institutions are relatively low. This finding is also supported by (population) research by Blondel *et al.* (1998), Cautrès (2001) and Cautrès and Reynié (2001), which show that the directly elected

European Parliament fails to promote feelings of European/EU identification among the European citizenry (all cited in Saurugger, forthcoming 2009). In addition to this, Maloney and van Deth find that associational size and levels of involvement appear to be irrelevant to European attitudes, but associational type matters. In Aberdeen, family and general welfare groups are the most committed to Europe; religious, culture, sports and group-specific welfare the least. The pattern in Mannheim shows some similarity, but not symmetry. Finally, Maloney and van Deth hypothesize – on the basis of the social capital model – that citizens affiliated to associations should exhibit a greater attachment to, a higher level of political engagement with and a higher level of confidence in Europe and European institutions. The findings for the civil society activists are compared (in an illustrative way) with the general populations. The tentative conclusion is that, in general, attitudes towards Europe and European institutions among activists are not much more positive than those found among the populations.

The role and position of civil society associations in the European multi-level system are analysed from a different perspective in the next chapter. Hooghe (Chapter 4) combines the political opportunity structure (POS) approach and the multi-level governance (MLG) perspective in order to assess the impact that Europeanization has on the configuration of social movements in Europe. It is widely assumed that various features of the POS affect the development of social movements and NGOs. The ongoing process of European integration has created a system of multi-level governance that, according to most interpretations of the POS model, should lead to a proliferation of access points for NGOs. To better understand the interaction between social movements and NGOs, two (historical) cases are studied – first, the development of the environmental movement in Belgium and second, the proliferation of environmental groups operating on a global scale since the 1960s. Looking at the development of European civil society, Hooghe does not uncover any evidence of a massive proliferation of European civil society organizations. On the contrary, there is a strong tendency towards professionalized organized interests and an increasing professionalization of existing groups: within EU policy-making processes there is a 'surfeit' of professionalized representation. These bodies range from traditional interest groups and European federations to NGOs and civil society organizations (Saurugger 2007). Hooghe hypothesizes that European processes and structures may inhibit the formation of mass membership groups and encourage more professionalized representation. In his research on the Belgian environmental movement, he finds that the POS had no impact on the make-up of civil society. Civil society groups are not simply reactive to political changes but respond to 'cultural dynamics' that affect the structure of the social movement sector as strongly as the POS. In short, social movements affect the structure of governance as much as governance configurations impact on social movements. Similarly, global environmental organizations are not simply responsive to changes in the POS: no 'evidence of a top-down logic' can be found. The evidence drawn from these examples supports the claim that an overly deterministic use of the POS concept should be avoided when analysing the strategic interaction between the political system and social movement organizations. Finally, and turning to the core issue of this volume, Hooghe notes that while the EU has been an important driver of environmental policy throughout the member states, there is 'little evidence for the existence of a flourishing environmental movement at the European level'. He concludes that the scarcity of mass membership organizations active at the EU level may have serious implications for the integration process. In essence, Hooghe sees the Europeanization process as 'elite-driven' and the bottom-up dimension as 'weakly developed'. His findings raise serious questions about the extent to which European unification can or will lead to the development of a truly European civil society.

In the last few years, no European issue has attracted more public attention than the proposal for a 'European Convention and its Draft Treaty establishing a Constitution for Europe'. In a detailed case study Cook (Chapter 5) examines the involvement of civil society in Wales in order to develop an understanding of the extent to which the Convention permeated citizens' lives. Cook considers institutional discourses, and structural and cultural opportunities and constraints (varying across levels of governance) and assesses the extent of group involvement in the European Convention, as well as the system of multi-level governance (involving Welsh, British and European institutions in the policy-making process). The analyses demonstrate that Welsh civil society organizations played a relatively minor role in the Convention process and participation was concentrated among a minority of groups. Like Hooghe (Chapter 4), Cook finds that the groups involved are a relatively small component of Welsh civil society and it is the highly professionalized groups that are included. She also notes that Welsh civil society groups are linked to the EU through the sub-national authority: EU participation is brokered through the Welsh Assembly. In terms of input into the Convention itself there are structural barriers to participation: that is, those entities with expertise, EU knowledge and so on are best placed. In Cook's view the Convention failed to (re-)engage civil society on the ground and local citizens were bypassed by the 'continued prominence of the Member State and above in this instance of EU high politics'. Accordingly, the findings cast doubt on the Convention's ability to reconnect citizens through civil society, and also highlight the continued lack of awareness of the Convention among British citizens.

Whereas the debates about the Convention are based on direct links between local civil society and plans developed at the European level, these relationships are usually characterized by more complex interdependencies in the European multi-level system of governance. An important example of these interdependencies is studied by Parau and Wittmeier Bains (Chapter 6), who explore the impact of the EU on public accountability in the domestic arena. They provide evidence from three case studies: the first focuses on an EU member state (the UK), the second involves (at the time of writing) a leading candidate for accession (the Czech Republic), and the third is a 'poorly performing' candidate (Romania). They define public accountability as

> a series of political proceedings whereby the general public seeks to double-check the representativeness of democratic government against such criteria as transparency of decision making; public access to information in the possession of government; the adequacy of the government's consultation of the public, and of the public's participation in the myriad workaday decisions which government takes in between infrequently occurring elections.

Parau and Wittmeier Bains assess the impact of Europeanization and, in particular, they focus on which actors get empowered, what use they make of these opportunities and how they circumvent any EU limitations that operate in the domestic polity. They argue that the participatory procedures authorized by the EU have 'the potential to empower civil society'. However, if or when empowerment is realized and which civil society groups are empowered depends upon domestic factors beyond the control of the EU. Parau and Wittmeier Bains argue that the nodal and influential position of member state governments in their domestic arenas means that they are well placed to counter 'the empowerment of civil society through EU tools like the Environmental Impact Assessment'. In their case studies they also found that the usual suspect (business) was the best organized civil society actor and that the EU-level 'opportunities and constraints' did not dramatically alter government–civil society relations: it tended to reinforce existing power differentials.

The final contribution to the first part of the volume continues the debate about the impact and relevance of EU policies for domestic politics in various member states. Following a revised political opportunity approach Chabanet and Giugni (Chapter 7) analyse the claim making of migrants and the unemployed in four European countries (Britain, France, Germany and Switzerland) that diverge in their institutional approaches to these issues. The claim making of underprivileged minority groups such as migrants and the unemployed is presumed to be constrained by domestic political opportunity structures. These groups lack the necessary resources, skills, expertise and collective action wherewithal to mobilize effectively. Chabanet and Giugni correctly hypothesize that the unemployed would face greater obstacles to pressing their political claims than migrants (confirmed by their empirical evidence). They find (akin to Hooghe, Chapter 4) that political institutions are 'less important' to these groups and have 'a minor impact on their (political) behaviour'. They partly attribute this to the marginalized status of both movements. Chabanet and Giugni's findings highlight the greater importance of specific contexts (specific opportunity structures) and discursive contexts vis-à-vis the more general political opportunity structures that are normally identified as crucial. The mobilization level of these social groups 'varies in important ways from one country to the other according to the institutional and discursive settings in which they are located', and their claim making is dependent on a set of opportunities specific to the relevant political area. Both the opportunities and constraints on political claim making are context-sensitive and vary from one country to the other.

The second part of the volume contains four contributions dealing with the consequences of Europeanization for democratic decision making from a top-down perspective. In the first chapter, Leconte (Chapter 8) addresses the persistent non-Europeanization of domestic political spaces at the mass level and speculates on how likely this is to continue in the foreseeable future. She also examines the extent to which Europeanization empowers domestic party elites at the expense of citizens and the alternative proposition that Europeanization may actually create opportunities for citizens by providing them with new points of references, enabling them to play a more active role in the structuring of political conflict and public debate in national arenas. Leconte argues that three theories (liberal intergovernmentalism, consociative theories and Europeanization theories) aptly depict the attempts of domestic party elites to use Europeanization in an instrumental way. Domestic actors seek to benefit from the emergence of a European party system and prevent the emergence of direct channels of communication between the European level of political representation and domestic electorates. In addition, Leconte demonstrates that these theories tell only one part of the story, since they are based on the assumption that domestic party elites are still able to retain the position as gate keepers between the domestic and the European levels of political representation. She notes that, theoretically, Europeanization could have a significant impact on the power of local political elites. For example, multi-level governance could lead to the emergence of a European electoral arena that could challenge domestic parties and possibly cause a change in domestic party systems leading to new Europeanized cleavage structures. Potentially, Europeanization poses a threat to national party elites – it could increase the perception that domestic parties are less relevant. Accordingly, Leconte argues that national party elites use a variety of strategies and tactics to weaken the vertical links between the EU and the national levels. She argues that 'to a large extent, domestic political elites have been able to prevent the crucial challenge which the development of a European party system could have posed to their authority'. However, Leconte also notes that Europeanization is not always a top-down phenomenon; it can empower (and work from) the bottom up. For example, in Poland a large majority of voters believe that Europeanization can be an effective mechanism for reforming domestic political practices. Holzhacker (2007: 5) also notes how organizations draw on European policies and institutions to bolster their claims for domestic reform. He argues that organizations can remind governments of their implementation obligations vis-à-vis EU directives.

Instead of looking at parties and party elites, Mahoney (Chapter 9) examines how, through the use of outside lobbying strategies and tactics, interest groups can encourage and facilitate citizens' political engagement. In her words, the crucial question to answer is how do 'interest groups foster civic engagement through outside lobbying tactics?' However, the degree to which civil society organizations perform their role as mobilizers is likely to vary on any given issue. Thus she seeks to understand how and why organizations foster citizen engagement in some issues and fail to do so in others. Mahoney considers the (political) institutional structure within which advocates operate, the characteristics of the relevant issue, and the interest group itself. She argues that (in line with the cursory observations of several EU scholars), EU interest groups use 'outside lobbying', and consequently mobilize citizens to a very limited degree. Beside, she finds that civil society groups are most likely to use 'outside lobbying', whereas business interest groups are relatively less likely to draw on such strategies and tactics. Her findings provide support for the theory that several factors contribute to the decision of lobbyists to 'go public': the extent to which civil society organizations act as mobilizers varies according to institutional, issue and interest characteristics. Mahoney concludes that 'EU advocates are not mobilising European citizens' as much as they possibly could via 'outside lobbying'. She argues that the absence of pan-EU media partly explains citizens' detachment and that a lack of political responsiveness from elected representatives also needs to be addressed.

The possible impact of EU regulations on specific policy domains in various countries is analysed by Adam, Jochum and Kriesi (Chapter 10). They provide extensive empirical analyses of policy-domain-specific coalition configurations in six EU countries and one closely associated state

(Switzerland). Their main conclusion is that, despite common EU regulations and policies (in the areas of integration, immigration and agricultural policies) resulting from EU integration, there remains significant variation between 'nation states in terms of the national context that these EU policies are confronted with at the domestic level. This variation is assumed to be responsible for different responses to EU integration.' This finding is in line with the Europeanization research of Risse *et al.* (2001: 1), who conclude that in many instances Europeanization is ' "domestic adaptation with national colors" in which national features continue to play a role in shaping outcomes'.

The final chapter deals with the archetypal top-down attempt to link EU policies to civil society associations. Stewart (Chapter 11) assesses the EU's activities that have affected the development of civil society in the Baltic states of Estonia, Latvia and Lithuania since the early 1990s. Her analyses focus largely on the 1998–2004 period; that is, on the period during which the Baltic states were candidate members of the EU. She explores the implications of multi-level governance in the EU through an analysis of the channels of communication and support between EU institutions and local/national civil society organizations, among these bodies in their respective national contexts, and between civil society associations and the relevant national and local governments. Stewart finds that the EU funding of civil society has 'tended to privilege a few large and well-connected NGOs . . . increasing their capacity and resources' (akin to Hooghe's and Cook's findings). Smaller and geographically dispersed organizations have effectively lost out. Stewart also cites work by Krzeczunowicz (2004) and Lagerspetz (2004) that notes the propensity of the EU to draw on large resource-rich NGOs as 'administrative partners'. The increasingly complex areas of policy making and funding largely exclude smaller NGOs that lack the necessary expertise and resources. She speculates that 'a more stratified and hierarchical civil society realm appears likely to emerge, especially since this development is convenient for many national government officials as well (see Lagerspetz 2004: 98)' (see also Saurugger 2007).

12.3 THE DEMOCRATIC DEFICIT

Do civil society organizations at various levels contribute to good governance in terms of democracy and efficiency? The evidence presented in this volume provokes a somewhat sceptical answer to this question. Realizing the aims and objective of the White Paper on Governance – increasing the democratic legitimacy of the EU – may be an even bigger task than initially thought. First, it is clear from several analyses that the prospects for bottom-up improvements of democratic decision making are limited. Local and national civil society associations do not seem to be able or willing to be involved in European affairs. Activists within these associations do not exhibit particularly positive attitudes towards the EU and professionalized groups appear best placed to take advantage of the opening-up of opportunities and thus seem to be able to have some impact. However, it appears that it is elites – not citizens or volunteers – that play a leading role in decision-making processes. Apparently, attempts to integrate citizens into European decision-making processes by strengthening civil society are hampered by activists' attitudes, distinctions between various associations, and elite behaviour.

Shifting the focus from a bottom-up to a top-down perspective does not generate a more optimistic picture. Our second main conclusion is that the interrelationships between various levels are highly dominated by national gatekeepers. This conclusion appears to be valid irrespective of whether we deal with political parties, lobby groups or social movements. Although differences between policy areas and different countries can be noted, it is clear that the national opportunity structures remain the most important determinants of decision-making processes. Even explicit attempts to reach civil society with specific EU policies appear in general to have been unsuccessful, or, at best, to have enjoyed limited success.

The two main conclusions outlined above share a common perspective: the key to understand decision-making processes in the European multi-level system lies neither at the EU level nor with grassroots civil society associations. Instead, professionalized groups and national gatekeepers appear to be the dominant players. Cumulative evidence from this volume prompts a rethinking of the relationships between (local, regional, national and trans-national) civil society on the one hand, and multi-level governance at the European level on the other. National organizations, policy networks and elites still play a crucial role in Europe, and voluntary associations appear somewhat under-utilized. Accordingly, we should be cautious about the extent to which we can expect civil society organizations to enhance EU democracy (or to Europeanize the EU citizenry).

While the Commission has made great claims for the ability of NGOs to stimulate and bolster participatory and representative democracy and to increase citizen engagement with and confidence in the EU, the findings presented in this volume – and the general conclusions presented in the text above – do not provide much reason for optimism. These findings are also corroborated by other research (see Friedrich 2007 and Greenwood 2007). In his study of NGOs in the development policy area, Warleigh (2001: 632) found that most NGO supporters were unaware of the group's EU-level activities and the group's leadership felt that they did not have any responsibility to explain to their members why it was important for the group to interface with the EU. He also argued (2001: 623) that these bodies were incapable of acting as 'catalysts for the Europeanization of civil society', largely because they lacked the necessary internal democracy and that policy was made by a small staff-based elite. On the basis of her research, Sudbery (2003: 93–4) concluded that: civil society was unlikely to decrease citizen alienation from EU governance; NGOs perceived their primary role as influencing policy; and involving supporters was perceived as 'desirable', but there were several barriers – communication was mediated through national associations, and members and supporters did not believe they had a role in policy formulation. She also noted a lack of resources (see the introduction to this volume). Greenwood (2007: 347) wryly notes:

> Any reality check would show that almost all the EU groups are associations of organizations (in the citizen field almost entirely associations of national or other European associations), and therefore unable to deliver on many of the traditional strengths for interest groups in democratic systems . . . EU groups are political action organizations, not service based organizations, because their members – often national associations, or in the corporate world sometimes large companies – do not need member services.

Greenwood (2007: 347) further comments that very few EU-related activities are built around 'the difficult task of mobilizing members from across Europe in Brussels-oriented events based activism . . . Greenpeace [has] . . . a Brussels policy geared to dialogue with EU political institutions and other stakeholders rather than a campaign office oriented towards engaging in mass activism'. These findings are clearly in line with the results presented by the contributors to this volume.

Improving democratic decision making in the EU multi-level system is crucial for the further development of transparent, legitimate and accountable governance in Europe. However, the evidence presented in this volume and elsewhere suggests that we should dispense with romantic notions (and speculation) about the benevolent aspects of integrating civil society into this complex system. Contemporary empirical research unambiguously points in the direction of the (continued) dominance of professionalized groups and national gatekeepers in European decision-making processes. Once this 'uncomfortable' situation is fully recognized, then a renewed and serious effort can be made to enhance democratic governance in the EU.

REFERENCES

Blondel, J., Sinnott, R. and Svensson, P. (1998) *People and parliament in the European Union: Participation, democracy and legitimacy*, Oxford: Clarendon.

Cautrès, B. (2001) 'La difficile émergence de l'électeur européen' *Politique européenne*, 64–85.
Cautrès, B. and Reynié, D. (2001) (eds) *L'opinion européenne 2001*, Paris: Presses de Sciences Po.
Friedrich, D. (2007) *Old wine in new bottles? The actual and potential contribution of civil society organisations to democratic governance in Europe*, RECON Online Working Paper 2007/08, www.reconproject.eu/main.php/RECON_wp_0708.pdf?fileitem5456965, last access: 19 November 2007.
Green Cowles, M. and Risse, T. (2001) 'Transforming Europe: Conclusions', in M. Green Cowles, J. Caporaso and T. Risse (eds) *Transforming Europe: Europeanization and domestic change*, Ithaca: Cornell University Press, pp. 217–37.
Greenwood, J. (2007) 'Review article: Organized civil society and democratic legitimacy in the European Union' *British Journal of Political Science* 37 (2), 333–57.
Holzhacker, R.L. (2007) 'Modes of interaction: Strategies of civil society organizations and their political environments', a paper presented at the CONNEX Thematic Workshop, Group 4:A3: *Social movements, interest groups and political parties as intermediators in the multi-level system of Europe and elsewhere*, Antwerp, 20–21 September.
Krzeczunowicz, P. (2004) 'European Union funding after enlargement: Blessing or curse for civil society' paper commissioned by: *Trust for Civil Society in Central and Eastern Europe*.
Lagerspetz, M. (2004) 'From NGOs to civil society: A learning process', in M. Lagerspetz, A. Trummal, R. Ruutsoo and E. Rikmann (eds) *Non-profit sector and the consolidation of democracy: Studies on the development of civil society in Estonia*, Tallinn: Avatud Eesti Fond, pp. 86–103.
Olsen, J.P. (2002) 'The many faces of Europeanizing' *Journal of Common Market Studies* 40 (5), 921–52.
Risse, T., Green Cowles, M. and Caporaso, J. (2001) 'Europeanization and domestic change: Introduction', in M. Green Cowles, J. Caporaso and T. Risse (eds), *Transforming Europe: Europeanization and domestic change*, Ithaca: Cornell University Press, pp. 1–20.
Saurugger, S. (2007) 'Democratic "misfit"? Conceptions of civil society participation in France and the European Union' *Political Studies* 55 (2), 384–404.
Saurugger, S. (2009) 'Associations and democracy in the European Union' *West European Politics* (forthcoming).
Sudbery, I. (2003) 'Bridging the legitimacy gap in the EU: Can civil society help to bring the Union closer to its citizens?' *Collegium* 26, 75–95.
Warleigh, A. (2001) '"Europeanizing" civil society: NGOs as agents of political socialization' *Journal of Common Market Studies* 39 (4), 619–39.

Index

Aberdeen
  attitudes towards Europe study
    mapping of voluntary
      associations 48, 50–51
    sectoral taxonomy of associative
      activity 49–53
    associations and their supporters
      53–5, 66
    socio-demographic characteristics
      of respondents 54–5
    attachment 56–7
    political engagement 57–8
    political confidence 58–9
    impact of associational life on
      62–6
    typology of attitudes 59–62
    conclusions 66–7
  basic characteristics 46–7
  democratic development 47
ACCESS 223, 224, 231
accession conditionality 110–11, 114,
  121
accountability
  multi-level governance 34
  see also democratic accountability;
    electoral accountability; public
    accountability
acquis communataire 225, 226, 227, 229
active citizenry 22
actors
  policy networks 194–6
  see also non-state actors; political
    actors; politicians
adaptational pressure
  Europeanisation process 110
  see also domestic adaptations
advertising, outside lobbying 180, 186
advocacy
  and service provision 225–6
  third sector organisations 14, 26, 27,
    36
  see also outside lobbying

advocacy NGOs 33
agency capture 114, 115
agency slack 153
agricultural policy
  conflict lines among coalitions 201,
    204, 207–209, 213
  power distribution among coalitions
    199, 200, 213
aloof attitudes towards Europe 59, 60,
  61, 62, 64, 65, 66
Amsterdam model, political
  opportunity structure 77
assimilationism 131, 136
associational impact on attitudes
  towards Europe study 45–67
  contextual layers 46–8
  mapping and research design 48–9,
    50–51
  sectoral taxonomy of associative
    activity 49–53
  associations and their supporters 53–5,
    66
  attachment 56–7
  conclusions 66–7
  political engagement 57–8
  political confidence 58–9
  typology of attitudes 59–62
  impact of associational life 62–6
    levels of associational engagement
      65–6
    sizes of associations 64–5
    types of associations 63–4
associational membership
  credibility problem due to lack of
    7
  participatory democracy 6, 13–14,
    23–4
  third sector organisations 38
Athens programme (EPP, 1992)
  158
attached attitudes to Europe 56–7, 60,
  61, 62, 64, 65, 66

253

254 Civil society and governance in Europe

attitudes towards Europe *see* associational impact on attitudes towards Europe study
Austrian Freedom Party (FPÖ) 157, 161, 163
Austrian People's Party (ÖVP) 157, 163
Austrian People's Party/Austrian Freedom Party (ÖVP/FPÖ) 157, 158, 163
Austrian Social Democratic party (SPÖ) 157, 158

Bache, I. 34, 35, 36–7, 38
Baltic States, civil society 218–35
　EU efforts to support 222–33
　　consequences for multi-level governance 234–5
　　developments in NGO sphere 224–9
　　Phare 222–4
　　value and norm transfer 229–33
　historical context of development 219–22
　historical legacies and civic engagement 218–19
　NGOs' connection with EU funding 233–4
bargaining 31, 195, 201, 212
Bechtel 120, 121
Belgium
　consensus building and consensual decision-making 77–8
　environmental movement 80–82
belongingness 26
Berlusconi, Silvio 158, 163
big government
　civil society championed as a means to defeat 5
　US initiatives to reduce 24–5
biotechnological research, Czech Republic 113
Biotrin 113–15
Bismarckian (insurance-based) welfare states 132, 136
bottom-up approach, democratic decision-making 4, 9, 11, 12, 249–50
bottom-up Europeanisation 111, 160–62

see also Europeanisation, case studies
Bourdieu, Pierre 22–3
Britain *see* United Kingdom
Brussels bias 96
Bundesrepublik 47
business groups, accredited as NGOs 13

Cardiff conference (2002) 98–9
Catalan Convention 100
Central and Eastern Europe (CEE), Europeanisation, research 109, 110
chequebook participation 7
Ciampi, Carlo Azeglio 163
citizen groups, outside lobbying 185, 187–8
citizens
　control over political elites 153
　distance from EU institutions and decision-making 10, 12, 251
　interest groups *see* interest groups
　perceptions of Europeanisation 161
　rarity of links between EU institutions and 11
　transnational fora 165
　unwillingness to engage in political life 3
citizenship
　and claim making 130–32, 136
　community action programme to promote European 5
　political rights in EU 165
civic dialogue 32, 33
civic engagement 28
　Balkan States 218–19
　role of interest groups in fostering 170–90
civic mindedness 21, 22, 28, 37
civil service, confidence in 58
civil society 20–22
　as an encompassing concept 28–30
　Baltic States *see* Baltic States
　citizen alienation from EU governance 251
　conferral of legitimacy on NGOs 12–13
　core of 29
　definition of 93

development, path dependency 219–20
empowerment 109–24
multi-level governance
  democratic challenge 4–9
  Europeanisation 241
  from governing to governance 31–2
  social capital, third sector and further development of 34–8
  need to stimulate a more engaged and vibrant 45
  as a point of reference 29
  research on role in Convention on the Future of Europe 91–2
  see also Wales
  toward a European 85–8
civil society contact groups 95, 96
civil society organisations (CSOs) 4
  activists, attitudes to EU 250
  attractiveness to policy makers 4
  deliberative tradition type of definition 13
  EC argument for stronger involvement in decision-making 71
  and EU governance 32–4
  flourishing of, later 19th century 21
  involvement with Convention on the Future of Europe, Wales *see* Wales
  role as mobilisers 171
  use of outside lobbying 189
  see also interest groups; non-governmental organisations; social movements; voluntary associations
civil society plenaries 95
Civil Society Programs 223
claim making *see* political mobilisation
coalition structures
  analysis of power and interactions in conclusions 211–14
  empirical findings 199–211
  operationalisation and data 196–9
  domestic policy networks 194–6
Cockfield, Lord 159
Cohn-Bendit, Daniel 164
Colloqium on civil society and governance 99

Commission Registry of Civil Society Organisations (CONECCS) 178
committed attitudes towards Europe 59, 60, 61, 62, 64, 65, 66
The Commission and Non-Governmental Organisations: Building a Stronger Partnership 33
communication
  CSOs as channels of 33
  gap, EU and domestic political spaces 151–65
  see also civic dialogue; social dialogue
Communist legacy, adaptational pressure, Europeanisation 110
community action programme, to promote European citizenship 5
community concern associations, attitudes towards Europe study
  attachment levels 64
  distribution and respondents 53
community method, governance 32
competition, in policy networks 195, 206
Conference on Environment and Development (UN) 84
Conference on the Human Environment (UNCHE) 84
conflict, in policy networks 195
conflict lines
  among coalitions 201–202, 213
  agricultural policy 207–209, 213
  European integration 202–207, 213
  immigration policy 209–11, 213
  policy change 211–12
conflictual issues, outside lobbying 176, 182, 183, 184
consensual decision-making 78
consociative theories, communication gap, EU and domestic political spaces 153–4
constituent mobilisation 182
Convention on the Future of Europe 91, 94–7
  research on civil society role in 91–2
  see also Wales
Conventioneers 95–6
cooperation, in policy networks 195, 201, 202, 207, 208, 210, 212

cooperative movement 21–2
Copenhagen criteria 225, 226
corporatist model, welfare 47, 136
Council of Ministers 32, 153, 165
courts, confidence in 58
Cox, Pat 163
credibility, lack of membership participation, NGOs 7
cultural conditions, citizenship 131–2
cultural difference dimension, political mobilisation 136
culture associations, attitudes towards Europe study
   attachment levels 64
   distributions and respondents 53
Czech Commission for Genetically Modified Organisms and Products (CCGMOP) 113, 114, 115
Czech Republic, legislation on GMOs 113–16

Dahl, Robert 29
Dahrendorf, Ralf 29
decision-making
   communication gap, EU and domestic political spaces 153
   consensual 78
   federalism and opportunities for oppositional groups 77
   majoritarian style 78
   social movement organisations 74–5
   see also democratic decision making
Delors, Jacques 22
democracy
   dependence on social capital 6
   EU grass-roots approach to promotion of 228
   need for active citizenry 22
   see also participatory democracy; representative democracy; schools of democracy
democratic accountability 173–4
democratic decision-making
   EC argument for stronger involvement of CSOs 71
   establishing and improving at EU level 4–9, 251
   horizontal and vertical dimensions 9–12, 31
   prospects for bottom-up improvement in 249–50
   role of NGOs 12–14
   unwillingness of citizens to engage in 3
   within Europe 3–4
democratic deficit 37, 151, 164, 249–51
democratic legitimacy
   of European Union 45, 151
   and multi-level governance 34
Deptford residents association 117, 118–19
d'Estaing, President 94
developing countries, unconvinced about need to be involved in environmental protection 83
Development and Strengthening of Civil Society in Latvia 227
DG Employment, Social Affairs and Equal Opportunities 9
Diffusion thesis 112
discursive context, claim making 128, 131–2
   migrants and unemployed 137–8
distributive policies, research 31–2
domestic adaptations
   European Union 193–4
   see also adaptational pressure
domestic policy networks
   applied to coalition structures 194–6
   as determinants of policy change 211–12
domestic political elites 159–60
domestic political parties
   attempts to limit Europeanisation 158–9
   gains from a European party system 157
domestic political spaces
   and EU political space
      limited interactions between 151–2
      explanations for disjuncture 152–5
   Europeanisation
      new perspectives for 160–64
      selective 156–60
domestic power relations, effect of EU on 111–13
dominance, in policy networks 195
Don't Make a Wave 82

economic interest associations,
    attitudes towards Europe study,
    distributions and respondents 53
economists, interest in non-profit
    organisations 26
Eder, Klaus 161
educational reform 20
efficiency, judging governance
    arrangements 32
electoral accountability, outside
    lobbying 181
elites *see* political elites
Emergency Ordinance (60/2003) 120
employment-centred regimes 133, 136
empowerment
    contribution of third sector
        organisations 26
    Europeanisation and civil society
        109–24
Engström, Angers 232
enlargement, as a question of value
    transfer 230
Environment Programme (UNEP) 84
environmental groups, Soviet era 220
Environmental Impact Assessments
    (EIA), EU directive on 116–17,
    121
environmental movements
    Belgium 80–82
    Germany 73, 77
    see also global environmental
        movement
Estonia
    citizenship regulations 221
    discourses on role of NGO sector
        230–31
    introduction of democratic norms
        and values 232
    see also Baltic States
Estonian Civil Society Development
    Concept (EKAK) 224, 225, 226,
    230, 231
Etzioni, Amitai 24
Euro-Feds 33–4
Europe
    attitudes towards *see* associational
        impact on attitudes towards
        Europe study
    decision-making in 3–4
European Anti-Poverty Network 9

European Commission (EC) 74
    argument for stronger involvement
        of CSOs in decision-making 71
    demand for inner democracy 45
    discussion paper on NGOs 13
    EU governance and civil society
        organisations 32–4
    funding regimes for citizen interest
        groups 4, 8–9
    governance arrangements, judging
        32
    highlighting of importance of
        voluntary associations 32–3
    integration of social capital and
        third sector approach 30
    intervention, Bechtel motorway
        120–22
    perceived mission 32
    social partners 32
European Commissioners 159
European Council 74, 84
European democratic interference 158
European Economic and Social
    Committee (EESC) 33, 96
European Environment Bureau (EEB)
    7, 87
European and External Affairs
    Committee (Welsh Assembly) 98
European Free Alliance (EFA) 98
European integration 87–8
    conflict lines among coalitions 201,
        202–7, 213
    consociative theories of 153–4
    power distribution among coalitions
        199, 200, 213
European Network Against Racism 9
European Parliament (EP) 74, 158,
    159, 163, 165, 173
    see also Member of the European
        Parliament
European party system 152, 156, 157
European People's Party (EPP) 157,
    158
European People's Party – European
    Democrats (EPP–ED) 158, 162
European politics, interest in 57
European Public Affairs Directory
    (2004) 178
European Public Space, lack of 174
European Social Platform 9

European Union (EU) 165
  confidence 58, 59, 61–2
  democratic legitimacy 45, 151
  Directives
    environmental impact assessment
      116–17, 121
    GMOs 114, 115
  domestic adaptations 193–4
  effect on domestic power relations
    111–13
  efforts to support civil society in
    Baltic States 222–33
  establishing and improving decision-
    making 4–9
  governance
    arrangements and civil society
      organisations 32–4
    network structure 31
    research 31–2
    see also multi-level governance
  institutions, comparison with US
    172–5
  lobbying *see* outside lobbying
  political space and domestic political
    spaces
    explanations for disjuncture
      between 152–5
    limited interaction between 151–2
    rarity of links between citizens and
      institutions 11
    as weak multi-level political system
      74
  White Paper on European
    Governance (2001) 5–6, 33, 45,
    71, 72, 88, 104
Europeanisation 109–24
  adaptational pressure 110
  case studies
    conclusions 123–4
    legislation on GMOs in Czech
      Republic 113–16
    South East London Combined
      Heat and Power Incinerator
      116–20
    Transylvanian motorway in
      Romania 120–23
  communication gap, EU and
    domestic political spaces 152–3,
    154
  domestic political spaces

  new perspectives for 160–64
  selective 156–60
  domestic political systems 154–5
  interdependency between civil
    society, multi-level governance
    and 241
  research 109, 110–11
  structure of social movements 73
Executive Empowerment thesis 112
expertise
  advantaged over mobilisation, in
    policy-making 8
  Euro-Feds as transmitters of 34
external participation, Welsh CSOs'
  contact with Convention 100, 101

family associations, attitudes towards
  Europe study
  attachment levels 64
  distributions and respondents 53
federalism 47, 73, 77
Federation for a Better Environment
  (BBL) 80–81
Filer Commission 25
financial resources, outside lobbying
  177
Flemish environmental groups 80–81
Flinders, M. 34, 35, 36–7, 38
focusing events, outside lobbying
  175–6, 183
fonction tribunitienne 164
formal institutional structure 77
Forza Italia 157, 158
France
  coalitions
    conflict lines among 201, 202, 203,
      205, 206, 207, 210, 213
    power distribution among 199,
      200, 201, 213
  political mobilisation study
    individual equality dimension,
      citizenship 136
    migrants
      discursive position towards 137
      findings 141
      predictions about extent of 139
    unemployed
      discursive positions towards 138
      findings 142
      predictions about extent of 140

Friends of the Earth (FoE) 83
funding
   citizen interest groups 4, 8–9
   EU support for civil society development 227–8
Futurum 95

general welfare associations, attitudes towards Europe study
   attachment levels 64
   distributions and respondents 53
genetically modified organisms (GMOs), legislation on, Czech Republic 113–16
German federalism 73, 77
Germany
   coalitions
      conflict lines among 201, 202, 203, 204, 205, 206, 207, 208, 210, 212, 213
      power distribution among 199, 200, 201, 213
   confidence in parliament and government 58
   democratic development 47
   environmental movement 73, 77
   political mobilisation study
      individual difference dimension of citizenship 136
      migrants
         discursive position towards 137
         findings 141
         predictions about extent of 139
      unemployed
         discursive position towards 138
         findings 142
         predictions about extent of 140
      use of CSOs to tackle social question 21
   see also Mannheim
global environmental movement 82–5
good government 23
governance
   EU White Paper on 5–6, 33, 45, 71, 72, 88, 104
   societal explanation for good or bad 23
   see also big government; good government; multi-level governance

Grant, W. 12–13
grassroots approach, democracy promotion 228
grassroots lobbying tactics 174, 180, 182, 183, 185, 186
Greenpeace 82–3, 113, 115, 116, 119
group-specific welfare associations, attitudes towards Europe study
   attachment levels 64
   distributions and respondents 53
Guterres, Antonio 157

Habermas, Jürgen 29
Haider, Jörg 158
Hain, Peter 97, 99
history of issues, outside lobbying 176, 183–4
horizontal communication flows 165
horizontal dimension, decision-making 10, 11, 31
human rights
   EU support for watchdog organisations 226–7
   international associations 85

Ilves, T.H. 229
immigration policy
   conflict lines among coalitions 201, 205, 209–11, 213
   power distribution among coalitions 199, 200, 201, 213
Incinerator Monitoring Group 117
indirect empowerment 230
individual equality, political mobilisation 136
informality, of governance arrangements 31
information dissemination, by EU, through NGOs 228–9
inner democracy 45
input legitimacy 20, 32
instigators 171
Institutional Choice Approach 27
institutional level, citizenship 131
institutional reforms, to address communication gap 165
institutions, influence on outside lobbying 172–5
   research findings 179–82
   see also political institutions

insurance-based welfare states 132, 136
integration *see* European integration
interactions
  in coalition structures *see* coalition structures
  policy networks 195
  social movements and political institutions 79
interest groups
  funding regimes for 4, 8–9
  impact on European system 86
  influence on outside lobbying 176–7
  research findings 185–8
  perceived as a force derailing democracy 170
  role in modern democracies 171
  tendency to overlook the positive side of 170–71
interest representation, third sector organisations 38
interested attitudes towards Europe 60, 61, 62, 64, 65, 66
intergovernmental cooperation, transformation of JHA sector 161
intermediary sphere 22, 23, 24–5, 28, 29–30
international human rights associations 85
international politics, interest in 57
Internet Forum 95
interwar phase, civil society development 219, 220
issue advertisements, outside lobbying 180, 186
issues, influence on outside lobbying 175–6
  research findings 182–5
Italy
  conflict lines among coalitions 201, 204, 205, 208–209, 210, 213
  good government in 23
  power distribution among coalitions 199, 200, 201, 213
  public administration reforms 23
  public finance reforms 160

John Hopkins Project 30
judicial review 77
Justice and Home Affairs (JHA) sector 161–2

Kocka, Jürgen 21
Kriesi, Hanspeter 77

Laeken Council (2001) 94, 95
Lamy, Pascal 159
Latvia
  citizenship regulations 221
  NGO development 234
  see also Baltic States
Latvian Ministry of Welfare, NGO survey (1995) 226
Laveau, George 164
Le Pen, Jean-Marie 163
lebenswelt 26
Lega Nord 158, 161
legislation, on GMOs in Czech Republic 113–16
legislature, comparison of EU and US 173
legitimacy
  domestic political parties 157
  see also democratic legitimacy; input legitimacy; output legitimacy
Lewisham Planning Department 117, 118
liberal intergovernmentalism 152–3
liberal welfare regimes 47, 132, 133, 136
LIEN Program 223, 225, 231
Lijst Pim Fortuyn (LPF) 210
listening phase, Convention on the Future of Europe 94, 98
Lithuania
  Civil Society Program 223
  NGO development 234
  zero option, citizenship question 221
  see also Baltic States
lobby sponsorship 9
lobby-cracy 6–7
lobbying *see* outside lobbying
lobbying groups 6
Lobbying Reports (1996) 178
lobbyists 36, 170
local politics, interest in 57
Luxembourg Council 222

Mair, Peter 152, 154
majoritarian style decision-making 78
Making Democracy Work 23

Index

'Man And Biosphere' research
  programme 83
Mannheim
  attitudes towards Europe study
    associations and their supporters
      53–5, 66
    attachment 56–7
    conclusions 66–7
    impact of associational life on 62–6
    mapping of voluntary
      associations 48, 50–51
    political engagement 57–8
    political confidence 58–9
    sectoral taxonomy of associative
      activity 49–53
    socio-demographic characteristics
      of respondents 54–5
    typology of attitudes 59–62
  basic characteristics 46–7
  democratic development 47
media
  significance of, US lobbying 174
  strategies, outside lobbying 180–81,
    186
  see also newspapers; pan-EU media
    system
Members of the European Parliament
  (MEPs) 159, 162–3, 164, 165
  see also European Parliament
membership *see* associational
  membership
MERCI project 134
Method of Open Coordination (OMC)
  31
migrants, political mobilisation *see*
  political mobilisation
minimalist welfare 47, 132, 133, 136
minority rights, EU support for
  watchdog organisations 226–7
mobilisation
  expertise and technical knowledge
    advantaged over 8
  see also political mobilisation
mobilisers 171
multi-level governance
  civil society
    democratic challenge 4–9
    Europeanisation 241
    from governing to governance
      31–2

  social capital, third sector and
    further development of 34–8
  civil society organisations 32–4
  EU support and consequences for,
    Balkan States 234–5
  horizontal and vertical dimensions
    9–12, 31
  political opportunity structure
    (POS) 72, 73–4
  research area 92–3
  roles and functions of NGOs 12–14
  schematic overview of relationships
    10
  study of political representation in
    the EU 151
  weakness of 35
  see also Wales
multi-level political representation
  164–5
multiculturalism 131, 136
multifunctional character, third sector
  organisations 25–6, 33
mutual influencing 79, 85

Nastase, Adrian 121
nation-building, creation of social
  movements 85
National Assembly for Wales 93–4,
  97–8, 99, 101
national awakening, civil society
  development 219, 220
national gatekeepers 250
national political elites
  instrumental use of the European
    level 156–8
  insulation of political competition at
    the domestic level 154–5
national politics, interest in 57
National Socialism 47
neo-corporatist arrangements, third
  sector organisations 37, 38
neoliberal revolution, Washington
  24–5
neoliberalism 19, 47
Netherlands
  conflict lines among coalitions 201,
    202, 203, 204, 205, 207, 208,
    210, 213
  consensus building and consensual
    decision-making 77–8

power distribution among coalitions 199, 200, 201, 213
Network Governance thesis 112–13
new issues, outside lobbying 176, 183
'new' politics associations, attitudes towards Europe study
  attachment levels 64
  distributions and respondents 53
newspapers, portrayal of Convention on the Future of Europe 99–100
non-distribution constraint 25, 26, 27
non-governmental organisations (NGOs) 6–7, 21
  Balkan States
    connection with EU funding 233–4
    developments 224–9
  global, main problem for 83
  letters urging Romanian government to halt Bechtel motorway 122
  multifunctional character 33
  role
    in democratic decision-making 9–10
    and functions 12–14
  Stockholm forum 84
  supporters
    passive role of 7
    unawareness of EU-level activities 250–51
non-profit organisations
  micro-economics and study of 26
  multifunctional character 25–6
  political science and sociology research 26–7
  start-up incentives and motivations 26
  voluntarism 30
non-state actors
  organisational set-ups and opportunity structures of 36
  role and legitimacy 34–5
normative element, civil society 28
norms *see* values and norms

Observers 95–6
Ohne miche 47
older issues, outside lobbying 183–4
Open Society Institute Network 225
operational NGOs 33

oppositional groups
  more opportunities, in federal states 77
  political elites
    routine responses to 77–8, 79
    support for, to promote self-interest 78
Orange Revolution 161
organisational membership, outside lobbying 177, 187, 188
organisational set-up, and opportunity structures 36
organisational structure, outside lobbying 187, 188
organisational survey, attitude towards Europe study 48–9
organised civil society 4, 19, 33
O'Rourke, John 224
Osiatynski, Wiktor 225
output legitimacy 32
outside lobbying
  citizen engagement 171
  comparative study, EU and US
    data collection 177–9
    empirical findings 179–88
    conclusion 189–90
  factors influencing
    institutions 172–5
    interests 176–7
    issues 175–6
  United States 171

pan-EU media system, lack of 174, 189
parent bodies, Welsh CSOs' contact with Convention 100, 101
participation
  of public in consultation on GMOs, Czech Republic 115
  of Welsh CSOs in Convention on the Future of Europe 100–103
  see also chequebook participation; civic engagement; voluntary participation
participatory democracy 5
  associational membership 6, 13–14, 23–4
  civil society and possibility of linking policy analysis with 22
  contribution of NGOs 33

current attractiveness 20–21
  judging governance arrangements 32
Party of European Socialists (PES)
  157, 158, 162
party networking 156, 157
passive involvement 7
path dependency, civil society
  development 219–20
patronage, EU norms and erosion of
  162
people's fronts 220–221
Phare 222–4, 227, 229, 230, 232, 233
Phare Democracy Program 223
pluralist models, citizenship 131, 136
Poland, perception of Europeanisation
  161
police, confidence in 58
policy analysis, linking with
  participatory democracy 22
policy entrepreneurs, third sector
  organisations as 37
policy implementation
  linked to social capital 23
  third sector organisations 36
policy networks *see* domestic policy
  networks
policy-making
  civil society, Wales and EU 93–4
  contribution of NGOs 14
  expertise advantaged over
    mobilisation 8
  multi-level governance, EU 92–3
political actors, outside lobbying
  176–7, 185–6, 187–8
political confidence, respondents,
  Aberdeen and Mannheim study
  58–9
political culture research 23
political discourse, re-entry of civil
  society into 20
political elites
  as beneficiaries of two-level game
    153
  citizen control over behaviour of
    153
  power configuration 78
  protection from potential impacts of
    Europeanisation 154
  responses to oppositional groups
    77–8, 79

see also domestic political elites;
  national political elites
political engagement, respondents,
  Aberdeen and Mannheim study
  57–8
political institutions
  conclusions 143–4
  confidence in 58–9
  critique of interaction between
    social movements and 79
political mobilisation, migrants and
  unemployed 127–44
  citizenship and claim making 130–32
  findings
    migrants 140–42
    unemployed 141–3
  political opportunity approach
    129–30
  research
    data retrieval 134–5
    hypotheses 138–40
    operationalisation 135–8
  theoretical framework 128
  welfare state and claim making 132–4
  see also outside lobbying
political opportunity structure (POS)
  72–6
  concept of 76–80
  criticism of 78
  differing definitions 73
  importance of 86–7
  multi-level governance 72, 73–4
  political mobilisation 127, 128,
    129–30, 135–7
  problem with 73
  social movements
    creation of new 86
    environmental movement,
      Belgium 80–82
    global environmental movement
      82–5
    study of 71–3
political parties
  confidence in 58
  see also domestic political parties
political representation
  access at European level 152
  control of communication between
    national and supranational level
    158–9

from two-level to multi-level 164–5
hampering of links between European and domestic level 160
multi-level governance research 151
two-level game 154, 165
political science
  interest in non-profit organisations 26–7
  replacing of term 'governing' with 'governance' 31
  social capital approach in 23
politicians, confidence in 58
politicisation, Europeanisation and acceleration of 162
politics associations, attitudes towards Europe study
  attachment levels 64
  distributions and respondents 53
post-Putnam social capital debate 5–6
post-Soviet period, civil society development 220–21
power
  in coalition structures *see* coalition structures
  configuration, political elite 78
  see also domestic power relations
power distribution
  among coalitions 199–201, 213
  policy change 212
  policy networks 195
Presidium, Convention on the Future of Europe 94
pressure groups, third sector organisations as 36–7
Prodi, Romani 45, 159
professional associations, outside lobbying 181, 186
project management, NGOs' contribution to 14
Promoting the Role of Voluntary Organisations and Foundations in Europe of 1997 32–3
protests/rallies, outside lobbying 180, 186
public accountability 109
public administration reforms, Italy 23
public education/PR, outside lobbying 180

public sphere, civil society as 21
Putnam, Robert 6, 23–4, 28–9

Raik, K. 230, 231, 232
Reagan, Ronald 24
reflection phase, Convention on the Future of Europe 94
Registry of the European Parliament (2004) 178
RegLeg (Regions with Legislative Power) 97
religious associations, attitudes towards Europe study
  attachment levels 64
  distributions and respondents 53
representative democracy 20
republicanism 131
The Role and Contribution of Civil Society Organisations in the Building of Europe 33
Romania, Transylvanian motorway 120–23
Romanian Academic Society 122
Romanian Think Tank 122
Ruddock, Joan 118

salience of issues, outside lobbying 175, 179, 183, 184
Sbragia, Alberta 160
Scharpf, Fritz 20, 32, 33, 195–6
schools of democracy 14, 37–8, 62
Scientific Conference on the Conservation and Utilisation of Resources (UNSCCUR) 83
scope of issue, outside lobbying 175, 182, 183, 184
Scotland
  confidence in government 58
  see also Aberdeen
Scottish Parliament 58, 100
segregationism 131
selective Europeanisation 156–60
self-actualisation 26
service delivery, third sector involvement 27, 36
service provision, advocacy and 225–6
Smet, Miet 81
social capital 4
  anti-modern form, Russia 220
  post-Putnam debate 5–6

social capital approach 22–4
  democratic governance research 30
  development of multi-level governance 35, 37–8
social dialogue 32
social milieus 21, 27
social movements 20
  adaptation to growing influence and impact of European decision-making 74–5
  facilitated by nation-building process 85
  growth of non-profit organisations 26
  mass-membership based 86
    absence in Europe 75, 87
  political opportunity structures
    creation of new 86
    critique of interaction between 79
    environmental movement, Belgium 80–82
    global environmental movement 82–5
  study of 71–3
social networks 194–5
social partners, European Commission 32
societal interests, NGOs as counterbalance to 14
sociologists, interest in non-profit organisations 26–7
solidarity 26
Soros, George 226
South East London Combined Heat and Power (SELCHP) Incinerator 116–20
South East London Waste Disposal Group 116, 117, 118, 119
Soviet era, civil society development 220–21
Spain
  conflict lines among coalitions 201, 202, 203, 204, 205, 206, 207, 208, 210, 213
  power distribution among coalitions 199, 200, 201, 213
Spanish People's Party 157
special interests 170
sports associations, attitudes towards Europe study
  attachment levels 64
  distributions and respondents 53
staff characteristics, outside lobbying 186–7, 189
Strong, Maurice 83–4
study phase, Convention on the Future of Europe 94
sub-protecting regimes 133
Sudbery, I. 251
Swedish government, push for more active role for UN in combating pollution 83
Swiss People's Party 206, 209
Switzerland
  coalitions
    conflict lines among 201, 202, 203, 204, 205, 206, 208, 209, 210, 212, 213
    power distribution among 199, 200, 201, 212, 213
  political mobilisation study
    individual difference dimension of citizenship 136
    migrants
      discursive positions towards 137
      findings 141
      predictions about extent of 139
    unemployed
      discursive positions towards 138
      findings 142
      predictions about extent of 140

Tarrow, Sydney 23, 79, 85
tax reform, Washington 24
Taylor, Charles 29
technical knowledge, advantaged over mobilisation 8
thematic approach, EU support for civil society development 229
think tanks, outside lobbying 186
third sector approach 24–8
  democratic governance research 30
  development of multi-level governance 35–7
The Third Sector and Domestic Missions 24
third sector organisations 25–7
  interest representation 38
  membership *see* associational membership

welfare domains 35–6
see also civil society organisations
Tilly, Charles 79
Tocqueville, Alexis de 5–6, 23, 24
top-down approach, democratic decision-making 4, 9, 11–12, 250
top-down Europeanisation 110, 162–4
transitional societies, civil society development 219–22
transnational citizens fora 165
Transylvanian motorway, Romania 120–23
Trenz, Hans-Jörg 161
turbo-capitalism 19, 21
'two-level game' metaphor 153, 154, 165

Ukraine, Orange Revolution 161
unemployed, political mobilisation *see* political mobilisation
unemployment-providence regimes 133
UNEMPOL project 134
United Kingdom
  coalitions
    conflict lines among 201, 202, 203, 204, 205, 206, 208, 212, 213
    power distribution among 199, 200, 201, 212, 213
  confidence in government 58
  political mobilisation study
    individual difference dimension of citizenship 136
    migrants
      discursive position towards 137
      findings 141
      predictions about extent of 139
    unemployed
      discursive position towards 138
      findings 142
      predictions about extent of 140
  South East London Combined Heat and Power incinerator 116–20
United Nations
  Charter, conformity of NGO aims with 13
  confidence in 58
  involvement in environmental protection 83, 84

United States
  analysis of intermediary sphere 24–5
  expertise advantaged over mobilisation in policy-making 8
  institutions, comparison with EU 172–5
  lobbying *see* outside lobbying
  significance of media in lobbying 174
universalist model
  citizenship 136
  welfare 47
Use of Genetically Modified Organisms and Products Act (2002) 114
utopian programme, civil society and 21, 22

values and norms
  EU attempts at transfer of 229–33
  introduction of EU and erosion of patronage 162
  third sector organisations as transmitters of 27
vertical dimension, decision-making 10, 11–12, 31
vertical integration OMC 31
Vilnius 221
voluntarism 30
voluntary associations 21, 23
  Baltic States 220
  as channels for societal integration and political participation 37
  civic engagement 28
  EC highlighting of importance of 32–3
  importance for interest articulation and aggregation 28–9
  intermediary sphere 29–30
  see also associational impact on attitudes towards Europe study
voluntary participation, non-profit organisations 25

Wales, civil society
  Convention on the Future of Europe conclusions 104
  formal structural opportunities open to 96–7
  scope for involvement 97–100

participation 100–102
  non-participation 102–103
 EU policy-making 93–4
Wales European Forum (WEF) 94, 98, 101
Walloon environmental groups 80–81
Wallstrom, Margot 189
Washington, neoliberal revolution 24–5
Washington consensus 19
watchdog NGOs 225–6
weak state structures 73

welfare associations *see* general welfare associations; group-specific welfare associations
welfare domains, third sector organisations 35–6
welfare regimes 47, 132–3
welfare state
  crisis, and shift to input legitimacy 20
  and political mobilisation 132–4
White Paper on European Governance (2001) 5–6, 33, 45, 71, 72, 88, 104